Prepare for a rocky journey!

I thank God that when the going got tough I am
sure He gave a helping hand to negotiate the road.

Catherine ER Ellison

Acknowledgments

I would like to say a big thank you to those who supported me and made suggestions for improvements while I wrote this book especially; Brenda, Su, Ruth, Valerie and my family.

I would also like to acknowledge everyone who has influenced my life, whether that be good or bad, as without those characters there would be no book.

To protect the identity of individuals, I have changed the names of people and some of the places.

Disclaimer

If you wish to apply any ideas contained in this book, I will not be held responsible for the outcome. It is therefore understood that you will take full responsibility for your own actions.

ISBN-13: 978-1986353762 (CreateSpace-Assigned)
ISBN-10: 1986353761

Email: **catherineerellison@gmail.com**

CONTENTS

A CHILD OF THE 50s

N ow I am not going to make this chapter into a history lesson, but I am going to write a few lines to give you a quick flavour of what life was like growing up in the 50s. I also know that many 1950s children were born and raised in loving, secure homes, but I wasn't one of them. I was born in 1953, a time when very few people in our area had cars, telephones, indoor toilets, central heating, freezers, automatic washers or televisions. Even toilet paper was a rarity or a luxury, as most working-class people used newspaper, posh people cut the newspaper into squares and hung the pieces on a nail in the toilet.

For women in the 50s the equivalent to the modern-day gym meant participating daily in weight lifting activities as they carried the family shopping from the town centre, and lifted young children up and down, thus building strong biceps and shoulders. Checking in at the equivalent of two hours on the tread mill was: walking to the shops, taking the kids to school, and searching the streets to find them at bedtime. Shovelling coal for the open fire also improved the arm, stomach and back muscles. Sweeping the floors helped to shape the waist line along with improving their poise and posture. Tummy tucks were executed as they crawled around the floor with a scrubbing brush; this also exercised the spine and built neck muscles. The Sunday matinee to produce more offspring kept the reproductive system in good order along with improving the cardiac system. For many, it was also considered negligence if they did not smack their children, as they would grow up unruly and answer their elders back. This activity also improved coordination and increased ability to hit moving objects with precision. Sunday was a special day, not because we went to church like the 'Waltons', but it was the only day we were likely to get a cooked meal. Sunday night was also bath night whether we were dirty or not.

Equal rights had not been invented, as a result our schools prepared us accordingly. That is, girls had lessons in cookery, domestic science, darning, sewing and knitting. In other words, we were trained to look after our future husband, children and the house. Boys were given lessons in woodwork, metalwork, and how to become labourers, tradesmen, or get a career. As a result, many women were financially dependent on their working husbands.

Well now that I have given you a flavour of the environment I grew up in, let's look at the lifestyle that laid the foundations for the years of chaos to follow. I was a skinny, unkempt little girl, with straight dark brown hair, large brown eyes and a heart-shaped face. I usually wore a thin cotton dress, and if I was lucky a cardigan would keep me warm. Everyone said I looked like my mother. Can you imagine telling a four-year-old they look like their mother? I felt horrified. I couldn't quite understand the resemblance. To me my mother looked old, and so she was at twenty-six. To be fair, my mother was a good-looking woman, with straight, thick, dark brown hair, beautiful skin and an oval shaped face.

By the time I was three and a half years old I had two younger sisters and an older brother by eighteen months. We lived in a two-bed-roomed, brick built, terraced house on a council estate. The house had a large overgrown back garden, to the front was a yard with a combined outside toilet and coal house with a concrete roof. The roof doubled up as a playground for young aspiring dare devils. Yes, we would dare one another to see who could walk the seven-foot-high walls and jump the gates. After playing on the roof we would jump down from the top; now that certainly got you street cred. Of course, this was an extremely dangerous pastime, but I don't think any of the adults in my life were too concerned with safety issues.

It was amazing how almost every nook and cranny of the house could be used as a playground. When things were good we would swing from door posts, race down the stairs on our stomachs and walk up the recess in the bedroom wall to touch the ceiling. That is, you stand with your back against the wall and then lift your feet onto the opposite wall and slowly push yourself up the wall until you touch the ceiling.

Yes when things were good it could be fun, but the reality was that it was seldom good. So I must tell you that earning beatings in my house was very easy. In fact, there was seldom a day went by that I failed to get into trouble and clouted for something. Even when at five years old I put something pink in the twin-tub washer turning everything a dirty pink and cleaned the sideboard with a brillo pad. The woman had no appreciation of my dedication to duty. My mother, like many of the other mother's in those days, chastised us with blows; any part of the body was a target that could be whacked with not only her hand, but anything she had in her hand at that time. This included shovels, shoes, tins of soup and pans all bounced off my head at some time during my childhood. How I didn't get permanent brain damage I will never know. Perhaps I did! She was not a malicious woman who thought about ways to hurt us. No, she was just a thoughtless woman who didn't think about ways to hurt us.

I even had a couple of baby teeth removed with the slamming of a door. Now for those who don't know what this means I will explain. You take a long piece of thread and tie one end to the door handle and one end to the child's tooth. (That's my tooth) You then slam the door hard and the tooth flies out of the mouth. This is called a 'simple dental procedure' without the fuss!

Now as children it was important for us to learn how to do jobs correctly. So one day my mother told me to scrape the potatoes. I was about six years old and did not know the difference between old and new potatoes. Shame on me! When my mother noticed I had peeled the potatoes instead of scraping them, what a smack in the head, I went reeling. Now as you can imagine my mother's teaching methods left something to be desired, but I learned quickly the difference between old and new potatoes!

Nevertheless, I had principles, and was prepared to take a beating if I felt I was in the right. On a rare school trip with ten shillings, I spent every penny on a present for my mother. I bought her two 'gold' horses with black manes and tails, which took pride of place on the sideboard. The one I had cleaned with the Brillo pad! I came home from school one day and the manes and tails were missing. I asked my mother what had happened and she replied, "Ronnie Green came in with his mam and pulled them off." Ronnie was a very destructive boy of about eleven, not some two-year-old who didn't know any better. I was disgusted with my mother that she could allow this to happen. I put what was left of the horses in the middle of the floor and jumped up and down on them, knowing full well that I would feel the back of her hand. Sure enough I did, as she also swung me off the horses by my hair and belted me. It was worth it!

As a child I had all the normal childhood illnesses as well as frequently suffering from severe bouts of whooping cough and bronchitis. If I had to stay off school for any reason, which could vary from being too ill to attend, or I was needed at home to do jobs or messages, I never in my life went to bed. It was just the norm to continue with my errands and chores as if I was the picture of health. Yes, TLC was not high on the agenda; it would probably have produced spoilt, pampered children, and we could well do without that! Wouldn't it have been lovely to be tucked up in bed with someone attending to my every need? Dream on.

To be fair, there was one day I felt really spoilt; my mother told me to go to the shop. She said, "Go *straight* there and come *straight* back." As I walked to the shop my four-year-old brain reasoned that if I walked there forwards and walked back backwards, that would be *straight* without turning around. So, after getting her shopping I walked backwards out of the shop. An unsuspecting nurse driving her car knocked me over, obviously believing that like any normal person I would walk forwards away from her, and not backwards into the path of her oncoming car. Silly woman!

A CHILD OF THE 50s

Given she was now a bumbling wreck, the coal-man picked me up and carried me home as she followed. I savoured the experience, being showered with all the attention, as I lay on the settee concussed after the blow to my head when I hit the ground. My mother put the kettle on, as the cure for shock was a cup of hot sweet tea. That did the trick, after their tea they felt much better and returned to work. I was quickly brought back to reality and up on my feet again seconds after their departure.

In the picturesque Northumberland town where I lived I regularly went shopping from a very young age. Just in case you hadn't noticed that four years old was quite young to be out shopping. I was probably a very familiar face in the shops and liked to do things better than other people. I oozed with pride when I was able to carry all the groceries home for my mother. I would run all the way to the shops, and hurry back as fast as my little legs would carry me. One day she might notice my effort if I tried harder and harder; I should be so lucky. She had a talent for spotting with great precision only the things I did wrong, rather than when I did something right. These were the days when praising a child meant they would grow up conceited with a high opinion of themselves and it would have been a cardinal sin to raise a generation of narcissistic brats! Well there was little chance of that happening for me.

A CHILD OF THE 50s

Sometimes, she would send me repeatedly backwards and forwards the two mile round journey into town and back for shopping. It made no difference to my mother what the weather conditions were when she sent me to the shops. She would often send me out in the thick snow, or in the thunder and lightning. The rain would be hitting so hard off the ground it would bounce up as high as my knees. There was often no one else on the streets except me. The sky would light up, as the lightening zigzagged across the black clouds. The thunder would roar as if God was angry with everyone. I would be soaking wet in my thin cotton dress, but I did not care. There was something awesome about being under those black clouds all alone; in a funny sort of way there was a peace. I suppose it was an escape from the constant flow of chaos, anger and violence from my home life. Nothing used to make very much sense to me as a child; there was no predictability at all. Half the time I did not even know what I was getting hit for. That is certainly a recipe to make a person feel stupid. I couldn't even work out what I had done to get into trouble. How stupid was I?

Shouting and fighting between my parents was also a regular occurrence. My mother would get really upset and angry when my father didn't come home from work, and just went straight to the pub. This was most nights when he was on day shift. It was scary listening to them as they fought and rowed. Blows were often thrown and sometimes my mother would hide us in the bedroom with her and jam the door with the chair and the sweeping brush. Many of the rows were about my father's drinking and womanising. This really upset my mother as she believed in faithfulness and did not drink; he believed in nothing other than himself.

Probably a sign of the times for some families but unfortunately my mam made a stark difference between how she treated girls and boys. We would watch on hungrily as my brother was given more food, and sometimes he would be the only one who was fed along with my father. My mother would send me to bed and allow him to stay up late to watch the new black and white TV. However, if she needed anything done, like going to see where my father was when he did not return from the bar, she would get me up to do it. I would trail the streets at some unearthly hours looking for him, knowing full well when I got back home that it would be my fault if I'd failed to find him.

My brother could hit me, but if I retaliated my mother would usually hit me, as girls mustn't fight. I had to do the housework: wash dishes, scrub floors, light the fire, fetch the coal, do the shopping and cook meals. My brother did nothing; everything had to be done for him. He had to be waited on hand and foot; sitting there like lord and master gloating at his good fortune; while I seethed with jealousy at the favouritism bestowed upon him. Don't think being the product of a favoured upbringing did anything to provide him with an endearing personality. No, he was a wicket, brutal child with no ability to understand the feelings of anyone. To be fair, I don't know if being devoid of feelings was a legacy of that generation or just our household. I can assure you that we were certainly not sitting around the dinner table discussing the events of the day and how we felt about them.

On one occasion when my auntie was in our house chatting to my mother, she noticed my brother had his foot stuck in my throat, and I was turning blue. She said, "Heather, that lad is choking that bairn." My mother turned to look. She turned back, said, "Oh it's only Catherine," and carried on chatting. Would she come to my rescue when it involved my brother? Not a chance, fairness on any level did not exist in our family. One thing was for sure; if I had been hitting him she would have jumped up and belted me.

I was repeatedly bombarded with: 'Girls don't do that'. It was as if all girls were allowed to do was housework, and slave over everyone else, but they weren't allowed to do anything which was fun. They do not climb trees, do not run (unless it is a message for her) it's not lady like, do not fight.

A CHILD OF THE 50s

Even if we read, she would find something more suitable for girls to do. The kitchen floor wants scrubbing, this had to be done on our hands and knees certainly not with a mop. She once nearly knocked my head off my shoulders when I put the floor cloth under the brush to mop the floor; a trick I had seen another woman do. A trick I was not going to try again while she was around, the consequences were a bit too painful.

This story is going to contradict other stories which I tell about my mother, but don't worry about it, as I went passed the stage of making sense of the completely contradictory, unpredictable life style I was living. So here goes, I sometimes attribute my gutsy behaviour to my mother. I was five years old when my mother told me to go to the shop, I told her that I was scared because Julie Grey would hit me. Julie Grey was eighteen months older than me. My mother said, "Well just hit her back." I screeched, you know in that whiny voice children have, which without a doubt would get the response of, "Start your whining with me and I will give you something to whine about." This was the same response any form of crying received. "But her mam is always there." I continued. This did not deter my mother from sending me to the shop. No, she was a determined woman who would not be beat. Nevertheless a few weeks later I was crossing the back field with my mother, and this girl was also crossing with her mother. My mother said, "Well there she is, now go and hit her back." "But her mother is there." I once again screeched, and she said, "Yes and I'm here with you." I charged across the backfield and hit this girl. I think I received a message from my mother that at some level I was worth fighting for. However, she failed to teach me that when the odds were impossible you needed the wisdom to walk away.

Now my mother also had problems sleeping and regularly woke me up through the night to make her drinks of tea and go to the shop for five Woodbines. I know you are probably thinking how could you go to the shop in the middle of the night when there was not such a thing as all night shopping in those days? The explanation is easy, I had to go and knock the shop keeper up. The owners lived above their shop not too far from our street. I would imagine I was never a welcome sight but believe it or not the shop keeper usually got up and sold me the cigarettes. In those days they sold cigarettes to children no matter what their age. I would guess that they probably knew that if I did not go back with the cigarettes I would be in a lot of trouble. Although as a young child I was unable to work all that out and just felt so happy that they sold me the cigarettes, I could skip!

I loved my early years at school; this probably had something to do with the very wholesome school meals which were dished up daily. I would wolf down my first helping and pray that there would be seconds. I ate more than any child in the school, but instead of being fat, I was as thin as a rake. I put my huge appetite at school down to the fact that it was hitty-missy whether I got fed at home; more missy than hitty I may add. Never mind, I was great on the school yard apparatus, and loved our PE lessons in the infant school. I had a natural aptitude for gymnastics and sporting activities. Probably a result of the gymnasts I was preforming every day at home.

In those days children in schools were often smacked over the hands or backside with leather straps, belts or canes. There was a child in our class, who was called out every day to be given the cane. My heart went out to this little girl; my brain could not comprehend why an adult would want to hit a child every day. One day the same teacher called me out for swinging on my chair. She then proceeded to take a leather belt several times across my hand. I was so distressed that I did **not** eat my school meal that day. That was a first, as I am sure you have gathered my school meals meant a great deal to me. I went home and told my mother what had happened. Guess what, she gave me another hiding, and said, "The teachers don't hit you for nothing." She was well deluded! Well that was the day I made a couple of very important decisions. I would never go home and tell my mother anything again. I also made a decision never to cry again. It was clear that no one was the slightest bit interested in my tears. This was a promise I was to keep until I was thirty-four years old and in a rehab for alcoholism.

You might be thinking, well if she was getting hit daily at home, why would it bother her to get hit at school? It was so different. I was so used to my mother hitting me it was just the norm, but I also do not think my mother was malicious; she just reacted to the situation with anything in her hand. Whereas the teacher went and looked for a weapon to hit me with, she thought about hitting me. In the years that followed I got many a belting from the teachers, but this too just became the norm.

I was very lucky, as the small town where I lived was surrounded by miles of countryside, woods, brooks, streams rivers and castle ruins, were all within a couple of miles of our house. During my early childhood years, sometimes on a Sunday, my mam and dad took us for walks into the countryside. I loved these walks, as there was so much to explore, discover and learn about. I loved playing in the old stone ruins of Black Beards Castle, bluebell woods and the surrounding streams. I continue to believe to this day that the countryside is by far the best ever playground.

A CHILD OF THE 50s

I am sure you will have gathered that my father had little to do with the child raising practices in our home. He was like most men in those days and went to work. He usually made quite good money in his line of work but of course, he gave my mother a meagre amount of housekeeping money while he spent the rest on his own pursuits. Nevertheless, on our walks he educated us about nature. He would tell us when to pick various plants, berries and mushrooms; he knew all the names of the birds and trees. He was in fact quite a walking encyclopaedia. He told us stories which were passed off as fairy stories about Sweeny-Todd the Barber, Black Beards Castle and Jack the Ripper. It was not until I saw the films when I was an adult in my thirties that I discovered that the fairy stories my father told us were actually horror stories. You wonder why I grew up confused.

My father was interested in the politics of the country and proud to be classed as a working-class man. Although saying that, my father's family would have been considered more middle-class than working-class, as his family were what we call quite 'well to do' in comparison to most of the people living in our area. As well as being well read he could hold his own in any discussion. He was about five feet nine inches tall, of medium build, with fine fair hair and large round piercing dark-grey eyes. He was always well-dressed, and never bought his suits 'off the peg'. People used to say he was one of the most intelligent people they had ever met. He had a fun loving personality when out and about and was never short of companions at the local pub.

Most of my father's family were professional people with clean, well-dressed, well fed children and good careers. We got the booby prize; my father was not interested in career success. He loved only himself, fully believing life was to enjoy with no consideration for anyone. That meant work for money to spend on drink, gambling and playing pool. He used to say to us, "You come from good breeding, your family and ancestors are the best and have all done well with their lives." It took a huge leap of faith and imagination to believe that we were the best, given that we were usually dressed in second hand, worn out hand downs. What is more, he certainly did not treat us as though we were the best. He could be a vicious and sarcastic man with a gift at humiliation and put downs. If I did not do something the way he believed it should be done his retorts would tear me to shreds. He was a genius at head games and knew how to have an impact. Yes, he was much more vicious and devious than my mother. My father would think through how he could hurt, whereas my mother didn't think.

A CHILD OF THE 50s

Nevertheless, during the limited time he did spend with us, he taught us how to play cards, dominoes and bought us comics. Our childhood was so stimulating we could all read, count money and tell the time before we went to school. These were prerequisites to manage our daily lives and conduct our chores. We were also all card-sharks, and when my brother grew up, he could beat most people in any card game. His winning streaks had more to do with moving his hand quicker than the eye could see. In other words, he was an accomplished, talented cheat. He probably picked some of this attitude up from my father who drummed into us, "You play to win." My father was also a brilliant snooker player and would leave most competitors, not only poorer, but also extremely impressed at his mastery of the game. That might account for our competitive nature, only thing was, there can only be one winner, and in our house the odds were well stacked in favour of my brother.

My forte was fighting, I had a reputation second to none as a fighter; I could beat my brother in any fight as long as my mother was not present, and he knew it. If my mother was there, I had no chance. I could also beat all his friends at fighting and most sporting activities, even though they were older. Yes, I got hard quickly, as it seemed the wisest option given the environment I was living in.

A CHILD OF THE 50s

It may sound a bit peculiar a girl bragging about their fighting abilities and achievements, but I suppose when I was young this is what I excelled at, so it was what I could boast about. I say boast, but my environment was really not conductive of boasting. In those days it would be seen as having an over inflated opinion and getting above my station; and without a doubt some overbearing adult would have said, "Who do you think you are?" In that tone which would shame me to the bone. That would quickly bring my bragging to an end.

Nevertheless, when my brother wasn't around, I used to play on his two-wheeler bike, girls in our house weren't allowed a bike. One day I fell off and split my knee wide open, right through to the bone. The gash looked really nasty, as the blood streamed down my leg onto my dirty grey, supposed to be white, sock. I knew there would be no mileage in going home, even though I was only about two hundred yards away. I cycled the one and a half mile to the hospital and watched as the nurse sewed it up with eight stitches. Fortunately, or unfortunately, as the case may be, I was familiar with the process of having cuts stitched up, as I'd previously split my chin open and my finger. She gave me a lolly for being brave. Yes, a lolly was the reward for bravery in the 50s. They obviously hadn't made the connection between sweets and rotten teeth or obesity.

I did manage to have another couple of catastrophes while playing on my brother's bike, probably something to do with the brake blocks being non-existent. So, when my younger sister asked if I would give her a go on the back. Of course, I would, we went belting down a very steep hill at rocket speed, straight up the woman's garden path and stopped when the bike smacked into her kitchen units. She did look surprised at our undignified entrance, as we fell onto her kitchen floor. I don't know why my sister never wanted to ride a bike again! Another time my friend and I were whizzing down an extremely steep hill at the speed of light; of course, once more there were no brakes on the bike, and we couldn't stop. We had gathered up so much speed that the mudguard got caught in the wheel, and as it smashed in half, the two of us were flung head first straight over the handle bars into the middle of the road. Now I was stuck with a bike with a front wheel smashed in two, it looked like a large bent banana! How would I talk my way out of that one?

The reality is that all the above paled into insignificance in comparison to my biggest fear, which was my mother's 'nervous breakdowns'. Unfortunately in the 50s and 60s the atmosphere around mental illness was very different to what it is today. There was no such thing as 'talking therapies' people were just put into mental hospitals and forced to undergo their brutal treatments. One of the things most people don't know is that numerous studies have found that people with higher IQs often develop mental illness. If we look back through time many great thinkers and gifted people have had mental health problems. We have, Charles Darwin, Isaac Newton, Leonardo Da Vinci, Beethoven, and Van Gogh to name a few. We can also look at the countless celebrities of our day to see how many have been incarcerated against their will or needed medical intervention. I really admire Prince William for the work he is doing around mental health issues. I only wish it had been like this when I was a child.

Yes we lived in a society that was quite barbaric in the treatment of mental illness. Although I had no real understanding of my own feelings as a child, when I look back I was clearly in a state of terror. My mams breakdowns were horrendous, both for her and for us. She would lose all sense of reality and not even see me when I tried to get her attention. It was as though I didn't exist, it was absolutely awful to watch her disappear into oblivion and not even see us in the room. She would do things and not know what she was doing; it was as though she was walking around in a trance completely oblivious to the world. She'd just sit staring into space, this could turn to tears, screams and even change to laughter, but it was a haunting laughter. I knew when she was like this there was no way to reach her, no matter how much I tried. I know it might not sound like it, but I actually loved my mother, there was a warmth about her and when she was her normal self, she was an interesting woman.

My state of terror was not just about the breakdown my mam was having, it was about how she would be treated when they took her by force to the psychiatric hospital, or the asylum as they were then known. She would be forced to undergo electroconvulsive therapy, also called electroshock therapy (ECT). This involves sending electrical shocks to the brain to change the way it functions. It is a completely barbaric treatment which can often damage the person's memory. Whenever I try to even look into this treatment on Google I feel ill, it's as though I am reliving the brutality my mam experienced when she was forced to undergo this treatment

There was a man in our street that used to laugh at my mam when she was having a breakdown. I hated him with a vengeance. It was bad enough that as children we were dealing with this, but to have an adult man standing at our back door laughing was really rubbing salt into the wound. I hope you've heard the saying, 'Be careful of stones that you throw'. Well only a few years later his daughter experienced a breakdown and was hospitalised for a number of years. This taught me an important lesson!

Now because my mother was often taken by force to the local psychiatric hospital, I had to take some responsibility. So, by the time I was seven years old, I would sign the family allowance book in three places. Yes, I did say I forged two other signatures along with my own. I signed her name as the authority on the book. I changed the signature and signed as a witness, then put my own signature as the messenger. In other words by the age of seven I was an accomplished fraudster. I would collect the money from the post office, then get on a bus and take the money twenty miles to the mental hospital where they had taken her.

In a strange sort of way I was desperate to see my mam and make her proud of me for taking her money and going to see her in the hospital; the reality was the hospital was horrendous. The patients lined the corridors and wards with vacant eyes and blank expressions. They were fed a cocktail of drugs and forced to undergo electric shock treatment. When I found my mam she was often vacant and the money or my visit would have very little meaning.

You might wonder how a seven-year-old was doing this by themselves. I wondered about this too as an adult looking back. I feel disgusted with the authorities; nurses, doctors, health visitors, social workers and teachers, who repeatedly turned a blind eye to the plight we were experiencing. So yes, I had to get her family allowance and take it to the hospital, or when she got out, I would be in deep trouble. That would be unusual!

FOUNDATIONS FOR DISASTER

Wow I have just turned eleven and on my way to the senior school. On my first day my friend Anna said, "Nuw we ha tu start smokin or we'll git bullied by the ader kids if we divin't fit in." She clearly lacked any degree of self-awareness, as she terrorised anyone who was foolish enough to cross her path. Nevertheless on this note she produced some of her father's 'John Players Navy Cut' cigarette ends out of his ashtray, ready for our initiation into senior school. Well I'd hate to look like a wimp, so I proudly took my first draw of a cigarette and blew the smoke straight out. I was told, "Na yu ha tu let the smoke gan rite doon yu throat into yu guts." So I took my second draw of a cigarette and inhaled as though I was having a three course meal. That was more like the thing; I was now joining an elite group of rabble at my new comprehensive school.

I continued smoking as though I was having a three-course meal for the next thirty years. However, as I didn't like my friend's cigarette ends, me being particular and all that, I brought my own Woodbine dumps to school, stealthily taken from my mother's ashtray. We felt like millionaires if we had a whole cigarette to ourselves. If I had been babysitting for a neighbour, I might have a little bit of money, which I hadn't handed over to my mother, so we could afford a full packet of five woodbines. Wow! How rich were we?

FOUNDATIONS FOR DISASTER

Even as a smoker I continued with my keen enjoyment of sport, it did not matter if it was hockey, netball, trampoline, or gymnastics I usually excelled. I'm sure you wouldn't be surprised if I told you my mother went to the school to say I was not to participate in sports, as it was for boys and not girls. I was gutted. Fortunately, I was able to convince the school teacher, who I really liked, to allow me to attend the lessons. At the senior school we had a lot more equipment than at the previous school, and it was here I was to experience throwing the javelin. Yes, I was a natural, probably a result of all the stones we threw when out playing. I won a number of the school competitions and was eventually entered into the area sports, where I continued to excel and reached the county sports.

It was a big deal getting into all the sporting events in the region. Nevertheless, I remember walking home from school with a leaflet that had my name printed on it. I felt so proud, other than our school reports we never got our names in print. I just longed to be able to take it home and show my mother, but I knew this would be expecting too much. I never forgot the feeling, as I tore it into little pieces and watched it blow away in the wind. It was a bit like a part of me blowing away. I later threw the javelin far enough to get into the All England competition, but yes, you have guessed, I would not dare go home and tell my mam. My sporting career story didn't have a happy ending like Billy Elliott, she wouldn't be running up the street shouting, "*She did it, she F……..g did it.*" If she'd known she was more likely to be running me up the street shouting, 'I know what I'll do with you when I catch you.' That was the end of that dream.

  We now also had a three-year-old younger sister, and when my brother reached eleven the council provided us with a three bedroomed house. This was a semi-detached house in the same area. It had a small front garden with five steps leading up to the front door. There was a cherry tree in the centre of the garden and marigolds grew under the window area. Sounds like a fairy-tale house, I don't think so. Around the back of the house was a large uncared for garden, which doubled up as an adventure playground. The hedges, which we could hide in and jump on were huge; there was also quite a large old wooden shed as well. We could be like the lovely children in Enid Blyton's story books. My friend and I could use our old shed as our secret den that would be exciting. Although the down side being it was a grotty old shed. We did once set it on fire while playing, and I got a right hiding. It was not unusual for the cows, from a nearby field, to take a shortcut through our garden, this added to the natural look. It was great if my mother was in a good fettle when I got in from school on sunny days. Sometimes she would sit on the front step and chat with us and be pleasant. I loved my mother being happy; she was actually a warm, interesting, funny woman when she was in good form. Just she wasn't in good form often enough for me.

Well I suppose now at senior school we had to establish some street cred, so the next thing we had to do was play truant, obviously part of being a credible teenager. Playing truant was quite an exciting activity, as we had to find ways to spend our days and avoid getting caught by the adult population. In those days everyone knew everyone else. There would also be times I wanted to make sure my mother was all right without her knowing, so I would sneak back to the house to check on her. Sometimes we would turn up at school for the PE lessons, or even just for our lunch and disappear again. As a result, we spent many a day running over the moors. In the summer we went swimming and diving in the local river. The "school board man" used to often spot us, but he was no match for such accomplished runners. If we did get caught, we usually got the belt across our hands, or detention. This was another learning curve, as I had to master writing with three pens, '*I will not play truant*'. That is, you hold three pens together in your writing hand. You have to space them so that each pen hits the lined paper perfectly and then place them on a gradient. With practice, this becomes so easy, in fact just as easy as writing with one pen! Gosh what a lot we had to learn at school.

Anna, the friend I mentioned before, was what one would call 'rough'. She also came from quite a destructive background; her mother once broke her arm with a sweeping brush and threw her down the stairs more than once. How lucky was I? Anna and I used to practice boxing with one arm behind our backs, so that our stomach muscles would get hard. This was so that when we got hit at home, we would be so tough we would not feel the punches. We had heard this is what boxers do to make their stomach muscles hard, so they don't feel the pain. To any onlooker it would appear that we were preparing at eleven years old for a professional boxing career.

When we were children it was a rare occasion if we ever received presents on our birthdays or Christmas. I remember when it was my first teenage birthday that would make me thirteen! I was so looking forward to it, and thought being thirteen was really special. I was clearly the only one, as it was not even acknowledged, never mind being selfish enough to think I should get a card or a present. I do remember when I was about five years old on Christmas day, my mam said there was a present in the pantry for me on the top shelf. I climbed up all the shelves in the pantry with great agility to find one of those tiny pianos. You know the ones with about twelve keys. I can still remember the delight I felt at getting this present. Years later, as an adult I bought myself a real piano, it did not matter that I lived in a flat and was tone deaf!

Although we never had a holiday in our life, when my mother was in hospital, we were often sent to my auntie's who had eleven children. It was quite some household when the five of us landed on her doorstep. Because there were so many, some of us had to sleep at the top of the bed, and some at the bottom. I always felt so safe and secure at my auntie's. When I arrived, she would usually be sitting by the fire with a baby in her arms. She would look up and say my name, in her beautiful soft voice, "It's Catherine, now here is trouble." My heart would melt with the love I felt for her; I would smile as I crashed through the house to see everyone. There was usually food to eat, she made porridge in a pan as big as a bucket. There might sometimes only have been a loaf of bread and some margarine or even chips, but we did know we would get something to eat. That all too familiar feeling of hunger disappeared when I was there. It did not matter that I probably didn't have a change of clothing, what mattered was the love I felt.

FOUNDATIONS FOR DISASTER

Certainly a very painful experiences during my childhood was when I was told to take my dog to the vet and get him destroyed. I called my dog Blacky after Black Beauty because he was black, with a tip on each paw, and on his nose. I chose him from a litter of mongrel puppies someone was trying to give away. I spent hours house training him and teaching him to do all manner of brilliant tricks. He used to run through the fields with us, with a loyalty surpassing any human being. When Blacky was about four he started barking at the new 'milk woman' and she was frightened to come up the street. That day I am sure he knew he was going to be destroyed. He whined and struggled on the lead all the way to the vet. I was gutted, but given I had promised myself I would never cry again, I did not shed a tear.

Although for years my mother had serious mental health problems, she also started to experience quite serious physical health problems. It was really sad, as when my father discovered my mother was dying from cancer, he told no one; he walked out leaving us to look after her and ourselves. He had already been working away from home for a number of years before this. What we did not know at that time was that he had found himself a new family, which he obviously liked better than ours. My mother struggled to cope with five children and very little money. In those days almost all families had two parents. She also believed strongly that marriage was for ever, so when she found out there was another woman, she struggled with the hurt she felt that he had walked out and left her for someone else. I don't think any of us knew then that my mother had cancer, I don't think she knew herself. In those days, they told the next of kin – my father - but not the person themselves. She was in pain all the time, she went back and forwards to the doctors, they told her, she had an obsession with the doctors and took no notice of her complaints. How insulting was that? Can you imagine going to the doctor because you are really ill and being told, you have an obsession with the doctor?

During this period my mother was swelling up and looked bloated. One day, when the home help was at our house my mam was very ill. The home-help ran to the telephone box, two streets away and called the doctor; when he arrived, he could hardly believe what he saw. The packing, which is used to pack the body during operations, had not been removed after the operation. Obsession indeed!

They had to send her back into hospital to sort out the mess they had made. Needless to say, this caused major problems to her internal organs. I spent many a day travelling to the RVI with my mother as the doctors tried various methods to rectify the problems they had caused. This went on for a few years as the situation got progressively worse. They decided to do another major operation which was very risky, but needed to be done if any progress was to be made to improve her health.

It was during this period of hospitalisation that one of my aunties on my dad's side of the family came to look after us. I liked her, she was pleasant and sang songs. She made our breakfast before school and cooked regular meals. When my mother returned from hospital, she did not look good; I can remember feeling distant from her, she looked very thin and pasty, not like her normal self at all. Needless to say the operation did not improve her health, the hospital visits were now increasing.

The cancer was clearly spreading, and on many an occasion my mother would be crawling around the floor screaming in pain. As children, all we could do was to look on helplessly and watch her suffer. It was quite horrendous listening to her screams of pain. She would say to God, "What have I done God that is so bad that you need to make me suffer like this?" She would pray to die. I hated seeing her in pain and just prayed that God would make her better. While she was in the depth of these experiences we would not dare breathe; playing or laughing would have been the ultimate betrayal of her suffering. The house would fall into a deadly silence, essential to accommodate her agony and provide space for only her cries of pain.

Because of my mother's health problems, she experienced disturbed sleep. During the night she would wake me up every couple of hours to make her a cup of tea. You'd be right in thinking this certainly resulted in me having disturbed sleep too! It was not enough that she woke me up almost every couple of hours for tea - she used to make me get up at five a.m. to go down to the post office sorting office. She sent me down there to collect a letter from my father with her 'housekeeping money' in. Only thing was, most weeks he did not send any money, housekeeping or otherwise. Reluctantly I had to trail through the isolated dark streets, although I really didn't want to go, I wouldn't dare not go. I knew only too well from experience that if a letter came later in the post, she would know I had not been, and I'd get a belting. I knew also if there were no letters at the sorting office, I would get into trouble too, and accused of not going! In this situation she would often send me out again, in case the letter was late in arriving. Yes, you have worked it out, I really couldn't win. I just got used to the craziness.

I did once swear at her when she came into the bedroom to wake me up at 4am. I shouted at her "F... Off," and slammed the bedroom door. When I eventually went down stairs she was in floods of tears, she could not believe that she had a daughter who would swear. What had she done wrong in bringing us up? I won't answer that, as I am sure you would work that out too! In all fairness I really felt so sorry for her, and said I was sorry and would not do it again. I just wanted to make her feel better, as I hated seeing her upset.

During this period going to school was hell. I worried so much about all sorts of things: what she was doing, or whether she would even be alive when I got home. If I was not worrying about that, I would try to think about anything I had done wrong that I would get a hiding for when I got home. I would wonder if there would be any food in the house. On most occasions there would be none or very little. No, I did not worry about getting the highest grades that was the last thing on my mind. It was also guaranteed if my brother got home from school first, he would hit the kids. I hated him doing this, so usually tried to get home before him. Given I was more of a match for him, I could get the focus from the kids and on to me. Although, now he was a lot older and stronger, he had the upper hand and unfortunately I usually came of worst. But what the heck!

Although I am painting a bleak picture of our family life, I need to add that I loved my mother and sisters. I used to pray all the time for God to make my mother better. I always imagined that I would get married to someone with a big house, and my mother and sisters would come and live with me. We would leave my brother where he was and live happily ever after. Well I did say imagine! I know too that she had her work cut out with five kids, and I was not always the best of teenagers.

For instance, one night a gang of us, who usually hung out together, all got on a bus to another town and went to the fairground. We played on the bumpy cars and the other rides My favourite was the waltzer I used to ride this standing up and walking the platform. I did the same on the merry go rounds, often standing on the backs of the animals and riding the side railings. Thank goodness there weren't all the health and safety rules in those days, as that would really have ruined our fun. We had a brilliant time that night. In fact, it was so much fun we all forgot about the time; that is until we realised we had missed the last bus home. The police were soon to pick us off the streets and put us in a police cell until they could arrange to get the eight of us home. Eventually, that is two in the morning, a police van took us home and dropped us off. We were met by a brilliant reception, all of our mothers were standing on the corner of the street waiting. I guess the local police had been contacted and paid a call to all of our mothers.

FOUNDATIONS FOR DISASTER

What a hiding we all got, as we were chased up the street and into our houses. It was a good night though!

By now it was rare that our father ever came home to see us. After my mother discovered he had gone off with another woman she made numerous suicide attempts. That was another reason I had to run home from school or play truant. I had to get home first to make sure she was alright before my siblings got home. More often than not she was far from all right. For instance, I would arrive home to find the house full of gas fumes, as she lay unconscious on the floor by the cooker. Other times she would overdose on her medication and be unconscious. She was no light weight, which made it very difficult to try to help her from where she had fallen to some more respectable position before anyone came home. She did end up in hospital several times, as these episodes were now frequent occurrences. I think the pain she felt on every level was just too hard to bear; that is the emotional pain of my father leaving her for another woman and the physical pain she was now experiencing night and day with the cancer.

On one occasion my mother took me with her when she decided to pay my father a visit and confront him with regard to what she should do with us children. We took a train, my first ever train ride, to the place he was working. I remember standing there when my mother asked him, "What will I do with the bairns?" In his patronising uncaring voice he said, "Put them in a home." Those words rang loud and clear in my ears. My father did not care about us at all. I suppose, there was until then a part of me that so wanted him to be at home to help the situation. It was like he was rejecting a faulty ornament, not his five children. And he said this with no shame or guilt, as I stood there looking at him with hope in my eyes. This registered big for me, not to say I carried a grudge, but I did. Many years later when my father was very ill, I was able to say the same thing back, when the doctor said, "What will we do with your father? I said, "Put him in a home." I felt good saying it, I thought if you wait long enough what goes around comes around. Nevertheless, I couldn't and didn't put him in a home. I was just pleased I had my moment. Now in all fairness to my mother she would never have put us in a home. Although I am sure she felt like it at times when we were all giving her grief and fighting with one another.

The older I was getting the worse my behaviour was becoming. You know how they say we get wiser with age, well I certainly didn't. At school I was playing truant, fighting, swearing, smoking and always in trouble. I spent more time in the head master's office than in the classroom. I was certainly building a reputation; but it was not for being a studious, sweet fifteen-year-old. We once put glue from the science lab, all down the school handrails and waited until the bell went. Ugh! If I got caught smoking, I would blatantly stand and admit it, whereas all the other kids in the school would deny it. When I left school at fifteen, they were pleased to see the back of me, although I got a good reference. Yes, you did read that right, I got a good reference. They said that although I got into trouble, I was always honest and admitted what I had done without denying my misdemeanours. As a result of the reference I got a job with my friends in the hotel trade. This was great fun, we had many an all-night party. I now had constant access to alcohol and made the most of it. I was always drunk and went to all the dances. I was now also hanging out with older women whom my mother classed as 'whores', I thought they were great. In the hotel where I worked, I was sacked every weekend for being drunk, and every Monday someone would come knocking on my door, "Catherine, a've been sent tu see if yu cumin back." "Aye am cumin a'll be there in a jiffy." I would screech. I did enjoy my work; it was just so tempting when we worked on the functions with sherry on arrival not to drink all the sherry that was left over. This meant before they started the wedding, I was usually drunk. I remember someone years later coming to see me breaking her heart. "I've been sacked," she sobbed, "I've been sacked." The shame and humiliation were overwhelming for her. "Oh pet," I said, "When I was your age

FOUNDATIONS FOR DISASTER

I was sacked every weekend." Her pain dissolved quickly as we giggled and laughed at the outrageousness of the situation. She certainly left in a far better place than she entered.

When I was sixteen, I was frequenting the local bars a lot, as well as going to the town hall dances and the occasional night club. I was now old enough to buy my own clothes and had grown into quite a trend setter, moving myself away from that poverty stricken look endowed on us during our childhood. Believe it or not, but I tried to encourage my mother to join us and start getting a life. I was concerned that she sat at home every night of the week watching the kids. However, she was from the 'old school' and thought a woman drinking in bars was a disgrace. Eventually, with the power of persuasion she agreed to go out to a night club with us. It was quite a distance from home that is all of twenty-five miles! Commuting in the 60s was not quite the same as today. My mother knew all the other women who were going, as the majority were a bit older than me and they often popped in to see her. She had her hair done at the hairdressers and got dressed up for the occasion. She looked fabulous and wore a lovely dress. (She seldom wore trousers.) Whenever I wore my jeans she'd say, "It's not ladylike to wear trousers." Like I gave a dot!

In the nightclub we were all drinking heavily, that is except my mother! I tried to encourage her to join in the spirit, but that would have been far too optimistic. She thought it was appalling that these women were drinking and flirting with men. How bad does it get? It's just as well she wasn't born into today's society. My mother was not used to bars, never mind night-clubs. On the very rare occasion when she went out, the most she drank was a tia maria or a port and lemon. At the end of the night I said, "Come on mam we can get a lift home with Edith's friend." She grabbed me by the hair swung me around and said, "We will do no such thing; I do not associate with women like that." She dragged me to a taxi and paid a week's housekeeping money for the taxi fare home. I was not top of the popularity list for a while I'll tell you that.

As I had now left school and was working and staying in the local hotel I was out partying most nights. One night we went to a dance about eight miles from home. I loved drinking and dancing. At the end of the night we rang the local policeman up, from the phone box, to ask if he would come and take us home - he fancied one of my friends and she knew it. As you can imagine he was only too pleased to come to collect us and dropped us off outside the hotel. We'd left the window off the latch so that we could get in when we got home. Someone saw us climbing in through the window and contacted the police, that is the same policeman who had dropped us off. He knew it was us, but had to be seen to be doing something, he told us the next day. Lucky us.

This was a period when my mother was going through a good spell and things were looking up. Our house was always full of visitors, usually the local women would pop in for a cuppa and chat. Yes, when my mother was in good form our house seemed a good place to hold the local drop in centre. Although sometimes we did not have the money for the gas or food, she would boil the kettle on the coal fire, producing a steady stream of tea for anyone and everyone who called in. I know, given the stories I tell that she might sound like as awful mother, but she was probably no worse than most of the other mothers in our community during that era.

So, in any case, I was at work when I got a message to go and see her. I was seventeen and sat on the side of her bed, as she said in a very serious voice, "Hen I've had the death knock." "Oh mam." I said, knowing by the sound of her voice what she meant, "Don't worry I will go and give it to Mrs Howe across the road." Yes you guessed, I didn't like the woman across the road. "No hen," she said, "This is serious, a'm gona die." "Mam I will give it to Mrs Howe, and she will die instead." Yes, we did call older adults by their salutation Mr, Mrs or Miss and their surname. My mam continued to insist there was nothing I could do, and she would die soon. I was having none of it, and to be fair, I really wasn't taking her too seriously. I just thought she was probably going through another difficult spell. "Stop worrying I will go and do it now, you can watch out the window." I said, as I tried to calm her down. I went out and gave the death knock to the neighbour. I don't think my mam was too convinced, but she settled down a bit as I reassured her she would be all right.

  Nevertheless, a couple of days later I was going out to meet my boyfriend; I told her I would be staying at his house and wouldn't be home that night. She was in good spirits, lying on the settee. She waved, "A'll see yu the morrow hen." They were the last words she ever spoke to me. She was only forty years old when she died. I will never forget the next morning when two of my friends arrived at my boyfriend's house on the first bus to tell me my mother was dead. I just went numb, I got on the next bus home with my friends and hardly spoke. When I arrived home, our house felt like a morgue, my mother's brothers were arriving and beginning to take control. We all went to see my mother in the Chapel of Rest; that was the first dead body I had ever seen. My mother looked at peace. My youngest sister was only eight and not allowed to go to the Chapel of Rest, as my uncles said it was not the place for young children. I told her, "Mam loved us so much that she wanted to see everything we did, so she went to heaven to get a better view." I also went on and explained, "She was in an awful lot of pain on earth, and now all her pain had ended." The crazy thing was, in many ways I thought my mother was a good mother. O gosh I'm crying buckets. In fact, it was not until I had years of psychotherapy that I realised, that perhaps she had a few shortcomings!

As the funeral cars drove through the streets all the men stopped and took their hats off and the women stopped and watched the cortege as it passed. It was as if the whole town came to a standstill to show their respects. Everyone I knew and did not know said how sorry they were to hear about my mother's death. I think they were aware there were five children left on their own. I rather stupidly prided myself on the fact that I was determined not to cry. I was still holding that promise I had made to myself when I was seven. I also thought it would be wrong to cry at her funeral, because I had to show my sisters that I could cope with her death. In my head I was thinking, 'Well if I don't cry for my mother's death, I will never cry for anyone's death, as long as I live.' It was amazing the messages I told myself which I always believed I had to carry through.

My father's sister, the one who I said I liked, who came to look after us when my mother was in hospital, reminded me that she called at the house to see if there was anything the family could do to help with my mam's funeral. I told her there was nothing she could do, and we did not want her or any of their family at the funeral. Because of the pain my mother felt when my father had left us; my mam did not have a good word to say about him or his family. I was also aware that there would probably be bad feelings between my father's and my mother's family, as they were sure to blame my father for her death. My auntie had offered to prepare the tea, and make sure there were plenty of cups, plates, food etc. I impolitely told her to get lost with a few swear words scattered throughout my colourful bombardment of verbal abuse. We needed nothing from her or any of her family. She did tell me I was a very forceful character to deal with at that time in my life. I think that was an understatement, to be fair she must have been blessed with a very understanding nature.

Apparently, my father did come back to the house a few weeks after the funeral and spoke to my brother saying, "I will come back if you allow me to bring the woman I am living with, and her two children with me." My brother told him to leave without consulting any of us. That was the last thing we heard about my father for many years. In fact, when people asked about him, I just said he was dead; as that was easier than saying he did not want us, and as far as I knew he could have been dead.

FOUNDATIONS FOR DISASTER

I hit the drink heavier after my mother's death; I was a very angry person. I looked at older women and wondered why they did not die instead of my mother. There was an old woman who lived across the road from us; she used to burst our balls if they went into her garden. She had no family and I really did think she should have died instead of my mother. Yes, it was her who I gave the 'death knock' to. I was now furious with God. How could he let my mother die when she had five children? I swore, I would never be like my mother; a good woman who devoted her life to looking after her children. I had learned an important lesson. If you are good God makes you suffer and kills you prematurely. If he was going to kill me then I would make sure I had a good time before he did.

We were all now left without any parents around. My brother worked down the pit, and believed his wages were his own, to be spent solely on himself. I was a hotel waitress and earned about £4 a week, plus tips. For weeks I was unable to get any money to keep my sisters in food and clothing. Because my mother was dead, all the money even the family allowance was stopped. All the benefit departments said we were not entitled to any money because no one was in charge; there were no parents or guardians to claim the benefit. Officially, I was too young. To add to this my father had stopped sending any payments. At the time I was wearing a pair of shoes which had no soles, the top looked fine! We had very little food, or anything else for that matter. My brother was certainly not prepared to spend any of his money on helping towards feeding the kids. After weeks of trying to sort out some financial help, I shouted at the benefits officer: "My father has worked all his life and paid tax. My brother and I are working, but we can't afford to keep a house and my sisters with our wages." The man I was dealing with had a reputation for being a mean, stingy, hardnosed sod, who thought the money he was expected to organise for a payment was coming out of his own pocket. I did politely tell him this too. I was eventually able to organise a payment through the social services.

My very spoilt brother did not have a personality transformation after my mother's death. He continued to be extremely wicked both psychologically and physically. His friend, who worked in the butcher's used to regularly give him a big bag of steak. He would make one of us cook the steak, and then make us sit lined up on the settee while we watched him eating it. He would sit there slurping saying, "Watch me eat this delicious succulent steak." He would hold it up to his mouth and put it in very slowly so that we would watch in slow motion. He knew that the kids would have very little or nothing to eat for days unless they were at school. He often beat my sisters quite badly; I was always a mass of bruising from his thumps and kicks. He would often hold my arm up my back, twisting it so that the pain was shooting right through me. He would shout at me, "Say give in." Even if he had twisted my arm off, I would never give in. He would come in from the pub at all hours in the morning and make us get out of bed to cook his supper and listen to him drawling on about the latest film he'd seen, usually Clint Eastwood and a 'Fistful of Dollars or A Few Dollars More'.

I got pregnant not long after my mother died and he threatened to, "Kick the illegitimate b….. out of my stomach." which I had no doubt he would do. In order to protect my unborn baby, I stayed with an auntie and uncle who had one child, a son, Graham who was a few years younger than me. He was a great kid, quite a jack the lad who loved sport and football. He was also blessed with a very interesting and entertaining personality, telling stories about his escapades with all the drama that any gifted story teller would envy. When my mam was alive, she often looked after him, and never passed him on the street without giving him 'thrupence' that was three old pennies. While at my auntie's there was no shouting or fighting; that was a bonus, to not be going home to wait on the next beating. Nevertheless, because money was scarce, I had to hand over most of my earnings for board and lodgings. I also had to wait until Graham came in from school before I was allowed to put a match to the fire. That was one cold winter given my son was born in the March. My auntie also brought the tea home with her after work, so other than a sack of potatoes there was no food in the house through the day. When I went into labour I almost died; I had eclampsia and my son was born with forceps. I did not see him for a couple of days after he was born, as I was unconscious. The same doctor who brought me into the world also delivered my son. He said, "I have not seen a body as malnourished as yours since during the war." I think that about sums up the level of malnutrition I experienced.

It was difficult caring for my baby son David at my auntie's house, as my uncle, who was now getting on a bit, found having a tiny baby in the house hard to cope with. My auntie also used to say, it was like living with the Mafia, as my friends were always at the door looking for me, especially if there was any trouble they wanted help with. I was in my glory helping out whenever I could. Nevertheless, I decided to move back home with my own family. My brother actually loved my son, he would tell me I could go out and he would babysit. He looked after David with a real gentleness. Oddly enough, they shared the same birthday. I was obsessed with making sure David was well fed from the beginning, I promised myself that he would never go hungry; I would buy best steak for him and put it through the food blender. I prided myself in turning him out really clean and well dressed. I was trying to give him the life I wished I'd had.

When David was about twelve months old, I'd be just turned nineteen, I married his dad. We had a lovely house in Rothbury which was provided by his employers. (It was up for sale not long ago at three quarters of a million pounds.) I worked so hard to make it really nice; I decorated most of the rooms and bought really good furniture. The first chair I bought was a rocking chair which I enjoyed playing on. I bought a lot of ornaments of horses. I loved horses I thought they were so beautiful. As a child I always imagined having my own horse; we could keep it in our garden, there was plenty of room there. I would clean and feed it, after which I would gallop around the streets and through the fields, the envy of every child in the neighbourhood. Sadly, this was a figment of my imagination rather than a reality. Wouldn't it have been great if it was a reality?

It was around this time when one of my sisters went missing off the face of the planet and a nationwide search was unable to find her. But I will tell you more about this story in the last chapter on miracles. By now the only two left in the family home were my brother and youngest sister, who I knew was having a terrible life. He was beating her regularly and there was seldom food in the house that she could eat. Although she did spend a lot of time staying with me, she had to return home for school. I also knew it was no good trying to take her to live with me, as my brother would have been on the doorstep fighting and I mean physically fighting to get her back. Not because he cared about her, but because money was going into the house to keep her. You would probably guess that it certainly was not being spent on her.

Fortunately, I got to know a teacher from her school who I was able to liaise with. I told the teacher what was going on at home for my sister and how difficult things were. I explained how useless it would be to take her in with me, not because I did not want to, but because it would only add petrol to the fire. Without my brother knowing, we were able to arrange for my sister to be given a place at a boarding school outside of the area. When she was taken into the boarding school, she had serious malnutrition. They had to feed her on special food and extra vitamins for three years until her body recovered. There was no one left at home now and my brother went to live in London where he stayed until he died in 2000.

During my short lived married life, I worked part time as a waitress and barmaid at a hotel not far from where I was living. When I went for the interview the German woman, who owned the hotel asked, "Are you the person who called me a money grabbing murdering b…..?" I did not think there was any point in lying to her, so I said, "Yes I am." She had recognised me from one of my drunken visits to the town, with quite a crowd of my equally inebriated friends. Nevertheless, she still gave me the job, because I told the truth. Well done me, I was still living my life according to my reference. That is, getting into all types of trouble and having the audacity to blatantly admit that I had done what I was accused of doing. I must admit I was very proud of my honesty, pity about my behaviour!

I enjoyed working in this hotel and stayed there for about two years. After I finished waiting on in the dining room, I would go to the bar and serve drinks. I was always rotten drunk by the time I had finished the shift. I did not feel happy with my marriage even though I do not think my husband was to blame for this. He seemed settled and responsible; I seemed unsettled and irresponsible. We could not agree on child rearing practices. If David was not well, he would not allow him to be cared for in our bedroom. My son's bedroom must have been twenty-five feet by twenty-five; it was a huge room; his cot looked dwarfed standing in the corner.

One night, David was unwell, he was only about fifteen months old, and had not developed the art of speech yet. I went to bring him into our bedroom to comfort him and my husband said children should not be in the bedroom with adults. That was just a start of the disagreements. Every time I came home from work trouble would erupt. David would reach out to be cuddled by me, and my husband would smack his hand. I would shout at my husband to leave him alone. On one occasion I got home when they were having their Sunday dinner, my sister was there. As David reached up for me to pick him out of the high chair, where he was eating his dinner, my husband took his little knuckles and rattled them on the chair side and said, "Eat your dinner." I picked my husband's plate of food from the table and threw the whole lot over the top of him, as I said, "Eat your f...... dinner as well." Some of my family and friends thought I was totally unreasonable because I would not allow anyone to smack my son. If anyone hit him, I would lash out at them. I came home one day, and my husband had put David in the bedroom with the curtains shut, making it dark, because he had been naughty. How naughty can a child under two get? I walked into the dark bedroom, picked him up from the bed as he sat sobbing, walked back into the sitting room, took my foot and kicked my husband right between the legs. I then ran out of the house, got on a bus back to my home town and never went back. That was the end of that marriage for quite some time.

WOULD I EVER ESCAPE?

When I left my husband and my job in the hotel I had nowhere to go. What would life hold for me now in the early 70s, as a single woman with a young toddler to raise? I got a job at the Royal Station Hotel in Newcastle and found a registered child minder to look after David until I could sort out some accommodation.

I saw an advert for hotel accommodation at a very reasonable price and thought this would keep me off the streets until I found somewhere to stay for the two of us. I booked into the hotel believing it was like the hotels in the town where I grew up, which were clean and 'respectable'. That night I left the hotel and went to work. When I returned after my evening shift it was about 11p.m. As I entered the foyer I was met by a large, bleach blond haired woman, obviously the gang leader of the group of inebriated riffraff who were sitting around the foyer. She shouted at me in her ruff, drunken, uneducated voice, "Yu sleepin wi him the night" as she pointed to a beady eyed man with her glass of beer. In the middle of the table were bottles of Brown Ale, cider, Guinness and other drinks. I conjured up enough courage to say in a threatening voice, "And who is going to make me?" "Us" she said in a drunken slur. "It will take more than you lot." I said in a strong threatening voice. I warned them that no one would dare to bother me that night. Deep down I was bricking it! Remember this is my first experience of the sleazy side of city life.

When I got up to the room it was evident the door had been kicked in on numerous occasions. The wooden panels were all splintered and the lock area badly twisted. I pulled the bed in front of the door, and jammed it so that if anyone did try to come in they would have had to completely break the door down. Needless to say, I was quite worried that night. Nevertheless, I did sleep and no one bothered me. I was pleased with myself, because I had obviously come across strong enough to back this rabble off. At this time in my life I was hot tempered, and if I was crossed my eyes immediately changed to something more like a wild animal than a human being.   When I went to work that morning I told the manager at the Royal Station Hotel about my ordeal, and they quickly got me a room in the hotel. I enjoyed working in the hotel; the majority of the staff drank and went to night clubs after their shift finished. They struggled to convince me that it would be a good idea to join them, about all of five seconds. I was soon drinking and nightclubbing almost every night. Sometimes I was so drunk that it was impossible to wake me up. Yes, I would fall into a deep unconscious stupor rather than a deep peaceful sleep.

WOULD I EVER ESCAPE?

Fortunately for David it was not too long before I was provided with some accommodation from a housing association. This was a one roomed apartment with a shared bathroom and toilet in Newcastle. In one of the upstairs apartments, a fourteen year old girl lived with her grandmother. Her mother was dead; it was never clear if she had been murdered or if it was suicide. The girl called Susan was tall and well-made, she was a breath of fresh air, and frequently knocked on my door to see if I needed a baby sitter. I usually allowed her to look after David while I went out. Shortly after meeting her I gradually got to know the rest of her very large family. One of her uncles, called Jeff, asked me out. I accepted and we agreed that he would call down for me on his way out that evening, while his niece babysat. He arrived hours later than agreed; I was getting quite wound up waiting on him. Little did I know then that this was going to be how my life would be for the next fourteen years. Although my childhood was dire, the next fourteen years with this man were worse. He was ten years older than me, and took advantage of my naivety. I even believed that in a fight it was not fair to cheat; that is, I had to fight fair with my hands. Needless to say I didn't have a chance, he was almost 6ft and 14 stone. I weighed in at 5ft 1inch and 8stone. The odds once again stacked against me.

WOULD I EVER ESCAPE?

Shortly after we met we were invited to a function at the Mayfair in Newcastle. While at this event I lost contact with him, and as I couldn't find him I decided to make my way home. When I returned to his mother's flat he was waiting. He called me all the sluts and accused me of meeting someone else and having sex with him. He punched me in the face and chased me out of his mother's house. I went to my own apartment downstairs. I locked the door and swore to myself that I would never have anything more to do with him, or any man who ever hit me.

It was about 10 am the next day when he came knocking at my door. I refused to open it and said I wanted nothing more to do with him. I heard a thud, then another. Gosh he was kicking the door in, I was terrified. He burst into my flat and beat me up quite badly. He said, "*If you go to the police they cannot give you twenty four-hour protection. I will find you and make such a mess of your face that no one will ever look at you again.*" This man was frightening. He said he was going for a pint and would be back, a bit like Arnold Schwarzenegger. I was in a terrible state and too frightened to contact the police. He was right, they could not give me 24 four hour protection. He came back hours later than expected, and just behaved as though he had a right to live in my apartment and for me to be providing for him.

WOULD I EVER ESCAPE?

What had I got into? This question never entered my mind. I did not know the meaning of reflection. Not only was the action not in my repertoire of behaviour, the word was not in my vocabulary. It was just a complete rebound from my childhood, the only skills I had were for survival, which consisted of going from one catastrophe to another. Although I was already quite a heavy drinker I started to drink heavier. If he was out I would mix Brown Ale and Old English cider to make snake-bites, drinking this concoction until my mind was dull or obliterated. This was one sure way to avoid feeling the punches and kicks he would throw when he eventually returned from his night out. Many a time I would be unconscious before he got back, and if not I would try to pretend I was sleeping. I learned to sleep on my stomach to protect my face from the blows. Sometimes I tried to fight him back, but I was no challenge for him. After the first time this man hit me I did say to him, "You might have got away with that, but let me tell you, if you ever harm a hair on my son's head I swear I will leave you for dead." All the years I was with this man he never smacked or hit David. I think he knew that what I had said was no idle threat.

When I met Jeff I was still working at the Royal Station Hotel in Newcastle. He would repeatedly accuse me of having sex with the men in the hotel. I was naive and spent most of my time trying to defend myself. 'Whatever' or 'take a hike' were not words in my vocabulary at the time, but if they had been they would have been an ideal response for the jealous psychopath. Or better still I should have picked up a cricket bat and done to him what he threatened to do to me. Never mind this wasn't to be, hindsight is a fine thing, but like reflection it was not in my repertoire of behaviours. I felt trapped and violated in this relationship, with no escape. I now felt owned, a piece of someone's property to use and knock around. I had to work to give him money. One day he beat me up so badly that I was unrecognisable. I looked more oriental than English. My eyes were black and blue and so swollen they just looked like small slits. Whenever he hit me he would not let me out of the house to get medical attention. On one occasion I invited my auntie and uncle through for the weekend. I took them to some of bars I was drinking in. Although my auntie had lived in London for years, she had never seen bars like these. That night the locals were talking to the pictures on the wall, and to top the lot there were several fights. I learned later that my auntie went home and cried for two weeks after her visit.

My son attended a local nursery in Newcastle, fortunately in some strange way he was sheltered from most of the violence and aggression. Although it was impossible to protect him from all of the fights. On one occasion when he was staying at

WOULD I EVER ESCAPE?

Jeff's sisters' he heard us coming in from the bar. The snow was lying thick on the ground, Jeff and I started to fight. He punched me in the face and knocked me over the neighbour's wall. David was only four years old; he ran at Jeff with his fists flying, crying, "I hate you, I hate you." David was a quiet, gentle soul and from ever I can remember people would say, "If the world was full of David's we would have a really good world." I know you are probably thinking that he should never have been subjected to these experiences in the first place, and I totally agree. My dream for our ideal lifestyle had certainly been absolutely shattered.

The whole culture I was now involved with was one of violence and petty crime. Saying that, there was also a feeling of belonging; everyone knew everyone and in the bars where I was drinking there was a close community. Nevertheless I watched many a horror story where people were seriously hurt, and sometimes scarred and maimed for life. One night we were in a bar on Shields Road when a fight started between a married couple. The man left the bar to returned ten minutes later. He took a brown ale bottle from the counter, smashed it and rammed it straight in the woman's face. The blood was pouring everywhere. Jeff told me to stay at the bar and not to interfere or I would be the next one to get it. During this period, if I was not at work. I would drink night and day the same as him. I would take my son to nursery in the mornings, and would join him in some bar and just drink. Often on the way home from the bar he would call at the betting shop. He would ask me for all the money I had, and begin to gamble it away. Many times we were left without a penny, but I would always have a way of getting food; my son would never go hungry. Jeff would always find a way to get his drink money for that night. I would realise days or weeks later that he had sold something from the house. Usually someone would come up and say, "Oh that thing that you sold us is great." I would be surprised, as I had sold them nothing. Jeff would tell someone that I was selling some of my belongings from the house to get the money for his drink. He was a compulsive liar, time and time again I would find things out through other people. I never failed to be confused as to why someone might lie repeatedly. What an unshakable, foolish, faith I had in human nature.

We eventually moved to Scotland beside some of his family. I thought things might improve. I had to be the eternal optimist! Do I need to tell you there was no change? We stayed with his auntie on his father side, she thought he could do no wrong. She would hear the fights going on between us and never interfere. These were the days when women were not really protected by the law, and often the police would not interfere in domestic violence. A marriage was considered private for the couple to sort out themselves. He kept up his torrent of violent, physical and verbal attacks on me. He never stopped making accusation that I was having sex with anyone and everyone. On reflection many years later, it was obvious that he used this method of violent bullying, controlling behaviour to camouflage his insecure, cowardly personality. One day I was on a bus with him, I swept my long dark hair out of my eyes with my hand. He waited until we got home then accused me of waving to an ex-boyfriend. Would you be surprised if I said that was just another excuse to kick me all over? It was these experiences that made me really appreciate how lovely my mother was!

One night when we were fighting he punched me in the face and hurt my arm. The next day I went to the hospital thinking I had broken my arm, as it was really sore. The doctor asked me to move my arm in various directions which I did. He eventually said, "Your arm is not broken, but your jaw is." It is amazing how a more severe pain overrides a lesser pain. "No" I said, "It's me arm." thinking the doctor was stupid. Alas, he had hit me so hard in the mouth that my jaw was all broken. When asked how this had happened, I had to say, "I fell and hit my face on the edge of a pavement." Once again I knew only too well the consequences if I told the authorities what really happened. I was told in no uncertain terms that this injury was not caused by a fall on the pavement, and would more likely to have been caused by a very hard punch in the face. I was admitted to hospital, as the break needed an operation and I was unable to eat anything except strained food. I could only open my mouth a tiny bit, and if by accident I tried to open it too far the pain was excruciating, shooting right through me.

Another day when we were fighting he put all my clothes up the chimney and covered them in soot. I did just as well, I soaked his every possession in a bath of water with everything I could find in the bathroom. That included the bleach, vim, toothpaste, perfume, and anything else I could lay my hands on. Sometimes I could laugh when I looked back at the shenanigans. To be fair it was not all doom and gloom, although the good times were few and far between. Without a doubt he was the embodiment of misery, other than when he was holding the bar up. In this environment he was always the life and soul of the party. Everyone thought he was such a good bloke, a fun loving jack the lad. That is those who didn't live with him held this opinion. You will have guessed by now it is not the opinion I held of him.

On numerous occasions I ended up with nowhere to live, and was not unfamiliar with the procedure for applying for homeless accommodation. Sometimes the violence was so bad I could not go home. One night after we had been out drinking, and he'd started to fight I had climbed into an old car in a scrap yard to get away from him. That was fine until I woke up the next morning with a German Shepherd barking. I don't know yet how I got in there, but believe me I didn't dally on my way out or I would have ended up as breakfast for Fido. Another time I slept in the cemetery – well in the church doorway as I guessed that would probably be the safest place to be, as I did not imagine anyone would go there. This time I woke up to the sun shining. My luck was in!

Would you be surprised if I told you that eventually my health started to deteriorate? I went down to six stone in weight and began to go psychotic. I was having a complete breakdown. During this period David and I were staying with a family member in Scotland. I had lost touch altogether with reality. I found myself standing in a job centre just looking at the jobs board unable to read any of the words. Everything in my brain just seemed completely muddled up. When I tried to speak the words would not come out my mouth. I was hallucinating and imagined this man doing me all sorts of harm. Perhaps I wasn't imagining this! My brain had gone into a state of fear and shock. I did eventually get home and spent the night wondering around talking out loud without any idea of what I was saying or doing. Eventually they telephoned a doctor and sent for an ambulance.

They took me by force to a psychiatric hospital in Ayrshire. This was one of the biggest fears of my life; my nightmare was now happening. This hospital had all the echoes of my childhood when they locked my mother up in the psychiatric hospital. I had to escape. Not long after being admitted I was walking along a corridor on the second floor when I spotted a heavy table lamp. I picked it up and smashed it as hard as I could through the window. As the glass fell to the ground I followed it. Unfortunately I split my foot wide open and fractured my ankle. Still determined to escape I crawled around the grounds looking desperately for an escape route leaving a trail of blood as I went. Drat my luck was out, a hospital grounds man found me, and I was taken back to a ward. I lay for days with my foot three times its normal size. I was unable to stand because of the pain and practically crawled everywhere. It was days later when my sister arrived. As she walked into the room she looked with horror, as I lay with my leg up on a bed unable to put on any socks or shoes. She asked if they had taken me to a general hospital for an x-ray. She was furious when I told her in my slow, slurred, drugged up voice that no one had done anything. She demanded that they get me to a hospital immediately for an x-ray. After her intervention I was taken to a general hospital and my ankle, which was fractured was put in plasters. I was escorted back to the psychiatric hospital with a pair of crutches. I was held against my will in this hospital for months, with no more contact with my family. These were the longest months in my life.

Because the hospital was very difficult to get to, and most of my family lived in the North East of England I had no way of knowing what was going on. I was told nothing about my son or my family. I felt completely alone and cut off from the world. I also had none of my own personal belongings whatsoever with me, nor did I have any access to any money. Because of my frequent attempts to escape I was sectioned under the Mental Health Act. This meant they would not let me out of the hospital and could treat me against my will. They forced me to take medication which made my head feel as if it was in a cage. This certainly left me with a 'real' understanding of what people meant by chemical cosh. I discovered first hand that they did not need to hit me over the head with a truncheon in order to reduce me to a comatose state. They also used an electrophysiological monitoring method to record the electrical activity of my brain. I remember trying so hard to make my brain respond to indicate that it was perfectly normal in the hope that they would let me out. Fat chance! My brain couldn't operate normally under the ridiculous doses of medication they were forcing down my throat. While in this hospital the staff performed their obligatory duties in a very sterile, clinical fashion. There was certainly no warmth or the guardian angels we consider nurses to be.

I was desperate to get out of this place and made numerous attempts to escape. I must also have asked umpteen times to be released only to be constantly ignored. On one occasion they sent for a psychiatrist or psychologist I don't know which. This woman sat behind her desk asking question about my life; I must have made a face a couple of times when I answered her. At the end of the interview she said in her cold, patronising voice, "You were making faces when you spoke." Now remember I am very vulnerable, and trying to give my best impression so that they will allow me to go home. (To be fair, I don't think I had a home at this time in my life, but the streets would have been a better option than this hospital). I said in a quiet voice, "I thought everyone made faces when they talked." My best impression obviously did not impress her. Yes, she was going to keep me in this God forsaken place. I still do make faces when I am talking. In fact I had a brilliant recent one while talking on a TV programme, but I would not think this is an indicator of my sanity. If it is then I should be locked-up again along with everyone I know.

While I was there they admitted a young woman who had been using drugs and was in a terrible state. The hospital staff treated her appallingly, as I think she had a somewhat colourful background. These were the days when they looked down on you if you had an undesirable reputation. Personally, I thought she oozed personality and character. She came to me one day and said, "Catherine can I borrow your crutches?" "Yes" I said unwittingly. She took my crutch and started to smash the place up. She put nearly all the windows out, and smashed the furniture up. Needless to say a number of the staff eventually brought her to the ground. They must have injected her with massive amounts of drugs, as she was soon unconscious. No one saw her for weeks, and when we did she looked like a zombie, dribbling down the side of her mouth, with a vacant expression in her eyes, without a semblance of a human being. My heart sinks at the thought of what they did to such a free spirit.

I continued to make numerous attempts to escape, but because the hospital was in a rural setting it made my attempts so much more difficult. I would find some way to get out of the hospital grounds; and when I thought it was safe I would start to hitchhike along the road. A car would eventually stop and I would jump in delighted with myself. "Yes I'm free." The car would turn around and take me straight back to the hospital; I think the staff patrolled the highways looking for escapees. That's when you know your luck is out.

While in the hospital the drugs they gave me stopped me having dreams. Prior to going into the hospital I used to suffer from horrendous nightmares; I would wake up through the night, screaming and screaming. Sometimes I was being chased, or sometimes terrible things were happening. I would sit bolt upright and be unable to settle down again. Nevertheless, I still very much missed my dreams, and wondered how much damage the medication they poured down my throat had done to my brain.

I was beginning to think that I was never going to be released from this hospital. You know the stories you hear about young women being placed in these places because they had an illegitimate child? Well I was really beginning to think this is what had happened. I had not heard from anyone for months. I was just imprisoned in this hospital without a personal belonging in the world, and no way of contacting anyone I knew. I would reach my 60s and be completely institutionalised; and devoid a personality. This hospital so reminded me of those early childhood memories when they incarcerated my mam. I had to find a way to escape.

WOULD I EVER ESCAPE?

Eventually they decided I was well enough to be allowed out of the hospital for the weekend. How charitable! They provided me with enough medication to last the weekend and I had to return on the Monday. They gave me a bus pass for the journey from and back to the hospital as I had no money. I went to where my son was staying with family; they had been informed I was out for the weekend. During the weekend, I threw the medication down the sink, took my son for a walk and never went back. I hitchhiked over two hundred miles down through Glasgow and back to Northumberland. On my way through Glasgow I encountered a gang of Glaswegian teenagers. They asked why I was hitchhiking with a little boy. Of course I didn't tell them I'd just escaped from the mental hospital. Can you imagine it? Nevertheless, the few shillings they had they tried to force me to take to help with my journey. Now although I wouldn't take their money, they certainly left their mark in my heart. To be fair, at that time in my life I did not have much of a heart! When I got back to the North East I stayed for a few days with an auntie, before going back to live with my husband. We lived in a farmhouse surrounded by the Cheviot Hills. A few months ago I went back to see this cottage and stood spellbound by the beautiful surroundings. Surroundings which all the time I lived there I could not see. I never once noticed this amazing scenery. That is just an indicator of where my head was at during this period.

WOULD I EVER ESCAPE?

We had a couple of neighbours who lived in the farm cottage next door; they were young and good fun. I learned quite a bit about country life while living there. Sometimes the farmhands had to control the rabbit population which meant going out late at night with a shotgun. When the headlights from the car or the powerful torch lights fell on the rabbits they would freeze, and become easy targets for the rifle. One day my son came running home to tell me all the cows were marching down our driveway, they had escaped from the field. It was amazing watching cows jump back over the fences when the tractor rounded them up. Sometimes I would go out on the farm and drive the tractor with my husband to plough the fields. We made the big straw bales when the hay was being harvested. David was five years old now and had started school. He got his first bike with stabilisers on, and I remember the feeling of pride when I removed the stabilisers and he rode a two wheeler bike for the first time.

The thing I liked most on the farm was watching the calves being born, they looked quite cute and within minutes of being born they could stand up and suckle. Once, when a pheasant had been killed by a tractor we found the eggs she had laid. We built an incubator with some sacking and a low heat, a few days later the chicks began to hatch as we held them in our hands. During this period I used to cook some great meals. My neighbours thought my cooking was fabulous - I would make the best ever soups, broth, dinners, home-made quiches and bacon and egg flans. Family and friends would come miles just to enjoy my food.

I told no one what had happened to me in Scotland, not even my husband. I was so ashamed, and frightened of being caught that for the next twelve years I kept my ordeal a close secret. I also thought I would be on a missing person's file; which meant the police would be looking for me to return me to that God forsaken place. This seriously affected what I did, as the experience had really knocked my confidence and also left me doubting my sanity. That was due to their reluctance to allow me to live back in the community. One thing I did do was pray earnestly every day and night that I would never go through anything like that again as long as I lived. I could now understand what my mother meant when she talked about the horrors of mental illness.

Nevertheless, although our life style was quite good everything was not working out in our relationship. As a result of our differences my reunion with my husband did not last very long; although we did not fall out we agreed to separate again. My time in the area did last long enough to establish myself, and get a two bedroomed house in a lovely village near Berwick. In my new house on the outskirts of the village pheasants used to walk passed the door in the morning. When I walked up the street everyone would almost sing, "Good morning". This was such a contrast to what I was used to. My immediate neighbours had bought their council house and the majority of residents were from middle class backgrounds. In fact, as the village was so small there was not even a bad area. Had I gone up in the world?

I remember David's first day at school. The headmaster had asked me to make sure I accompanied him to and from the school. I went to collect him on his first day. David said, "Ma am walkin home wi ma new friends." He was so proud of himself. I felt embarrassed in front of all these 'well to do' women whose children were running up and taking their hands as they skipped home. I took hold of David's little hand as firmly as I could and said, "Now come along son." and marched him back home! I felt terrible for doing that, but I could not handle the embarrassment in front of everyone. I decided after that it would be wiser to let him make his own way home from school. We just lived about two hundred yards from the school and there were no roads to cross, so I believed he would be safe. Also one of the other children's mothers lived two doors away and said she would watch him home from school.

WOULD I EVER ESCAPE?

I felt good living in the village; it was a safe friendly and pleasant place. David was a shepherd in his first school play. On the day of the play all of the other children's mothers and fathers had arrived on time. I walked in after the play had started and tried to sneak into a back seat without being spotted or causing any fuss. David saw me as I entered the room and screeched with excitement. "There's me ma." Well if I could have crawled into a corner I would, as every head in the room turned to see who was so important that I got this special welcome. That day always brings a smile to my face. Nevertheless, you've probably guessed, I was soon to end our idyllic life style.

THE ROAD TO RUIN

It was now 1979; I was twenty-six years old and working as an extra on a Walt Disney film with my seven-year-old son. Yes, I did say a Walt Disney film. Things were going really well; I had my youngest sister and a girl from Scotland staying with me. One day when I was at my auntie's house, I noticed some letters lying and recognised the handwriting, they were addressed to me. I felt bewildered, as I asked what she was doing with my letters. She said they were from Jeff. I picked the letters up and said I was angry that she had thought it was all right to open my mail. My auntie and sister said they had done it to protect me from him, as they hated seeing me with black eyes and bruising all over.

Me being a sucker, I read the letters which were written with what appeared to be great affection and sincerity. They were written in a way that someone naïve or just completely stupid like me would be taken in by the flattery and seduction. Yes, they were 'love letters' at their best. He said, how much he was still 'in love' with me, and if only he could have another chance everything would be so different. He would never again abuse or hit me. If only I knew how much remorse he felt. He promised that if we tried again there would never be any fighting; he had learned his lesson. He would even make up for all the bad things he had done. Well I can hear you thinking, surely, she is not stupid enough to believe this baloney.

Guess what, me being such a trusting soul with great faith in human nature, you know the sort of person who believes people change, (without years of therapy or divine intervention) we ended up back together. He was sweetness and light itself for the first few weeks. It was not long before he moved back in with me, and it would not take Einstein to work out that the fighting and rows soon started all over again. He would drink in the local pubs and have lock-ins until about two in the morning, or sometimes not bother coming home. I found I was working all hours in three jobs to keep us going in food, drink and gambling.

One day he was going on and on about money for drink and I said I did not have any. Because I refused to give him money he threw a heavy mug at my face. I moved and the mug smashed off the wall and into the back of my head. I thought I was going to die because of the amount of blood I was losing. The blood had saturated my white blouse and was running down my underwear. I had to get out and get the split in my head stitched. That time, I did eventually get out of the house, even though he was trying to stop me so that no one knew what a b...... he really was. I think he eventually realised that this deep gash could not go without medical attention.

THE ROAD TO RUIN

Whatever you do, don't think that he bothered to come with me to the hospital; that would have been expecting too much. It was enough for him to let me out of the house. I walked from where we lived to the general hospital with the blood pouring out my head. They had to shave my head and stitch it up. The staff at the hospitals always asked how I had been injured. This was where I had to think up some excuse to cover his behaviour. I knew only too well the consequences if he found out I had told them what had really happened. That particular day I was really fed up, and knew he would have gone to the local pub while I was at the hospital. I deliberately walked into the pub on my way home, and sure enough there he was, the life and soul of the party. Well I burst his bubble that day, as I made such a scene exposing his brutality. I made it clear that the blood that saturated the blouse I was wearing was a result of him smashing a cup into my head. Believe me I was not top of the popularity list, but I was beyond caring.

I can hear you saying why on earth did you not get out of this relationship? Well I will tell you, I lost count of the times I tried. I moved house countless times, I would find somewhere else to live, and when he was out I would either pack up my belongings or just move with nothing. I would start building up a new life and be really pleased with myself, as things began to improve. My son and I would be living in a peaceful environment looking forward to a future. It would not be long before I would hear a knock on my door, when I went to answer it he would be standing. My heart would drop to my toes with disappointment, fear and resentment. I felt like Julie Roberts in the film 'Living with the Enemy'. All my dreams would be shattered once again. If I refused to let him in he would make threats, and if I shut the door on him he would just kick it in, or smash a window and come through that. I couldn't win. In those days few people had telephones in the house, so it was not as though I could phone the police as he was kicking the door in. Once he knew where I lived I knew there was no escaping him. I think he believed that I was his property because we had been in a relationship. A bit like women are something you own, not individuals in their own right. I felt alone with no one in my corner and no one caring a dot whether I lived or died. Unfortunately, I knew he was not going to leave voluntarily, that would be too much to expect.

Saying all that, I did go on my first trip abroad with him and my son David. We got the ferry to Calais and hitchhiked to Paris. We climbed the Eiffel Tower and did some sightseeing. Given we could not find anywhere to stay we stayed in the Paris Metro station overnight. I remember the rats sounded like full grown men as they ran around the station. David said he slept right through, I suppose he was probably used to sleeping through noise, as he would certainly have been accustomed to it. I know I mention all the fights, but there was seldom a week went by without parties going on to all hours in the morning. I don't think I had planned the trip very well. Or is that a massive understatement? Given I did not have a clue how to plan a holiday; I had certainly made a bad job of this one. Our ordeal in Paris was nothing compared with our journey back to Calais. We stopped at a camping place that also had caravans. I asked where we could stay. The owner spoke very little English but managed to say, "Any any." So, after handing in my passport, as is compulsory in many countries, away I went to find a nice caravan. I did, I found a lovely caravan. I fed David, as they supplied food too in the caravan! I tucked him in, and went to the site bar for the evening. I know you are probably thinking, you really should not have left your son, but I did show him where I could be found if he needed me, and it was only a few yards from the caravan. Later in the evening the owner of the caravan park was running around the bar with someone's passport looking horrified. Well do I need to tell you it was my passport? A young couple had come home to their caravan and found David tucked up and fast asleep in their bed. Bit like the three bears, "Who's been eating my supper and who is sleeping in my bed?" Needless to say they were very shocked and confused.

THE ROAD TO RUIN

We got thrown off the site with nowhere to go. We spent the night in a field, given we were not near any towns, and it was now quite late at night. I had to wake Jeff and David up when the skies opened. David took quite a bit of waking up and said he was in a good sleep; believe it or not, but he always remembered that night as special, as he talked about sleeping under the stars. The rain came down in torrents that night, we were drenched right through. I tried rather pathetically to dry us off on a hand dryer in some toilets. That was after hitchhiking to the nearest town.

Over the years I lost count of the times I hitchhiked around the country. Jeff would go off with the money we had with the promise of returning, or worse still I would realise he had disappeared and so had the money. He would usually have the week's food money in his pocket which I knew he intended to spend on his drink. I was lucky that nothing too dangerous ever happened during these journeys; other than one day an elderly woman gave us a lift. She had no windscreen wipers and there was a massive blizzard. After she stopped the car a number of times in the middle of the road, because she could not see, and needed to get out to wipe the windscreen. I eventually said, "Thank you but I will take my chances waiting in the blizzard." I have been so lucky in many ways, as my son was a gem; he was and still is so easy going and laid back.

THE ROAD TO RUIN

I think it was his way of keeping some equilibrium in a crazy household. Although he was not interested in books or academia he had and still has a wisdom which seemed to pervade every part of his being. He does tell his friends some of the things I did bringing him up, but never in a bad resentful way; although I am sure if he did he would have every right to. Sometimes if his friends are in the house he will say, "Mam tell them about the time …" I think most of his friends had more normal mothers during their childhoods!

Nevertheless I continued to work in both paid employment as a carer for the elderly, and for myself. I was quite an entrepreneur and sold all sorts of things, I bought kippers and fresh fish from North Shields fish quay and sold them in the bars around Newcastle. With the money I made I became more adventurous investing in a set of weighing scales. Now I could buy fruit and veg from the wholesalers. I would put about three pound of potatoes, a cabbage, turnip, carrots, apples, oranges, bananas and some salad in a bag and sell it for a £1 around the doors. At first I was restricted to delivering as many bags as I could carry as I had no transport. Never fear as help was on its way, some local kids knocked on my door with a railway trolley to help me to deliver the fruit and veg parcels. How good does it get? My business was now growing I could deliver even more parcels. This growth resulted in the progression to a bump start transit van. That is, I had to park it on a hill so that I could roll it into a start, or the alternative was the whole street had to come out to push it before it would bump start. Now the kids could deliver the railway trolley back to British Rail, and I could get on with a bit more serious business. What do they call it? Business development! Over the years I had umpteen cars and vans. Many, but not all were old bangers which needed a constant stream of parts which I would buy from the scrapyards. I became a dab hand at climbing over the top of car roofs in a pair of high heels, which I always wore! These were the days when you could buy an MOT for £40, and we could fix the exhaust pipe on the car with a beer can and two jubilee clips! Innovation and creativity in abundance.

My next venture was when the some lads came banging on my door really excited. "Catherine there's a shop for sale; it sells second hand goods, it will be a great business for you and Jeff." I went up to the shop and sorted out the finances. I think he was selling for a few hundred pounds which I was able to organise. It wasn't only MOTs which could be bought, in those days you could buy pay packets and pay slips. An authenticated worn look was achieved by scrunching them up as they were rubbed on to a dusty floor. This was the resourceful method used by the locals to organise loans.

THE ROAD TO RUIN

Fortunately I have always hated having debt, and was lucky enough to make sure I could work to pay for the things I wanted in life. I gave the guy the money he wanted, and started selling second hand furniture. I was now working night shift as a carer for the elderly, and running the shop through the day. I occasionally fell asleep when working alone in the shop. One day a man had looked in, and went to seek Jeff from the bar because I was lying with the door of the shop wide open fast asleep. The shop was in a very deprived rundown area of Newcastle; and certainly not the sort of place to be lying sleeping. However, I was so exhausted trying to work night and day to provide a decent living for David and myself. As well as bringing in enough money for this tyrant of a man who beat me up if I did not have enough drink money for him. If he stayed in and watched the television he would sit and shout obscenities at the programmes. His cascade of verbal obscenities was so disturbing to listen to I felt sick at times. I think this was his Neanderthal understanding of what it was to be a man. My take on his behaviour today was more in line with a psychopathic, narcissistic, low life prat.

   Often the young lads who weren't at school or working would ask to do jobs. If they saw me bringing a delivery in they would be there to give a hand. I used to give them money to buy food at the Greggs 'seconds' shop across the road. Jeff came and went as and when he wanted. He liked playing the business man, but was never there to do the work. As often as not I moved the furniture myself; this included every household item you could imagine: tables, armchairs, sofas, wardrobes, beds, drawers and mattresses. When I started this business I bought a transit van and progressed to a Luton. If I wasn't emptying houses, I was buying from Millar's auction rooms. I was also turning over enough money to keep us afloat and him off my back.

Sometimes after work I would go to the bar. One night a fight broke out. A young woman went to hit an older woman who I knew and liked, it was actually one of his family. I jumped over the bar table and grabbed her to stop her hitting this woman. Inevitably, we ended up in a fight which I won. I did not give it another thought. However the next night I was getting ready to go out when my friend came rushing in. "Where are you going?" she shrieked in a concerned voice. "I'm going out." I replied, surprised at the urgency in her voice. "You can't go out, there are about two hundred of them on the pub corner." She shrieked. "Well I'm not staying in, that's for sure." I told her. She told me to wait until she got her family to make some telephone calls. They telephoned a number of bars in the East and West End which included The Raby, Jacksons, The Bobby Shaftoe, The Cumberland Arms,

THE ROAD TO RUIN

Blue Man, Robin Adair, Dodds Arms, and the Chesterfield. I made my way to the pub where I was met by quite a reception. The bar was heaving with dozens of familiar faces. We waited on trouble starting, I sat with my back to the wall facing the door. This was in order to see anything that might erupt. Alas the night ended quietly, I must say I did not feel alone that night. Crazy as it may seem I think it was also this dynamic along with his family which kept me going.

A year after we got back together I realised I was pregnant. Yes, this left me in a dilemma, I really did not imagine spending the rest of my life with Jeff; yet on the other hand I was so pleased and looking forward to having another baby. I had always imagined myself with lots of children like my auntie, eleven would do! I bought in all the things I needed, as you can imagine there was nothing left from David's childhood. I felt quite excited during the pregnancy looking forward to a new baby. However, I was told by the consultant, that given the problems I had experienced at David's birth that there was a high chance of me dying during the delivery. He said, I would be better off having an abortion. I refused and said I would leave that decision in God's hands, as I did not believe I had the right to take my babies life.

The small village where I now lived was fifty-six miles from Newcastle. I was in Newcastle the night my waters broke, and

THE ROAD TO RUIN

I was rushed into the General hospital. Things started to go wrong, my blood pressure was soaring and once again the situation moved into dangerous territory. This time I remained conscious. I could feel the baby being born, although he came feet first instead of head first. After he was delivered they handed him to me to hold. What a precious little soul, he seemed to give me a little wink and his finger was sticking up as though he was telling me something. I had to smile. I felt absolutely delighted that everything had gone so well without any real complications. They took my baby away to attend to him, and Jeff's sister came to see me. She smiled as she said, "Catherine you look radiant." I felt radiant, I was so happy. I asked her if they were able to locate her brother Jeff. She said that they were trying, but had not been successful. No surprise!

It was not long before a nurse came to see me; she said we are putting you in another room. They moved me from the ward and put me in a room by myself. I did not think anything unusual and just waited for the return of my baby. Someone else came and told me that my baby was very ill. He had haemorrhaged during the birth because he had osteogeneses of the bones. In short, this meant his bones were very fragile, and during the delivery his head had been damaged. They said he would probably die. Well when someone tells you this about your baby it is hard to believe, especially as he looked perfectly normal and also healthy. Never mind, I still prayed to God to make him all right. The doctors told me I could sit with him as long as I wanted. I went along to the ward and sat by his incubator. He looked fine, I held him in my arms and chatted away to him, I really could not see a problem. They asked about his father, and as far as I know the police were sent to try and find him. That would be to the local bars! Some more of his family arrived and said they did not know where he was. That failed to surprise me, he was probably inebriated propping some bar up performing his lovely guy image to an audience of equally inebriated admirers.

  The first day passed and my baby was still alive. I still did not think he would die and continued praying. On the ward one of the nurses asked me what I was going to call him. I said, "I'm not 100% sure." I can remember thinking there was no rush he would be here for a long time. The stupid woman said something like, "Do you not realise that this baby is going to die and needs a name now." I was gob smacked at her lack of sensitivity and abruptness. I muttered something and walked out. Later a priest came and asked if I would like the baby to have a blessing and be baptised in case he died. I said, "Yes." And told the priest his name was Paul. Still not thinking that anything would really happen to him. I knew this was a formality if babies were not well. The priest gave him a blessing and baptised him. That was fine, as I continued to gently hold him while chatting away quietly as he slept. The next day I went to get something to eat and left him for a short while. I had not been away long when someone came to ask me to return to the ward where Paul was. I went back, and was taken into a side room where there was a doctor holding Paul. He said, "Paul is going to die soon and I would like you to hold him as he dies."

When you carry a baby full term and they look perfectly healthy it is hard to really believe that they will die. I took hold of him and nursed him close to my body. It was not long before I noticed the skin down one side of his body slowly turn navy blue; he looked terrible. I was still holding him when the blood spurted out of his tiny mouth; I got a terrible fright. I did not know that blood really spurted out of people's mouths until that day. The doctor said, "That's it, he's dead." I handed him over to the doctor without saying a word, and walked out of the room. I was frozen, raging inside with a bitter coldness.

The next thing I remember was his family arrived, they had eventually found him, too late as usual. He came into the room with his mother. I told them to f... off. It was not long before a priest came and said, "I bless you my child." I told him to f... off too, I said, "Don't bother me with your f...... God he has just killed my baby. Now f... off." I went to leave the hospital the nurse was running after me shouting, "You can't go out like that you have had stitches you need to rest. I told her to f… off too. I had no money on me, because Jeff had taken all we had that week for his drink money. I walked out of the hospital and hitch hiked the 56 miles back to the small village where I lived. I was one angry, bitter woman.

I organised Paul's funeral to make sure he had a good send off. He did not get buried by the church wall like a lot of new born babies who die. He had a proper funeral, all my family and friends, and all his family and friends came to his funeral. Remember I had said when my mother died that I would never cry for anyone. Well I did not cry, neither did I speak to anyone. I was just numb and raging inside. Every time I looked at other mothers with their children I was jealous and angry. I resented them having their children when mine was dead. After this I hated God; how could he do this? He had certainly gone down in my estimation after taking my child's life. I had now even managed to develop a tempestuous relationship with God. I would not speak to him; this lasted for over a year before I was able to put my bitterness and resentment aside.

Although I had drunk very little during the pregnancy, I now started drinking heavily again. The experience was another one which I pushed to the back of my mind, and did not discuss with anyone. I was living in an environment where feelings were not up for discussion, the drink served its purpose of obliterating the pain. I remember Jeff once saying to me, "If you looked at me like you are looking at that bottle of Brown Ale I would know you loved me." He was well deluded if he thought he was any competition at all for a bottle of Brown Ale. It won hands down, and was certainly the more desirable object of my love, clearly doing a lot more for me than he ever did!

Over the years I lost count of the people who came to live with us. One young boy stayed for about a year while he was on a curfew from the courts. He was a lovely lad, and no bother at all. My sister and her boyfriend also stayed with us for about a year when they were teenagers, but me being quite a prude I would not allow them to sleep together. We took in a homeless man who stayed for months, he had been a professor and his wife had died. He just left everything to his daughter who worked in India with Mother Teresa and hit the road. Jeff's niece, her husband and three children often stayed with us; I thought the world of this family. There was also another man who came from my home town who used to often arrive and stay with us for months. Then my brother turned up, who I asked to leave when he threatened my sister with a boiling hot kettle of water. Jeff liked people to stay, as it was leverage to get money for the bar. There was probably also less violence, but it did not stop altogether.

Well as life continued I got pregnant again; my GP sent me to see a gynaecologist who said, "*There is a high chance that this baby will die the same as your other baby, and if he lives he will probably have a life filled with problems and pain, as there is a high chance he will also have osteogenesis.*" He also said, "*We have not got time to hang around, if you are going to terminate this pregnancy you need to do it immediately. I can get you a bed now and we will do the operation straight away.*" I felt stunned; he did not give me the option of going home to think about it. I won't add discussing it, as this was not an activity that was ever participated in. The probability was that Jeff would be propping some bar up somewhere, and by the time I found him the baby would be a toddler. It was a now or never offer, like those salesmen who tell you, the offer only stands if you buy it right now. I struggled, as I did not believe in abortion. Yet I was being told that if I carried my baby full term the probability was he/she would die, and if they lived they would probably have all sorts of problems. I did not want my baby to live a life of suffering. I had to make this decision there and then before I left this doctor's consulting room. Can you imagine what that was like? I had gone to the hospital just for an ordinary check-up, not expecting any of this. Abortion had not crossed my mind. It was now on the table as a best option. As I stood reeling from this consultation I agreed to terminate the pregnancy. He ushered me to a room in the hospital. I was later very angry with the doctor, as he did not give me any options or time to think about what I really wanted to do. I looked back and thought his practice was totally morally and ethically an utter disgrace, but in those days 1980 they got away with this.

Life went on. I put this behind me and kept going, although I often wished I was dead. That was because he continued to plague my life. I would stand looking out of the multi-story flat windows where his mother lived and think about jumping out. I hated my life with this man, he rubbished all my dreams. If I had a good idea he would ridicule it and tell me not to talk so stupid. The only thing that made my life bearable was my work, and his family who I got along with and liked. I obviously had my own family who I loved very much but they were not having such an impact on me. The only person I had a problem with was him, as he was the only one I was living with.

I eventually went to a solicitor and told him I wanted Jeff to leave the house because of his violence towards me. This was in September 1982. The solicitor sent a letter to him at my address and a copy of the letter to the local police. The letter, which I still have, read:

We have been instructed by Catherine… who has informed us that as a result of your violence to her she is unwilling and unable to put up with your presence in the house. We therefore request that you leave the house immediately and take with you your personal belongings. If this request should cause you to offer any more violence to Catherine, then immediate application will be made to the court for an injunction and you will be reported to the police. If you are determined to cause trouble for her then she is determined to make sure through lawful means that you are prevented from doing this. A copy of this letter has also been sent to the police asking them to ensure that you leave the property without any further harm to our client.

The letter arrived and he would not read it. That was another attempt at getting rid of him which failed. Months later, one night as I was getting ready to go out with him, the police arrived at the door with a copy of the letter. I told them he had refused to read the letter, so they gave him the copy and asked him to read it. He said, I was completely stupid and was getting ready to go out with him. He told the police I did not want him to leave, as we got along well. He also added what he had said to me for years. How on earth did they think they could enforce the law and keep him from returning to my house and doing what he wanted without providing 24 hour protection which they were not going to do? Again I was beginning to feel frightened. He said to me in his threatening voice, "Tell the police you don't want me to leave." I conjured up as much courage as I could and said, "I do want you to leave." In an angry voice he said, "But you are getting ready to go out with me." I said, "I would rather stay in and would be pleased if you never come back to my house." It was as though he did not understand a word I said, "You don't mean that" he replied in a surprised yet sarcastic voice. For some reason, this man actually thought I wanted him around. The reality was I hated him. He was the most miserable, aggressive, insufferable person I'd ever known. Far from being a bundle of fun, he was a liar, a cheat, a womaniser, drinker and a gambler whose misconception with reality was ruining my life. He had nothing going for him; yet he was struggling to comprehend that I might not wish to see him, that in fact I was seeing him only under sufferance.

He eventually left while the police were there, but returned that night, put my window out when I refused to open the door, and came back in. He tried to get into the bedroom but I now had a plan, which short of him smashing the door down he would not be able to get in. I pulled the bed across the room and put a piece of wood between the bed and the door. This jammed it solid, as the wedge went from the door to the wall. I was finally save from him, until I came out of the bedroom.

Because of the constant bullying and putdowns I felt really stunted in this relationship. You know when you feel under employed? Well I certainly felt that. I knew I had potential yet was unable to get into a well-paid profession for a couple of reasons. I still had some fear of that psychiatric hospital finding me and taking me back! I also had no qualification. Me being the eternal optimist, I decided to do some "O" levels at the local college to see if I could change the course of my life. By God I certainly was a woman with ambition! Jeff as usual rose to the challenge like a true champ with his bombardment of obsessively jealous, abusive comments. He could not bear the thought of me bettering myself. "Oh who do you think you are?" "Are you trying to be clever? sneer, sneer. "You are too thick to pass any exams." His put downs were relentless. Never mind, I ignored them and continued with my course, as well as working in a well know very rough bar in Newcastle. During this period we had many a violent fight.

One day, I was in the shopping centre with my carrier bag full of books for college, and a black bin bag full of his clothes and belongings. He had been out drinking all night, and had not returned home the next day. I walked into the local bar and threw his clothes right across the bar top, smashing everything on the bar. I got into a verbal fight with the manager who was about six foot three, and built like a rugby player. He threatened to hit me if I didn't shut up and get out. I retorted with a loud. "Yea it would take someone your size as there is no one else in here big enough." That was my five foot one inch and 8 stone talking.

You will have noticed by now that when I felt wronged I really had trouble keeping my mouth shut. Even as a child I would rather take a beating than keep the peace, if I felt things weren't fair. Apparently this is the trait of Sagittarians, they are known for their sense of fairness. Without a doubt I certainly met this criteria. I told the bar manger to keep Jeff there, as he had better not come back to me. Jeff told me to get out and stop showing him up. I started to shout at him that all he was, was a woman beater and not worth a w--k. He ran at me, and by this time we were outside the bar. I kept dodging him, he liked to look the nice guy in front of everyone, but he was failing drastically that day. I would not shut my mouth. All the books, pens everything in the carrier bag (that was my briefcase) were thrown all over the shopping centre, as it ripped apart under the strain. He decided the only answer was to go back in the bar and ignore me. I walked in behind him and ordered three bottles of brown ale which I started to drink with a vengeance. That afternoon the bar clientele were coming up to me saying, "A've fund this in the shoppin centre hen is it yours?" "Yes" I would say as I added another item to my collection of lost goods.

Another night he came home and began hitting me. He went on and on and on with his ridiculous accusations. Eventually he fell asleep on the settee. It was a rare occasion when I was stone cold sober, but on this particular night I was. After he fell asleep I looked for the hammer to bash his brains in. Unfortunately, I was unable to find it, nevertheless I found the next best thing. The pressure cooker lid. You know the sort I am talking about. The big heavy metal lids with the pressure bit sticking out of the centre. I looked at his face as he lay there snoring and thought about all the years I believed I had to fight fair. I had spent years of my life trying to win against someone who was twice my weight and height in a fair fight. I decided there and then that he had cheated me for years. He had a massive advantage, there was nothing fair about the fighting we had been doing. Well here goes, I lifted the lid as high as possible above his head and brought it down as hard as I could. Smack it landed, it was the strangest feeling, as each time it landed, it suddenly stopped. I kept hitting him over the head with it. I can remember each downward blow as if it was yesterday. I then took it across his knees and ran out of the house. This time I had opened the door ready for my escape. I hid behind a wall on the estate and watched the house. About half an hour later he staggered out the house and walked towards his sister's house. I went back in and locked the door. I did not see him for days. I met his sister and niece a few days later, and she angrily said, "You could have killed our Jeff hitting him like that." Now although most of his family had been in court for malicious wounding and could be violent people, I responded with. "You didn't interfered all the years he battered me. Now don't interfere now." She walked away and there was nothing more said.

He returned after a few days and said he had never felt as much pain in all his life. I was so pleased, I told him if he ever hit me again I would do the same again because he had to sleep. I waited for him hitting me again. It never happened he had received the message loud and clear. Now I know that sounds all well and good, but the reality was that it took years before I had the confidence to believe the fighting wouldn't start again. I do not think the fear ever really left me, as I always thought, will he start tonight when he comes home. This is something I fully understood when working as a psychotherapist. People do not just feel frightened the day they get beaten, they live in the constant fear of being beaten, as they never know when the next stream of blows is going to come. Will it be tonight or tomorrow? The unknown is often more frightening and anxiety provoking than the known. I do like the quote, "Most anxiety is caused by a projection into the future." This is so true, as most of the time we fear what might happen before anything happens. I would like to add that most of the yellow bellied, cowardly worms who hit women and children would not stand a chance with anyone their own size.

You might be wondering how I was able to go from one catastrophe to the next. Well I managed this really easily, it was all I seemed to know. When I studied psychology I gained a better understood of how the early years are repeated time and time again, until there is an opportunity to work through the old traumas held in the psyche. So far I had not had any time or opportunities to work through anything. I was too busy trying to survive the chaotic life I was determined to keep creating.

Jeff's niece Susan, the one who used to babysit, now had three boys who I loved to bits; they brought so much joy into my life. They learned quickly the ways of life for the environment they lived in. I had just started a new job and bought a new car to go with the job. Now given it was a sales job I was carrying a briefcase; a real briefcase this time and not a carrier bag! In the area where Susan lived anyone's car who was unknown would be highly likely to be broken into, especially if you were dumb enough to leave a briefcase where it could be spotted. Most professional people actually refused to work in the area, because of the level of car break-ins and violence. Guess what, when I went back to the car, surprise the car window had been broken, and my briefcase was missing. My niece's little boy, who was about three at the time said, "Auntie Catherine I will find out who smashed your car window and belt them." I felt touched by his loyalty and bravery. He was obviously oblivious to his limitations in size and strength, but certainly did not allow this to handicap his imagination.

Given my 'privileged position' as an insider, the children on the street told me who had broken into the car. I went around to their house on the next estate, and in my best 'gangsterish' voice said, "I will give you five f...... minutes to give me my briefcase back, and pay for the broken windscreen. If you don't I will demolish your f...... house." Within a few minutes a woman came to the door looking quite worried. In a rather timid voice she said, "It was our Ricky who broke in, he didn't know it was your car. He thought it belonged to one of the social workers." She followed through with, "He will be back soon and I will make sure he returns it and gives you the money for the window." At this point this big useless looking man came around the corner shouting obscenities at me. I was well dressed in a scarlet red Jacket and skirt looking ever so professional! I told him in no uncertain unprofessional terms, he had better move his arse back into the house and get my briefcase or I would wipe him of the face of the earth. He went back in and brought the briefcase out. He had sawn through it. It was not even locked, that was about the size of the mentality of the low life criminals in that area. Needless to say they quickly paid me for the damage to both the briefcase and the car window.

Just in case you hadn't worked it out the whole scene I was associated with, was one of petty crime, alcohol, gambling, parties and violence. The lads also always found ways to make money. Empty houses were stripped of their copper wire and other saleable goods such as, gas and electric fires, cookers, boilers etc. Scrap metal was found along the river beds where Vickers used to dump material from the factories. The old sleepers from the disused railway lines brought in a nights beer money, and collecting metal from the roadside or anywhere else always filled a few pints. They even paid the watchman to "watch" while they took the lead tiles off the roof. Shepard's scrap yard did a roaring trade.

THE ROAD TO RUIN

When I first went to live in Newcastle the teenagers used to steal from people's yards and houses; they would also steal clothes from washing lines. I drummed it into them that this was wrong, it was never alright to steal from anyone. I strongly imposed my moral values on many of the younger generation, and believe it or not they listened. Many of the teenagers stopped stealing from people as they started to understand that the people they were stealing from were like themselves; they were struggling to feed and clothes their own families and children. They also began to understand that it was never alright to steal from anyone no-matter how rich or poor they might be. I was always pleased with myself if I influenced anyone in a good way as my own behaviour certainly left a lot to be desired at this stage in my life, but I did have principles.

One day as I was driving down a quiet road in the country. There stood the most beautiful stone built house in its own grounds. A 'to let' sign on the huge wrought iron gate caught my attention. The first opportunity available I enquired about the property and was able to put a deposit down which secured it. I waited quietly and patiently until I knew Jeff would not be around to organise a furniture van. I collected David and made a quick escape. This was a really grand house, a farmer had built it for his family and moved out. The outside walls were made of new Cotswold stone, there was a huge living room with an open coal fire, and a beautiful oak beam mantel piece. There was also a large kitchen, separate dining room and four bedrooms. The bathroom was bigger than most living rooms I had lived in to date with a massive corner bath. The garden surrounded the whole house, and there was not another house within quarter of a mile.

I moved out of my house in an appalling area of Newcastle into this delightful large house, two minutes' walk from the beautiful Northumberland coast line. I had done it! Once again I was going to live happily ever after. Well that is really not too realistic. Yes, you guessed, it was not long before he had tracked me down and was knocking on my door. That once more was the end of my 'happily ever after'.

We were now on the home brew; I would wake up in the morning and look at the empty beer glass with scum up the sides. I was smoking 50 cigarettes a day and through the night. My fingers were all burned, as well as everything else around me. Through the day I was working in a rest home in Whitley Bay. In the mornings' I would walk down the drive to open the big wrought iron gate, vomiting every step I took. Sometimes I would collapse after I stood up, the colour would drain from my face, I would turn white and slide down the wall. If I had been doing this for effect believe me it wasn't working, no one ever took any notice. One morning I went passed my turn off on the roundabout and being such a bright spark, instead of going right around the roundabout I reversed back around the roundabout.

His niece, her partner and three children came to stay with us. They loved it in this massive house with all the outdoor space you could dream of having. I loved having them, they brought a real joy to my life. If I walked in and one of the kids was crying that they had hurt their leg, I would throw them on the table and shout for the knife followed by, "Don't worry if I cut it off the pain will disappear with your leg. They would scream, "It's better auntie Catherine its better." We'd giggle and laugh. Certainly not fitting behaviour for an eminent psychotherapist, but we did have fun. His niece would say, "You know this house is calm until you walk through the door and within minutes it is like a tornado hit it." In my life time I don't know how many times that was said to me; it seemed to be a natural talent I possessed. Again that house was always full, people came and went. We did make amazing home brew and on many a weekend there were up to fourteen cars on the driveway, while we partied and drank the night away. After a couple of years of country life I decided to move closer to Newcastle again; this was so that I did not have so far to travel to work. This time I 'bought' a flat in a sleepy little village not too far from Newcastle. I got a full mortgage as I had no deposit.

The sleepy village woke up, as we partied and drank to all hours in the morning. People would come from all over for the parties, and stay up drinking half the night away. I was getting worse and worse with the drink, my head was constantly in turmoil; my memory was going, and I really did think I had brain damage, either that or early dementia. I was holding down a dead-end job with no prospects. I'd travelled the road to ruin, and now at rock bottom I was falling apart at the seams.

COMING AROUND

I was thirty-four years old in 1989 when I was coming around from a three-day coma in a dull drab room. At first, I was unsure if I was alive, as my brain struggled to connect with itself. Yes, I am alive, I can feel my physical body as I move my arms. I opened my eyes slowly, I was in a room with tall bare murky yellow walls, surrounded by an old-fashioned cornice. I was lying on a high metal bed with white sheets, unsure if it was a jail or a hospital. I was aware of feelings I had never felt before running through my body. The only words I can use to describe them are sensual, I could actually feel my body. At the same time I felt somewhat shocked and confused as the feelings running through my body were so unusual. I also felt as though I had a soul. Now that might sound like a strange thing to say but it is what I felt. Before this experience I did not know people had souls. Now although I was fascinated by the sense that I actually had feelings in my body, my thoughts quickly turned to where I was and what had gone before. I really needed to work out how I had got there, wherever there was! I was not sure what had been happening to me, as I strained my brain to think, the memories of the days leading to ending up here slowly started to return. I must add that I did not know at this time that I had been unconscious for three days; so my memory took me back to what had been happening prior to this unconscious state.

I remember my evening drinking episodes (such an understatement) were really taking their toll on my physical and mental health. I had been drinking to obliteration every night of the week for over a year. Prior to that I had been drinking alcohol most nights for the past seventeen years with the occasional break. Whenever I drank, I got drunk; I can't remember ever being able to go out and have only a couple of drinks and return home sober. I recall trying to stop drinking, this was when the problems had started; as the drink was leaving my system it had catapulted me into a psychotic episode. I had once again lost touch with reality. Gosh this was getting scary, best leave it until I see where I am. I decided to get out of the bed and try the door to see if that would give me any clues as to where I was. I was on a hospital ward of some kind. There was a nurse just outside the door, "Oh," she said, "You have come around." I asked her where I was. She told me, "You are in St. George's Hospital Morpeth." I felt a streak of doom and terror run right through my body. I was in the psychiatric hospital – the asylum - where they used to put my mother. It was the most horrific place in the world as far as I was concerned; I would probably have been less worried if she had said I was in prison. At least in prison you would know when you expected to be released, but in these places they could keep you there indefinitely. My brain whirled, what had I done? How had I arrived there? What had been happening? How long had I been there?

I took a brief flash through my childhood memories, to those horrifying times I had visiting this place. From the age of seven I would negotiate the eerie hospital corridors to take my mother her family allowance. The corridors were scattered with zombie like patients making unrecognisable noises, mostly walking with their shoulders stooped and their heads facing the floor with eyes that either stared into the ethos or jumped around without focus.

My mind now had no choice but to brave the journey back to what I was doing before coming around. I can remember many strange experiences, which I later found to be what they call detoxing and going through the Delirium Tremors, better known as the DTs or cold turkey. Just to let you know, the DTs are a psychotic condition caused by the sudden stopping of the intake of alcohol or other drugs. When chronic alcoholics are going through withdrawals the typical symptoms they will experience are: tremors, hallucinations, anxiety and disorientation. This is the most severe form of alcohol withdrawal and needs to be medically supervised because there is a risk of death.

COMING AROUND

Well I had no medical supervision and had been swirling through the above symptoms with no connection at all to reality. I can tell you I'd rather fall off the edge of a cliff than go through that experience again. I can certainly understand how alcoholics die during this experience. My memory took me to the "Shop Front" on Westgate Road in Newcastle; this was a meeting place for alcoholics who were supposed to be no longer drinking. A friend took me there, as I was so far gone at this stage I was now incapable of functioning as a rational human being.

Lydia the woman who ran the programme for alcoholics was surprised, "Women don't normally come here." she said in her dulcet tones. No she didn't turn me away, as I just stood there looking glazed, and to be fair, I didn't really care whether or not women went there, I just needed help badly. My only interest was in stopping the mental torment and horrendous feelings that had taken over my brain and body. I felt so bad, death would certainly have been the better option. Lydia was a social worker, she was a very attractive tall woman, with large brown eyes and beautiful thick long dark hair. There was no doubt in my head she would have passed for a model had she chosen that for a career, over working with down and outs in the back streets of Newcastle. I liked her, and hung on to the hope that she would help me. It didn't matter that the place was stinking with the smell of men's stale alcoholic urine. Lydia said I would have to come daily to the unit before she could get me a place in the local detox unit. She explained, this was so that I could be given a supervised detox, as it would be too dangerous to detox me at home, given the amounts of alcohol I had been consuming. She worked with me for about a week before she could get me a bed in Parkwood House in Newcastle. The Friday prior to my Monday morning admission to the detox unit she told me to try to relax, and have a quiet time until she came to collect me on the Monday morning.

A quiet weekend was not on the radar, in fact I probably had not had a quiet weekend since leaving the womb. This weekend was no exception, there was a constant stream of trouble brought to my door. Some of my friends had been in a big bar fight and put the barmaid in hospital. It was touch and go if she would live or die. They sent someone to my door in the early hours of the morning, they wanted me to go up to the police station to bail them out. The police would not allow them out until they had word from the hospital that the woman would live, because if she died they would be charged with murder.

By the time I met the social worker on the Monday morning I felt as if I was not going to last the day. She took me to the detox unit and introduced me to the staff, then left saying she would keep in touch to see how I was doing. When I was taken to the ward where the patients spent their time I was surprised to find a number of people whom I already knew, from the bars in the city. This improved my ego and made me feel at home! I quickly made friends during my stay, mostly with people who were in the detox unit with drug addiction problems.

I don't suppose you would be surprised to learn that I did not really know what I was doing during that time. I had lots of tablets on me that had been given to me with good intentions by a woman trying to help me. I don't know who was the most deluded, I was taking the tablets to try to make me feel all right, as I was deteriorating by the minute. I think this was probably the worst I had ever felt, I felt as if I was struggling to survive. The experience was suffocating, like going completely under the ground, or like drowning. I felt as though it was taking every inch of the strength I had to try to stay alive. I remember my kidneys seemed to be excreting brown slush, I thought my insides were going to fall out. Every bit of my body and mind felt damaged. I had known for a while that the drink was killing me. My liver was swelling up every night with the alcohol so badly that I had to loosen my clothing. My memory was starting to go, and I thought I had brain damage, it was as though I would talk and fill in the gaps without any real thought to accuracy. In other words I had reached a stage where my brain and the words coming out of my mouth did not feel connected.

While in the detox unit I remember experiencing a feeling during the whole night in which my psyche seemed to be going down some sort of spiral. It was like some sort of unravelling of my memories but at high speed. I felt as if some sort of healing was trying to take place, but the healing was worse than the problem. I was also completely disorientated and hallucinating. However the terrible things I was seeing and hearing seemed real, yet they were as far from reality as the earth turning upside down overnight.

Trying to put a time scale to my memories was putting a real strain on my brain, which would not have been difficult at that time, nevertheless I was getting there. I worked out that I had been on the unit for about a week, when in my wisdom I decided to stop taking all medication. Little did I understand the serious consequences of this action. My body now started to react to this alien state, it had seldom been alcohol free for many years and was now unable to cope without alcohol in my blood stream. I remember beginning to go psychotic after stopping the medication too early. In my psychotic state I discharged myself from the unit, but did not know what I was doing or where I was going. It was now obvious that the stopping of the alcohol and the medication had triggered the DTs.

Oh my thoughts have just been interrupted by a young woman who is dressed differently from the nurses. Although at that time I hardly had the word psychologist in my vocabulary, I assume she may have been a psychologist or someone connected to the psychological profession. After I came around the nurse had sent for her to do an assessment on me. She walked into the ward and bombarded me with questions.

She wanted to know what year it was, and who the Prime Minister was. I thought - she thinks she is in the evening history lesson and I'm the lecturer. Nevertheless, I was not going to say this to her, as one experience of these people misusing their power was enough in this life time. And, although I talk with some bravado believe me I was so vulnerable and scared in case I had a repeat of the previous hospital.

Nevertheless, when she got to the part where she asked me to say the seven times table backwards from a hundred. I laughed, or rather sneered and said, "You have to be kidding. I can hardly tell you my name, let alone say the seven times table backwards from a hundred." This rather brash confrontation did not stop me from feeling somewhat inadequate, as if I could not do what I was supposed to be able to do. I now think it would have been more practical if someone had examined her head instead of mine. Only an idiot would ask someone just gaining consciousness to do such a feat. It would be likened to asking someone with a broken leg to run a mile.

Good, this ill-informed woman left, hopefully to study history and never to return. I was now free to go back to my thoughts and continue to recollect my memories. I remembered going home; David was now sixteen and must have gone through a terrible time with me during that period. Believe it or not he had always known me to be strong and in control. Maybe I'm still deluded! Well the point is that 12 years earlier, after I was locked up in the hospital in Scotland, I swore I would not drink through the day. The reasoning being that if I was sober through the day I would be able to take care of him and social services would not be able to take him from me. This was my ultimate wisdom, never thinking that if I drank so much in the evening I was probably drunk most of the following day, thus keeping my level of alcohol topped up around the clock.

Trying to resist drinking was a painstaking experience as many of those who have ever been on a diet or addicted to anything would know. I would start to watch the clock in the

early evening and tell myself, 'I will not have a drink tonight.'
It was like having two heads, one egging me on to drink, and
the other trying to get me to stop; 'Well, I will just have a little
drink.' 'No it is starting to really damage you.' 'One more
won't hurt' 'Well you never stop at one.' 'Well I will, I swear
to God I will not get drunk.' 'You know your brain is starting
to go and so is your liver.' 'You must stop drinking it is
killing you.' 'Well it might be better if I were dead.' This
internal dialogue would go on and on tossing from I will to I
won't, until I would make that last minute dash to the shop
and get enough alcohol to knock out a horse for the night. I am
sure many of you reading this will know too well this
experience. Only hope you had more success than me in your
fight against temptation, because I certainly wasn't winning
mine.

Nevertheless, I had gone back home to David, who I have no
doubt was pretty scared and confused as he watched my
completely insane behaviour. Fortunately, even though he was
sixteen, that age when young people often go off the rails, he
had his feet firmly on the ground. He needed them there, as I
was telling him to do things which were off this planet. I also
thought the dog was the devil, and was planning vicious
attacks against me. I'm not sure what the dog thought about
me, as I chased him around the streets, shouting and locked

him out of the house! Perhaps he thought I was the devil planning vicious attacks against him. It would have been more accurate. I was talking to the pictures on the wall; that was because they were talking to me! Every programme on the television, even the news bulletins were addressed directly to me. Now would that be paranoia or narcissism? Everything in my head seemed intensified, as though there was some deep meaning in every little detail.

I left home and managed to make it through to my sister's house in a completely psychotic state of mind. I can vaguely remember that the car seemed to be going all over the road. I imagine my sister was extremely concerned given I spent the night talking to the pictures on the wall shouting, "Alleluia I have been given salvation." I did not know the meaning of salvation, never mind shouting it around her house. I was refusing to eat food because it belonged to the devil. I was telling my sister she needed to get the children out of bed as they were in danger. In short, I was causing complete disruption to her normally sane household.

The next day she 'kindly' took me to Gosforth near Newcastle and dropped me by the roadside. She made a quick departure back home, where she could forget about her horrendous ordeal with me. I know she would never forget this experience as this must have been a complete nightmare for her. Nevertheless, it was clear that she just wanted to get me away from her door, and hope that someone else would help me out. We later laughed about this. Another important issue here was that she could not find it in herself to telephone a doctor; this would have brought back the nightmare memories of our childhood with our mother. I completely understood this.

I can remember doing the strangest things in Gosforth that day. I was walking to places I did not know existed, and looking for a Church. I talked to a number of people on my travels. God only knows what I said to them. The longer I was remaining alcohol free the crazier I was getting. I was perfectly sane when I was drunk. Now sobriety brought me insanity, life did not make a lot of sense. It was becoming obvious that my memories of the lead up to "coming around" did not look good. You know when that overwhelming feeling of shame and humiliation pervades your body; well that is how I felt, as though the ground would swallow me up. Never mind I had to brave more memories to try to get to where I was in terms of coming around. A horrible thought came flooding back; I remember standing in Jeff's house. I will never forget the amount of terror that went through my body that day when he walked into his apartment. I violently shook uncontrollably from head to foot for about half an hour. I was shuddering in every sinew of my being. Again, I think this was some kind of healing experience my body was going through, but it was a scary ordeal. At that point I had a white bible in my hand which I had bought before I reached his place. I was holding it up to protect myself from this man's evil presence. He said he would try to help me; I knew that his help would drag me further into the mire, as it always did. I told him how all these years I had only been with him because if I asked him to get out he would beat me up. He promised that would all change, and he would stop drinking in order to help me. I had listened to his lies, promises and threats for fourteen years and was beyond being conned any more. I walked away from him, swearing that he would never come back into my life. I told him I would rather be dead than continue in a relationship with him. For some reason this experience felt final, as though the Bible had acted as some form of deterrent placing a barrier between us which would last forever! Nevertheless, I still felt weird as I recalled the events in his home.

Next I went to a local metro station in Shiremoor with the white bible which had now turned evil and into a Bible written by the devil. I threw it on the metro line along with my bag, my money and all my belongings. Talk about turning on a sixpence! The next day the police had returned them to my son who was still at home wondering where on earth I had disappeared to. I ended up on the Sunday in the Haymarket in Newcastle and I started the nine mile walk home to my sleepy little village. It was beginning to get dark, I thought all the cars were spying on me; they were using radio control to keep in touch with each other to monitor my moves. I was totally paranoid and psychotic. I walked up to two women talking at the bus stop and told them in no uncertain terms, "I worked for it and paid for it!" Now that is paranoia at its best. God only knows what they thought.

At about eleven o'clock that night I remember starting to collapse. I'd had no food or drink for a couple of days, as in my head this was related to the devil. It's amazing how crazy the mind can get when not connected to reality. My body could not go any further. I had reached the railway crossing at Seghill. I collapsed on the crossing. I can remember a man being there, and helping me through, he looked brilliant. He had the most beautiful face. Where I was lying on the crossing, I could feel a cross on my back. I was choking it was as though I was being strangled. Someone must have telephoned for an ambulance; this man told the ambulance drivers I had to go into the ambulance head-first. He was placing importance on the way things were done. I seemed to be going through some crazy sort of God the devil fight. When people say before you die your whole life goes before you, it certainly did. I can remember my life just going before my eyes. Strangely enough, it was the events that I had a conscience about that were going through my memory like a video, such as bits of crime I had been involved in. I was making some attempt to apologise to God for my sins and swearing not to do these things again.

After this, I started to catapult back through life, I remember hitting certain ages; 30, 24, 16, 8, 2, and birth. My body then curled up into the foetal position at which point I went into a coma. There did seem to be some strange memories during this coma, both of evil and good. I remember thinking someone was the devil, but I also thought there was an angel there. But alas I have no explanation for what really did happen during that period. This was the three day coma I was just coming around from on the hospital ward. I found out later that this was the point that many alcoholics die. I also learnt that this part of my experience is what they call past life regression, which people go to therapists and hypnotists to experience. The only thing was I did not have a therapist or hypnotist controlling my experiences.

Well reflections over, now I had completed my recap, throwing some light on my situation, and how I had got to where I was, I felt better informed. Believe me being better informed certainly did nothing to make me feel any better. I felt horrified at the thought of some of the crazy things I had done during my 'accidental' alcoholic detox.

After my recap I was on my feet quickly, and eager to try to get out of this hospital. I am sure you would have worked that out for yourself. I still found it quite disturbing that many of the patients looked pathetic, were lethargic, and walked with stooped shoulders, looking at their feet. I was terrified in case I was going to end up like them. They would find out that I had escaped from that psychiatric hospital in Scotland twelve years earlier and I would now have to spend the rest of my life locked up in this hospital. I was sure they got paid extra for keeping patients in long term.

After I settled down a bit, I tentatively approached a nurse to explain that I had been dealing with Lydia the social worker from the Shop Front. I asked if she could 'please' arrange for her to come to see me to organise my release from this hospital. At least I now knew that the only way I would get out of this place would be if I had someone official on my side that was batting for me. They did get in touch with her, and she came to see me within a couple of days. I felt much better after speaking to her, as she said she would make some enquires as to what help was available for me and would return in a couple of days.

COMING AROUND

The staff here must have undergone a heart transplant, as they allowed me to go for a walk in the hospital grounds. Believe it or not, I did not try to escape, as I believed that Lydia would come back and help me to move forward. I can remember walking through the grounds and being aware of my experience, it was the first time since I was a young child that I could feel the breeze blowing around my face. I could see the green grass, trees and flowers. I could smell the air and the scents from the flowers dancing on the breeze. The sky was a bright blue with the odd fluffy white cloud moving slowly in the warm autumn breeze. I could feel my feet as they hit the ground when I walked. All my senses were alive for the first time since I was very young. I savoured the experience. Yes the alcohol was out of my system and I could feel again. This was one of those very special moments in my life; it was the beginning of things to come, which I did not know at that time.

While on the hospital ward there was an elderly woman who had been in the hospital for over forty years. One of the nurses told me she had been admitted as a teenager because she was pregnant and had been kept there ever since. She just fitted in with the hospital routine as she was completely institutionalised. At the ward round she just took her medication without question and did not say a word to anyone. Apparently, she had not had a visitor for years; after her admittance her father came in a couple of times and then stopped. I know we hear cases like this, but it just felt so sad that this woman's only company for the past forty years were the staff on the hospital ward. It was also clear that they really were not interested in forming any kind of real relationship with her.

Well this woman started to quietly follow me around the hospital. Now don't start to think I was going to stay there to keep her company. No, that was far from my intentions. Nevertheless, I did not think she was taking too much notice of me because she didn't speak. I had tried to speak to her, and all I got was a shy smile. She was never far from my side during the day; she would shuffle along as fast as she could to keep up with me. When I was aware of her shadowing me I would slow down to allow her to come alongside. She never came alongside, she dropped in behind me, and was obviously happy just staying in the background.

I often quarrelled with the nurses over having to take my medication. Then one day we were all sitting in the ward waiting for the meds trolley to come, and I did my norm, which was to object to having to take any medication. When it came to the old-timer's turn, she said to the nurse, "I am not taking any tablets." The nurses on the meds trolley could not believe their ears - they made such a scene. They shouted on the other nurses on the ward to come in and hear her. Here was a sweet old, institutionalised woman, who always obeyed orders actually arguing with them. I felt so touched by her behaviour, as she was obviously emulating my behaviour. I was never the best example of good behaviour in the world, but I was chuffed to bits.

However, it was not long before my body started to crave the alcohol it was missing. I had been told by the psychiatrist in the hospital that I had damaged my liver. My body was not in good condition as a result of the enormous amounts of alcohol I had drunk over the last seventeen years. The damage to my liver was reversible if I stopped drinking. I was told, "If you continue to drink you will be lucky if you last six months. Make a choice - **change or die**." I could not envisage life without drinking, just in case you didn't guess, it was one of the most important things in my life. Everyone I knew drank; my life had also revolved around bars for the past seventeen years. How on earth was I supposed to give all that up? Nevertheless, there was a part of me that wanted so much to make it without alcohol. I knew how much drink was ruining my life. I felt deep in my heart that I could be successful if I could only escape the lifestyle I was so immersed in.

I was delighted when Lydia did come back to see me. She said, it would not be wise for me to go home as my drinking and behaviour was so out of control; I would be dead within months if I continued with the life style I was living. She too said, "You need to change or die."

Well I thought, that was quite some choice they were giving me. At that time in my life I really didn't understand the implications of my life choices. Nevertheless, she was at least going to help me to make the choice, as she suggested I go into a rehabilitation unit which she would arrange. I agreed to this, although I did not have a clue about what this meant. She explained that I would have to go for an interview, and be assessed by the residents and staff in the unit. I was told, as soon as she was able to arrange this interview and if I was accepted by the staff and residents I would be discharged from the ward and moved to the rehab. Gosh how times had changed, they were **not** going to try to keep me in this hospital against my will until I died! How happy was I?

REHAB –
THE BEST TIME OF MY LIFE TO DATE

Well now she kept her word and sorted out my interview for the rehab. What I did not know as I made my way up the garden path to the front door was, that this was going to be the happiest, most loving, insightful, educational and fun time in my life to date. Wow that sounds promising, does it not? I'd made my way to Whitley Bay and stood looking at the large old terraced house, feeling very vulnerable, a feeling I was unaccustomed to. I did not know then what I understand now about alcohol and how it had anesthetised my feelings.

Now without the alcohol in my system, unfortunately some feelings were beginning to surface. Yes, I did say unfortunately. In the early days of sobriety, I can assure you I did not really like having feelings and struggled to deal with this alien state of being. It would be fair to say I was certainly emotionally illiterate; and had no vocabulary whatsoever for what I felt. The word vulnerable did not even exist, although I knew I felt something different from the normal cut off, emotionless state I had operated in for most of my life. Nevertheless, you will have realised by now that I did feel anger and plenty of it. However, I must add that at this point in my life I had not completed a course in 'emotional intelligence'. I therefore lacked the articulation skills to politely say to someone, 'Oh I do feel angry with your inappropriate behaviour; and would prefer that you refrain from treating me this way if we are to continue with our relationship.' No at this stage in my life I possessed a vast vocabulary of offensive words which reeled off my tongue without a second thought. Yes I was still light years away from expressing my thoughts and feelings in an acceptable civilised manner. I digress as I explain a little about addiction and my emotions.

I took another step towards the front door, with my thoughts racing, as I did not know what a rehab was. In fact, I had never heard of a rehab until a couple of days before. If only Amy Winehouse's song "Rehab" had been around; I would certainly have been in the know, however, I was now just about to step into a whole new life.

After ringing the doorbell it was a few seconds before the door was opened. In the doorway stood a young woman who was dressed in boyish clothes. She looked intensely at me, smiled and invited me in. Before me was a long hallway through to the kitchen; and on the left was the community lounge. I was invited into the lounge and introduced to a number of people of various shapes, sizes, sexes and ages,

REHAB –
THE BEST TIME OF MY LIFE TO DATE

starting from about seventeen to fifty. The thing that caught my attention was how relaxed they all were, as they stretched out on the long couch and flung their legs across the sides of the chairs. A bewildering concept for me, I don't think I'd ever sprawled around a room in such a manner. Probably something to do with the high probability of someone swiping me as I lay there in my atmosphere of bliss. The house appeared very homely, there were eight men and three women. On a seat in the corner sat a drop-dead gorgeous man, probably in his late twenties; he had blonde, longish hair and stood over six feet tall. I found out later he had worked as a gigolo, he also worked out daily at the local David Lloyds. He certainly had a physique which would have been a resting place for even the most tired of eyes.

Oops steal your glare away from this hunk while being introduced to Marg the project manager; a bleached blonde-haired woman, with a shoulder length bob and pale blue eyes. Her lips had that peculiar shape, you know when you make the top lips pointy like two mountain peaks. This effect was emphasised by the bright red lipstick she wore. She was about five-feet seven, very slim and dressed in a refreshing style; trendy would appropriately describe her. She also had an aura about her which was quite scary. She stuck her hand out to shake my hand. That was a new one for me, I was more accustomed to "Helow how yu deein." In a distinctive high-pitched, yet firm voice she said, "Hi I'm Marg the project manager." Her eyes seemed to pierce my soul which I had only had for a couple of weeks. I can remember shaking a bit inside, probably outside as well. You know when your head tremors? Well it was like that. I took hold of her hand in return and said hello in a strong confident voice. Although that is not what was going on inside my body, as I made a feeble attempt to camouflage the fear I felt.

Marg said she would leave the residents to do the interview and wait for their verdict. The woman who answered the door took control of the interview, her name was Lucy. She was about five-feet-two inches tall with short straight dark hair. Lucy asked the residents who were lying around the community lounge to sit up and take part, or to leave the room, asserting her authority in a firm yet friendly voice. They all sat up and stayed throughout the interview. I think they had been waiting for me coming to check me out. It was a large pleasant room, quite tastefully decorated with high ceilings, and a big old-fashioned rose in the centre. There was a TV in the corner and plenty of comfortable chairs, as well as a three-seater settee. This room led into an adjoining dining room, where in place of a dining table stood a full-sized pool table; a guitar was standing against the wall and games were scattered all over. This place actually looked pleasant and inviting, very different from the hospitals where they had previously incarcerated me.

Lucy asked me a number of questions relating to what I hoped to get out of my stay at the rehab – what did I have to offer others in the rehab and so on. She told me there were house rules I needed to comply with if I was accepted as a resident. She discussed these rules with me, while other residents chipped in occasionally to reinforce anything she did not make too clear. I was asked if there was anything I would like to ask. I asked how long other people had been in the house. Lucy had been there for two years. I was horrified and concluded that she must be extremely mentally ill. When they asked me how long I expected to stay, I said, "I will be fine after three days and ready to move on." They looked at one another, you know with that look of, 'Is she for real'? But said nothing. After a lengthy discussion they agreed I could move in, on condition I obeyed the house rules or I would be thrown out; simplicity at its best.

The house rules, or conditions of residency were that everyone in the house remained completely abstinent from illegal drugs and alcohol during their stay. If anyone relapsed they would be required to attend a house meeting. The outcome of this meeting would determine whether or not the resident was allowed to remain in the house, or whether they would be requested to leave. All residents and a member of staff would be present at the meeting. Various factors would be considered such as; how were they relating to other residents in the house. How long they had been using alcohol or drugs without the staff or residents knowing? How deviant had they been during their relapse? What had they learned from their relapse? Could they be trusted again in the house? What were they contributing to the community? Did they wish to try again? If so what guarantee were they prepared to give to assure other residents they would not relapse again? If they did relapse again could they elicit the support of other residents or staff quickly before it got out of hand?

Sounded more like an interrogation to me! Never mind, I was going to give it a go, as there was little to lose at this stage in my life and a lot to gain. And yes, I was soon to find out that the meetings were tough for residents who had relapsed, and quite often it was decided that the resident would be asked to leave. This was always a sad time for everyone in the house, as no one really wanted to see another person in the same predicament as themselves fail. Neither did they know when it would be their turn to take the dreaded relapse seat!

REHAB –
THE BEST TIME OF MY LIFE TO DATE

I was told that, as a new resident I would not be allowed to go anywhere for six weeks without an escort. This meant another resident had to be with me wherever I went outside the house and also someone would be watching me in the house too. Apparently people have all sorts of strange ways of smuggling drugs and alcohol into these houses. This felt somewhat strange having someone tag along wherever I went.

If I did not know the residents prior to entering the rehab, I was quickly going to get to know them. If I opened the back door to go into the yard someone would ask me where I was going or bless me with their presence. I found this difficult to cope with at first, as I was unaccustomed to being shadowed. I soon adjusted to the idea and allowed it not to interfere with my stay. Sometimes it could be useful, at other times it could be a nuisance.

During this period my uncle died, and I had to have an escort to the funeral. I felt really uncomfortable as my escort for the day was a young lesbian woman, who looked like a young lesbian woman. Now I got along brilliantly with her, she was only eighteen years old and quite a refreshing tonic. However, the funeral was thirty years ago in a town devoid of any homosexuals. Yes, coming out in a small town in those days would have been the equivalent of declaring you had been a traitor during the war. Being two sensible souls committed to our mission of sobriety, we made a quick exit after the service. That is, in our ultimate wisdom we decided to give the wake a miss at the local bar where I would have no doubt everyone would have been well inebriated as they drowned their sorrows.

While in the rehab we were required to attend all house meetings. There were both therapeutic group meetings, and administration meetings. The therapeutic group work in the rehab never failed to fascinate me. Marg facilitated what we called the 'Happy Hour.' Most of the residents felt physically ill prior to the group starting. One resident said she never knew when it was her turn to be interrogated or humiliated. The groups were so unpredictable it was like walking into the lion's den. An atmosphere of fear pervaded around the house every Tuesday before the group started at 6.30 in the evening. I loved it. This atmosphere felt familiar, similar to the one I had grown accustomed to throughout my life. I loved the tension, and the fear that gripped the group. Now I know this may sound strange, but it is how it was. At that point in my life I had no understanding of why I thrived on fear. It took years of psychoanalytic therapy before I eventually had an understanding of my background, and how this influenced my behaviour and feelings.

REHAB –
THE BEST TIME OF MY LIFE TO DATE

During the 'Happy Hour' we were encouraged to discuss any personal problems: past or present or issues within the rehab itself. We were also encouraged to express our feelings verbally and confront each other's behaviour, but without acting out any physical violence on any of the other residents. That is, if someone upset us, we were not allowed to kick them all over. We were lucky, as the group of residents in the rehab had a wide range of experiences; there was usually someone who could help another resident to make sense of what they were going through.

Believe it or not, but sexual relationships between residents were strictly forbidden. If anyone suspected any of the residents of having a relationship this would be raised in the group. Can you imagine what this was like to have your love life scrutinised by a bunch of people? Yes, it was a very uncomfortable experience for anyone unfortunate enough to end up in this position. Sometimes they were not guilty of the accusations made about them, or they refused to admit there was anything in the accusations. Who was to know, bit of a difficult thing to prove don't you think?

On one occasion Marg asked everyone in the group if anyone in the house was drinking. Of course, everyone said, "No." She continued with her line of questioning; until it became apparent that she had evidence to suggest that someone was drinking and using drugs. The tension was building up rapidly, as this felt like a betrayal to all the residents. As the tension built there was a sudden outburst when suddenly someone jumped up and ran to the door. She punched the door full force with her fist, which rocketed through the wood panel and out the other side. It took her seconds to retrieve her fist from the other side of the door before making her escape. It was my young friend from the funeral; I went after her and asked her to return to the group which was now not a welcome place to be. She was bombarded with questions. How did she sneak alcohol into the building? Why had she spent weeks being nasty with everyone and giving people a hard time? Why had she elicited extra support from residents, and used them during this period in a deviant deceitful manner? Needless to say, the other residents were furious to learn that she had been drinking while they had been trying to support her.

Many of the residents in the rehab had been sexually abused from a very young age. The abuse was often carried out by their relatives or mother's boyfriends. Drink and drugs were their main escape from the trauma they'd experienced. After a very difficult evening it was decided to allow her to stay if she adhered to the conditions which were now going to be implemented. She was placed back on escort until such time as the group felt they could trust her again. Her mail was also to be checked, as she had been smoking cannabis and getting it sent in the post.

Sometimes residents shared horrific stories. One resident's parents had burned him with cigarettes if he cried. There was more than one resident who had been involved with gangsters and had to do the dirty work. This could mean anything; one man had to pour petrol on people who did not pay their dues for the drugs they received. On one occasion, my gorgeous hunk of a man told me he was told to break every bone in someone's body. He described how a gang of them had taken truncheons and metal bars and set about a man. Sometimes residents struggled with sobriety, as they had nightmares and flashbacks to the scenes of people screaming as they were brutalised, maimed and/or murdered. These sorts of stories were quite typical in some way for most of the residents. Women residents who sought help for their drink problems often had their children taken into care, as they were considered unsuitable mothers. I was so pleased I had managed to keep my own son during my drinking years. Hope he was too!

I must add, that regardless of how heartless some of the residents may sound by the stories they tell while on the drink, or using drugs, you really couldn't have met a better, more upbeat, funnier group of people. On one occasion two of the residents were trying to share very difficult experiences in their lives. Suddenly a group member's stomach started to grumble really loudly, the rest of us burst out laughing. We sat for an hour giggling and laughing while these two residents struggled to tell their stories. One resident had relapsed and during the relapse he became extremely violent and ended up with seven criminal charges against him for grievous bodily harm and damage to property. The other resident had lost access to his young daughter that day in court. Every time they tried to share their grief with us we burst out laughing. You know when you have those fits of laughter and begin to belly laugh, well that is how it was. We were rolling around the chairs in stitches every time one of them spoke. Shame on us. The two injured parties were far from amused; they glared at us each time they opened their mouths, and we burst into another hysterical fit of laughter. Well done to Marg who managed to keep her face straight, as she attempted rather unsuccessfully to facilitate the meeting.

During one of the meetings we were asked to make a chart of how our lives had been and how we imagined life would be in five years' time. Everyone did complicated drawings of their lives and how they imagined they would progress. They drew

REHAB –
THE BEST TIME OF MY LIFE TO DATE

babies in prams, children at school, and college courses and jobs. In other words they elaborated on how they imagined their lives would be in five years. I chose to draw three lines which adequately described my life. A member of the group once reminded me of the fact that my three lines had more impact than all their fancy artwork. The first diagonal line running up the page represented my progress from birth to seventeen. This was when my mother died. The second line starting at the top of the first line running down the page diagonally represented my life going downhill from seventeen to thirty-four. These were the two halves of my life to date and this was the age I stopped drinking and ended up in the rehab. A small stroke to say I imagined I would have started the climb uphill again represented where I would be in five years without the drink. I need to add that without the drink I felt like half the person I was. I felt so much stronger with the drink, and I often wondered if I would ever feel as strong again without drink. In fact, it was my goal to get to be the 'same person' but without the drink. How ambitious was I?

At that stage I would have preferred to have the drink, but given that I was advised to remain totally alcohol free or I would die, left me with little choice. Just shows from my three line image how low my self-esteem was at that time, but little did I know then that in five years' time I would have gone well beyond what I could possibly have thought was possible. In fact, I couldn't even dream big, as I thought I was worthless.

When I first arrived at the rehab I found the language the residents used peculiar. They used an alien language for so called alcoholics. They used words which I did not understand, like: "abstinence," "dynamics," "counsellors," "derogatory," "paranoid," "psychotic," "vulnerable," "narcotics," "boundaries," "harassment," "depressed," "barbiturates," "sexuality," "programme," "deviant," "relapse." They would say to one another, "Aren't I growing." I thought they were a bit too old to grow. I had little conception of what they were talking about most of the time. I think they became accustomed to speaking this way as regular service users. The people I associated with prior to the rehab had not progressed as readily as these articulate, seasoned service users. No, the people I was associating with prior to the rehab possessed a vocabulary consisting of, I yis and na, scattered abundantly with profanities. Whereas, the majority of the residents had been exposed to this language through the constant contact they had with health professionals, social workers and counsellors. As a result, their use of psychological jargon became second nature; you would have thought they'd been educated at the British School of Nursing, not the streets of life.

REHAB –
THE BEST TIME OF MY LIFE TO DATE

Also, when I arrived at the rehab, I found the way the other residents were thinking and behaving quite peculiar. It was as though there was no loyalty; the residents actually reported each other if they broke the rules. I found this so difficult to understand. If you did this sort of thing out on the street you would not survive to tell the tale. I struggled to comprehend their behaviour. However, I could not believe how quickly I was indoctrinated into the same brainwashed behaviour. It was certainly a process worth watching in the making. Unfortunately, at that stage I had no knowledge of psychology, and no knowledge of the process that was taking place. I did read about it years later when studying psychology. On reflection, I was fascinated by the similarities in the process we were exposed to, and the technique known as brainwashing or the more acceptable term of 'thought reform'.

I think you would find this interesting, if we just take a closer look at the similarities between the methods used in the rehab, and the methods used in 'Total Institutions' to change a person's thought processes and behaviour. It will probably be helpful to explain what is meant by a total institution. It is an enclosed social system whose main purpose is to control most aspects of its participants' lives. They include prisons, concentration camps, mental hospitals, convents, rehabs, boarding schools, boot camps, some religious cults and military training camps. They are places in which people are cut off from the rest of society and come under almost total control of the officials who are in charge. The idea is to remake the person by stripping away their identity and putting a new one in its place. A tall order indeed, it sounds like some science fiction horror movie.

I am going to take reference from the "Open University Course Readers" and look at what that book has to say about the process. Then compare this with what was going on in the rehab with the residents. Just to give you a bit of background it was the same method of thought reform which was used in the revolutionary colleges set up all over China in the late 1940s for reforming the political views of the population. It was also used much more brutally during the Korean War to attempt political indoctrination of Chinese prisoners of war. So here goes.

A total institution has total control over the lives of the people who live in them. They use a high level of psychological control over their residents, since they control their stimulation, their response opportunities and the rewards they receive. The inmates lack access to contacts, roles or reference groups. Whether membership is voluntary or involuntary does not determine the effect of the influence on new members. The

REHAB –
THE BEST TIME OF MY LIFE TO DATE

*coercive power can be used to rob individuals of normal
supports to their understanding of their own identity.*

*Members discuss their experiences and their hatred of the old
regime. They are given lectures on the new ideologies and
purposes. A change begins to develop after a few weeks. There
is a shift in emphasis from the ideologies and intellectual to
the emotional and personal. Their views and attitudes come
under scrutiny and the leader and other members of their
primary membership group exert pressure on them to adopt
correct views. Constant criticism of others and self-criticism
leads to confessions and reform begins to take place. If they
do not adhere to the group rules they are relentlessly
humiliated in the group situation. This creates feelings of
anxiety and fear.* The Open University. People in Groups Unit
19/20/21.

Now back to the rehab. From what I have shared so far
regarding my experience of the rehab you will have realised
that both the residents and staff used a high level of
psychological control over the newer residents. They
controlled their stimulation, their response opportunities and
the rewards they received. Residents were discouraged from
talking positively about their drinking careers and to speak
highly of their new life in the rehab. They were deprived of

access to contacts, or reference groups, as they were not allowed to go anywhere alone for the first six weeks and visits from friends or relatives were also not allowed during this period. Their previous behaviour was frowned upon and new desired behaviour encouraged. A great deal of this was done during the group meetings and through therapy. Our views and attitudes come under scrutiny from other residents while pressure was exerted to adopt what was considered '*correct views*'. If we did not adhere to the group rules we were relentlessly questioned and '*humiliated*' in the group situation. This '*created feelings of anxiety, insecurity and fear*' of rejection which were familiar feelings to many of the residents, feelings they really wanted to avoid at all costs.

Can you now see the similarities between my rehab experience and thought control? I can also assure you that after a few weeks the change does start to take effect. I was so surprised when I realised, I was starting to think, behave and talk like the 'brain washed' residents I'd heard when I first went to live in the rehab. Now, although brainwashing and thought control are usually considered negative, I can only say the techniques used were pivotal in my road to recovery.

While in the rehab we were given a small weekly allowance of £9 to buy toiletries, clothes and personal goods.

REHAB –
THE BEST TIME OF MY LIFE TO DATE

There was also a small cash flow for various activities for the residents. This provided money for one activity a week. I went ice-skating with some of the residents for a couple of months. It was great fun, I could skate forwards and backwards and do quite fancy turns. I loved the feeling of moving on the ice. I also fell down a lot, and I'm sure at times I skated more on my stomach than on my feet. When I realised, I was no Jayne Torvill, with no chance of being the best ice skater in the world I gave it up. I loved the rehab; I would dance on the tables and sing at the top of my voice and believe me my singing certainly left something to be desired. Much to my disappointment, singing like ice-skating was not my forte.

It was rare when we could organise any sort of outing as we did not have the finances. However at one of our meetings it was agreed that most of the residents thought it would be a good idea to try to organise a trip to the Lake District. Now as there were about ten residents wanting to go, we needed suitable transport. That is we had to get a bus! Although we didn't have a bus, we knew that, Phoenix House the local drug rehab in South Shields had their own bus for their residents. The residents who were very persuasive asked me to organise everything and drive the bus. Me being ever so willing to please, I did. I contacted Phoenix house and explained our situation. Lucky me, the project manager agreed we could borrow their bus for the day.

Away we went to enjoy a wonderful day in the Lakes. We sang all the way there and all the way back. While we were there we had a meal at McDonald's, which at the time I thought was posh! When we returned after our fantastic day out I walked into the office to hand the keys back to the project manager, who I may add had a reputation for being extremely harsh and strict. I chatted for a couple of minutes, as I do and said, how much I enjoyed my time in the rehab. Her face physically changed in seconds from stern to furious. She thought I was a member of staff and hadn't realise when agreeing to loan the bus to us that I was a resident. It was clear she was horrified and started to say at much. Yes, it was time for a quick exit. I left her in mid-sentence, as I thanked her and waved goodbye.

One thing which surprised me was the respect the other residents held for me. I was quickly given the position as senior resident, even though I was not senior either by the length of time I had been in the rehab or by age. Residents used to feel confident sharing their problems with me, and urged me to begin training as a counsellor. I embraced the praise they bestowed on me, I was in my glory! They said I

REHAB –
THE BEST TIME OF MY LIFE TO DATE

would be a great counsellor, as I had a depth of understanding that surpassed the majority of social workers and counsellors who they had met to date. Although I loved the praise I did not share their confidence in myself, as I did not think I was good enough. Nevertheless, I did tend to be a natural leader in the rehab. Most of the residents believed in whatever I said both in and out of meetings.

The rehab was a great place for learning about my strengths and weaknesses. When I later told people who I knew that I was in a rehab because of my drinking. They always said something like, 'I can't believe it, you were about the strongest person I knew.' I found this strange, because I had no real perception of myself during my drinking career. However, the intense group discussions were allowing me to see much more of my personality, and have an idea of how other people perceived me. With trepidation by the sounds of it!

Although at one level I played a highly responsible role as senior resident, at another level my behaviour was very immature. I was oblivious to the fact that I had not developed emotionally. On hindsight, it was also obvious that neither had the majority of the residents in the rehab. They had developed mentally, that is they could be as bright as anyone else, but they were lacking any emotional maturity. Most of us had suppressed our emotions as a result of traumatic childhood experiences. Just like a three-year-old we would act on the primitive feelings of anger and frustration without using the control more emotionally mature people would be able to put in place. It was this lack of maturity that usually resulted in inappropriate behaviour and the inability to take any control over our lives.

After studying psychology and training as a psychotherapist I would label the behaviour I have described as arrested development. This means that rather than regressing back to an earlier stage of life, as in regression, the developmental stages had not been negotiated in the first place. In other words, I couldn't regress back to a stage I had not been through. This made my stay in the rehab all the more pleasurable, as the other residents were usually up for a laugh and we did have some real fun times.

Nevertheless, during the first years of my sobriety inside my head felt like a pressure-cooker. Yes, that is the only way I can describe what my head felt like. I did not have a headache, I just felt a build-up of pressure inside my head, which was really peculiar. I was also becoming more aware of what I looked like; drat! I often looked something akin to a wild animal. My eyes were frightening, they had that raised eyebrow look of a person fixed in a permanent state of 'startle response'. People occasionally told me I looked frightening, especially if I was relaying a story from the events of the day. Fortunately they knew I was absolutely fine and wouldn't hurt a soul that is unless I was crossed. To be fair, I had gained the trust and respect of probably all the other residents. One resident who had spent time in jail for murder, often said in his broad Geordie accent, "When a hear yu cough in the mounins a pu the kettle on an mek yu tea ready fu yu comin doon the stairs." That about sums up the effect I was having on the other residents!

While at the rehab I had to undergo numerous brain tests, as I felt as if my drinking career had done serious damage to my brain. When you drink for years your brain becomes accustomed to operating at a particular level. When I stopped drinking my brain felt peculiar, as if feeling it was like a pressure cooker was not peculiar enough. Yes, I also felt as though it had been stuffed with cotton wool and someone had just torn all the cotton wool out and left it exposed. In reality my brain was working much quicker than it was while I was drinking, but that is not how it felt. When you drink everything is slowed down but I was unaware of this until I got sober. So for instance, when I was sober working on a till I would add up much quicker. But, because the speed was so fast I could not trust that my calculations were accurate; then I would do it again much slower and get the same answer. It became painfully obvious that I was now even brighter than I imagined! I was given an ECG and various IQ tests which took several months to complete. When I was due to go to the doctors for the results one of the female residents called me, "Stupid" just before I left. I can remember being so offended, even though it was in fun. On my way up to the doctor's surgery the heel on my quite high heeled shoe broke. Because I now believed I had brain damage and was stupid, I made every effort to walk as if I was intelligent! I walked on my tiptoes to make the shoeless foot the same height as the foot with the shoe. That would make me look intelligent! When the doctor called me to his consulting room I was nervous and scared to hear the results of the tests. He said all the tests showed that I was well above normal intelligence and I had nothing to worry about. I was absolutely delighted, it is amazing how quickly I could change. I left the surgery swaying from side to side with my one shoe off and one shoe on; and I did not give a damn how I looked because I knew I was a bright spark!

Bright or not I was certainly still prone to the odd outburst. On one occasion the rehab manager was trying to calm down one of my outbursts. She was shouting at me, "Catherine you are hurt. Can you not see you are hurt?" I screamed back at

REHAB –
THE BEST TIME OF MY LIFE TO DATE

her, *"You F...... stupid B..... of course I'm not hurt, I'm f.....
angry. Hurt means when someone punches you and hits you.
Are you stupid or what?"* That was my level of understanding
hurt, perhaps I also lacked a bit of subtlety! I did not know
that people could feel hurt by words or events. Another time,
when I felt betrayed by the project manager, I burst into my
bedroom which was shared with another resident. This resident
was in the room having a counselling session with a counsellor
from a different organisation. The project manager was also
there. On seeing her I was unable to contain the rage I felt. I
just burst forth with my bombardment of accusations regarding
her betrayal of my trust, although at that stage I would not
have used the expression 'betrayal of my trust'. I would be
more likely to scream at her that she was a 'sneaky, lying
snake'. I was told afterwards that the other counsellor had
never in all her life experienced such rage in a human being.
She said she just slid down the chair and wanted to disappear.
These sorts of outbursts were typical for me if I was upset. Yes
I had still not mastered the skill of politely articulating my
feelings. Can you imagine this? Everyone would think I'd had
a radical personality change. Well in any case I wasn't having
one that week.

During my counselling sessions with Marg when I was
talking about something deep or possibly painful, she would

say, "Catherine, stay with your feelings." I did not have a clue what she meant, as far as I was concerned I did not have any feelings to stay with. She would say, "Allow yourself to experience what is going on in your body." I would respond with, *"The only feelings I ever have in my body are feelings of hunger, so I really don't know what you are talking about."* One weekend when she was off duty I decided to try to find these feelings, which she seemed to think I held in some deep recess in my body. I went into my bedroom and thought about something distressing that had happened in my life, (I must say that was a struggle) and stayed with that thought. I say thought, as there were no feelings. I held the thought for quite a while and eventually started to feel what my body was experiencing. It took a while before I could really connect with my body, but I can remember gradually feeling a sense of darkness. This led me into a state of deep dark depression for three days. Try as I may I was unable to bring myself back to my normal, funny, cheerful self! I did not wish to socialise with the residents that weekend. I felt as if I just wanted to stay in the bedroom and die. It was terrible, I had ventured into the real pain of my past experiences. That was the first time I did that and I am sure you would guess it would be the last for a while. Although saying that, this experience intrigued me. At

REHAB –
THE BEST TIME OF MY LIFE TO DATE

least now I knew that there were painful feelings buried deep in the recesses of my body!

My time spent in the rehab was like an exciting journey. An appropriate metaphor would be that I started at the bottom of a mountain and began climbing up. As I climbed my view got bigger, things I could not see before I could now see. As my feelings started to unfold, I was fascinated. I learned to begin to listen to my body, to identify my feelings, and to express them verbally if appropriate! At this stage I still had little or no control over them. It was becoming apparent that the feelings I had put on hold from the age of seven were now slowly coming into being.

In the rehab when we had problems we turned to each other for support. The alcohol no longer played the role of 'best friend' with the answer to all our problems. In group therapy we were encouraged to share our deepest thoughts and feelings. This helped us to understand ourselves and the other residents. Complete honesty was encouraged, but I doubt strongly that it was not always adhered to. I also think it would be a bit fool hardy at times to be completely honest. Can you imagine it? A sure recipe for disaster, we would probably end up killing each other given I was not the only one with an out of control fiery temper.

REHAB –
THE BEST TIME OF MY LIFE TO DATE

Sometimes we would sit up into the early hours of the morning telling stories and having fun. We would share our most horrendous times, and things which gripped our consciences. Living in such a close therapeutic community gives you a different sense of yourself. It was inevitable as a result of the therapy that we would share with one another how we experienced each other. This can be tough at times if you have personality traits which are not acceptable to others. I was very lucky as it was rare when anyone took issue with me. Not sure if that had anything to do with my personality at that time, or if I was just absolutely perfect!

I loved it in the rehab unit. The residents consisted of murderers, armed bank robbers, drug dealers, alcoholics and criminals of all walks of life. Nevertheless, it was the first time in my life I felt safe. There were no locks on any of the bedroom doors and I did not feel as though there needed to be any. There was a sense of comradeship, trust and safety. We looked out for one another and had fun together. Now I know that may sound odd for the sort of people I'm describing but believe me that is just how it was. I felt alive and able to be me for the first time in my life. These people actually liked and respected me for me; they encouraged and supported me in everything I did. (Well almost everything!)

REHAB –
THE BEST TIME OF MY LIFE TO DATE

In the rehab most of the residents were on long-term sickness benefit and registered alcoholics. It was often suggested by the staff and residents that I also register. However, I had other ideas; I had no intention of putting my life on hold any longer than it already had been. I felt as though Jeff had stunted my growth and held me back from reaching any potential for years. I knew that if I was on long term sickness benefit that this would prevent me from trying to better myself. It would just lead to a dreary monotonous lifestyle which I was determined not to have under any circumstances. No, I would give this opportunity my best shot or go under.

On one occasion I tried to raise money for some activity for the residents at Christmas, so I decided to get some paid employment. I was interviewed by a woman who wanted a cleaner to clean her house three times a week. We talked for about an hour, she was obviously impressed with what I had to say. She asked for my address because she said I had the job. When I said, "I live in the rehab across the road." She almost fell of her chair, and as her mouth dropped open, she said, "Oh! I can't have someone like you working here." and asked me to leave. I was gutted, I couldn't even get a job as a cleaner, and so much for my honesty. I won't tell you what I thought of her.

REHAB –
THE BEST TIME OF MY LIFE TO DATE

Unfortunately, I had been told it was important to be honest when applying for jobs, and to tell my employer about my past. All this accomplished was lots of rejection for work. "Oh, you are an alcoholic, I'm sorry I can't employ you." Not as sorry as I was. I felt like throwing the towel in, as no one would employ me; so being honest was certainly not doing me any favours. I look back now with great pleasure at those times when I was refused employment by some small-minded prat, as the same people now couldn't tie my shoelaces. I excelled them all, much to my delight! Many times, I was on my backside; and just as many times I got up and won the next round. I am also aware that I was never meant to get those jobs, because if I had I would not be where I am today.

I remained friends with one of the female residents who I met on my first night at the rehab. She looked like a witch, with straggly black hair which was thin and lank, her eyes were drawn and popping out of her head. She was so thin she looked as if she had been in a concentration camp. I did not particularly like her when we first met. By the time she left the rehab she looked years younger, her hair was short and healthy looking, her eyes were lovely, she put on some weight and looked like a healthy normal human being. It was great to see people change and begin to look cared for and compos mentis instead of uncared for and deranged.

REHAB –
THE BEST TIME OF MY LIFE TO DATE

As you can imagine some of the residents moved on and new ones moved in. After about a year I felt as if the good strong residents had mostly gone and been replaced with a group of spineless wimps. During one of the administration meetings I suggested that everyone contribute to getting the house prepared for Christmas. A good spring clean, to which they all agreed. That evening when I came home from doing my voluntary work, a male resident came up to me and nervously said, "Catherine after yu left we had a group meetin and we would like tu tell yu in a group what we decided." I agreed to meet with them having no idea of what this was about, although I had a gut feeling that I should be somewhat apprehensive. The reality was it would not have taken Einstein to figure out it was something unpleasant. I met the 'eleven' other residents at seven o'clock. They started by saying they found me too powerful and were frightened to tell me when they disagreed with what I said. Like I should be responsible for their shortcomings! They did not really want to clean the house but were frightened to tell me during the group. Just in case you didn't know, when I'm attacked my defence can often be to attack back. Nevertheless, I calmly went around every resident in the group and asked if they had any more problems with me. Was I ever unfair? Did I not pull my own weight? Did I ever bully anyone? Was I ever nasty and so on?

REHAB –
THE BEST TIME OF MY LIFE TO DATE

Each resident said, "No I was not unfair, a bully or a problem in any other way other than they found me a very powerful person." I said, "In that case I suggest you move up to my standards and don't expect me to move down to yours." And walked out of the meeting. Did I feel pleased with myself for the way I handled them? It was one of those moments you know when your fist smashes through the air as you shout, 'Yes.'

Nevertheless, my eighteen-month experience in the rehab was the most productive time in my life to date, a time of growth, opportunity, learning and fun. It was a safe, secure environment where for the first time I was in an environment where I could thrive. This was the start of the rest of my life.

THE MOBILE PHONE SAGA

This is just a little story about my stolen mobile telephone. I was driving along the road when it started to rain. It was not long before I spotted a young man getting very wet, as he stood hitch-hiking by the road side. I pulled the car into the layby to pick him up, and as I did, I had a bad feeling about him. I realised that the previous evening I had given someone a lift and the passenger car door was not locked. As a result, he had the door open before I could pull away again. He jumped into the car with a cheerful, "Thank you." He was on his way to the metro station, which I was passing about eleven miles down the road. We engaged in a meaningless conversation, as he said he did a few local gigs in city centre bars. He chatted about the music he enjoyed and discussed the local night life in the city. As the conversation was in full swing he appeared fidgety, I remained suspicious, as there was something about him making me uneasy.

When he got out of the car at the metro station, I quickly checked to see that my handbag etc. were still where they should be. Within seconds I realised that my mobile telephone was missing. I quickly parked the car up and ran up to the metro line; he was still there and just as I was about to pounce, he realised and took off as fast as his scrawny legs could carry him. I was no match for him, as he quickly jumped a fence and ran off. Although unable to chase after him I shouted after him, "I want my mobile phone back you thieving scum of the earth, low life." When it was clear he was out of range of my verbal onslaught I give up on the chase and made my way to the Drs Surgery where I was seeing clients that afternoon.

On reaching the surgery I explained to the receptionists what had happened. Now I had worked quite closely with these lasses for about two years and had a great relationship with them. There was never a day went by where I did not part with some pearl of wisdom. I remember one day they were discussing secrets. They said they felt it was important to always tell people your secrets and asked my opinion. Well, I said, "I believe that you should only tell anyone your secrets if you can cope with everyone else knowing them! I explained the power dynamic when someone has something on you which makes you vulnerable to them; going on to say how this can be used against you when your relationship hits problems, as it often will. The look of shock and disagreement on their faces was obvious, when in walked a nurse who had heard what had been said. She now joined our conversation and said, "When I was first married, I told my husband a secret and he later held me to ransom in a relationship which I hated for four years before I felt strong enough to leave." I rest my case! I digress, the lasses in reception were only too happy to help me out in my moment of need. They suggested I call the stolen telephone from the surgery phone to leave a message. Fortunately, they knew me well enough to not be surprised at the message I left:

"You scum of the earth I want my phone back. The umbilical cord should have choked you at birth it would have done the world a favour. I did you a good turn and this is how you repay me, you are nothing but low life and shouldn't have the privilege of associating with decent people." I spoke firmly and clearly down the telephone with a tirade of abusive insults before I hung up, really satisfied with myself but still determined to get the telephone back. You might be wondering how I reckoned this was the way to get my phone back! I had always been told 'honesty is the best policy'. Well whoever had my phone was certainly getting their share of my honesty and I bet you they were not too impressed. Did I care? Not a bit.

After finishing work in the surgery with the clients I made my way home. I was advised to block the telephone so that it could not be used. Just as I was about to make this telephone call I thought I would give it one last try. I rang the number and surprise! Someone answered. I immediately went into my abusive rant. The person on the other end eventually got a word in edgeways and said, "I have just bought the telephone for £10 from someone in a bar and did not realise it had been stolen until I listened to the message you left." I asked if he knew the person, he'd bought it from. How stupid do you get? Of course, he said he didn't know him.

After a heated conversation, the man said he would bring the telephone into Newcastle the following Sunday afternoon and would meet me outside a rather seedy pub in the Grainger Market. Yes, I agreed to this without stopping to think of any possible dangers. He said he wanted £10 in exchange for the telephone. I am very uncomfortable telling lies therefore I avoided a direct answer. "Yes, I would pay him." Very aware that I did not say what I would pay him. When I told my friends what I was doing they were shocked. The response was, "Don't be so stupid, do you realise how dangerous this could be? "Just telephone the police and they will get your telephone." They obviously had no idea of the limitations of the police. I knew that if I contacted the police I would never get the phone. Can you imagine it? Hello this is PC Crimestopper could you give me your name and address so that I can collect Catherin's telephone? I don't think so. Nevertheless, everyone thought my hair brained scheme was ridiculous and dangerous.

As I was not one for caution at that time in my life I went ahead regardless. I arrived ten minutes early to wait for this man coming along with my mobile telephone. Right on time, a man walked along the street clutching a mobile in his hand. I walked up rather brashly and asked, "Is that my mobile telephone?" When he said, "So you are Catherine." I snarled, "Now give it back to me." I more or less snatched the phone out of his hand. There was no resistance as he asked for money. I said, "Go and get your money from the thieving git who sold you the telephone. It was not his to sell it was stolen property, my stolen property." He shouted, "I can walk into that F...ing bar and get people to turn you over." I retorted with, "Go and get who you f....ing like but I will guarantee I will have you turned over first." I gave him £5 to cover his bus fare into town but made it clear he was not getting another penny. He disappeared and I got safely home with my telephone, chuffed to bits with myself too. My friends were amazed I had actually got the phone back. Didn't I do well?

MY PROFOUND MYSTICAL EXPEREINCE

This week will always be remembered as the most important week in my life. To be fair I would like to prepare you a bit for this chapter, because when you read it you might be highly likely to think I am either absolutely crazy, psychotic or completely deluded. I can assure you this is one time when I was not any of the above, but as you read, you will see why I have said that. It might also be that you do not wish to read this chapter because you do not believe that strange and weird spiritual phenomena can happen. If that is the case then feel free to skip this chapter, and move to the next one, as I am sure you will pick up the thread.

Here goes! I had been sober for about three years when I started to go through a difficult spell; not that there were not difficult spells before this, but this was an extra difficult spell. There were several things happening in my life at this time which I was struggling with. This included issues of loss which may have been compounded by my father's untimely death. My shop, where I was selling miscellaneous goods and designing fancy stud work onto leather jackets, was also blown up in the Scotswood riots. On top of this, my car was stolen and found burned out. Last but not least I threw the undertaker out of the house when he was talking above my head. It was as though he had swallowed a dictionary and was now spewing it up all over me, I was not impressed. I'd certainly had better weeks!

Nevertheless, I got through this period; I survived the Scotswood Riots although my shop, where I was selling miscellaneous goods and doing designer work on leather goods and jackets, was completely burned to the ground, as it was inside the local post office. I was working in the shop as the rioters started to gather; they were coming in their droves and it was obvious by the expressions on their faces they meant business. I left earlier than normal and locked the shop up as the atmosphere was eerie and the local people were disappearing off the streets. When I returned the next morning my shop had been burned to the ground. The street was all cordoned off and the police would not allow anyone near the ruins that were left from where the shop had stood the night before. It was like a bombsite. That was the end of that business.

Nevertheless, my father did get cremated and the year was going reasonably well. I had left the rehab and was now living on the nineteenth floor in an apartment in Newcastle city centre. I went to bed on the Sunday night, it was the 6/10/1991. As I was dozing off a man's head appeared in my mind, it was as though it was on a television screen or in a box. He talked to me for about twenty minutes saying several things, such as, 'I will affect you through your feelings.' 'You need to do more good than bad.' Many of the things were about how to live my life. I was told to turn to the future and not the past, but most of what was said did not remain in my memory. After the voice finished talking the head disappeared; I fell asleep and never gave it another thought.

The next morning, I got up as usual, had a bath, dressed, ate and began to make my way to the drug and alcohol unit where I did my voluntary work. I did not get far when the voice seemed to appear back in my head as clear as day. It told me to go home. I said in my head, 'I need to go to work.' And continued on my journey ignoring the voice. I was again 'commanded' to return home. Me being me, and not the most obliging of souls, I kept on ignoring the voice and continued making my way to work. I did not get very far when my legs began to shake, then the strength began to leave them. I was unable to take another step forward towards work. This began to feel frightening, I was almost on my knees. I slowly turned around and began to walk back home. As I did, the strength began to return to my legs, and I felt fine. I immediately thought, I am fine, I will just turn around and go back to work. I tried this, and to my utter surprise, or more appropriately horror, the same thing began to happen, once again the strength was taken from my legs. Now I do know this may sound peculiar, but I am telling it just how it was. I quickly turned back around and headed straight for home, as whatever was happening was really scaring me and felt like a force to be reckoned with.

When I got home, I sat wondering what was going on, I felt really frightened, as if some great force had taken over my thoughts. As I sat trying to make sense of what was happening my eyes fell to a playing card lying on the floor, it was the king of hearts. I was instructed by the voice to place the card above a mirror quite high up in the hallway, which I did without question. After doing this I sat on the sofa worried and confused. It was not long before something compelled me to stand up, as I did there was a mirror on the side wall where I caught my reflection. I watched as my face changed from its normal self, to a contorted mess; it was as if all the evil in my body was pouring out through my face. I'm sure you can imagine the horror of that! When they talk about 'a purging of the soul,' that is what it must have looked like. My face became contorted, it looked evil, as if poison was pouring out of me. It felt as though all the badness in me was coming up from my toes and out through my face. I felt as though I had just stepped into a horror movie. This went on for a while, and believe me I was scared, eventually this settled down, as you can imagine much to my relief.

MY PROFOUND MYSTICAL EXPEREINCE

It was not long before the voice returned and told me to perform a number of rituals, one was to go through some sort of baptism and communion. Every time I tried to ignore what this voice was telling me to do, I would lose the strength in my legs and feel as if I was on the verge of collapse. I got through that day, but this was far from over. This experience continued throughout the week in various shapes and forms. At one point it was as though I could see the amount of good or evil in each person I saw. Certainly, an experience I could have done without.

You know by now that I am not the most obedient of people, and as the expression goes, 'would argue with a saint.' Well I was still trying to argue against what was going on, even though I was absolutely terrified. The dialogue in my head at the time went something like this, 'God please leave me alone, there are people out there sitting on a mountain looking for you and I'm not one of them.' God was not interested in what I had to say, he seemed to have his own agenda. Drat! By now I was referring to this voice as God, as it was my only explanation for the power and nature of the experiences I was having. I was told to kneel down, ask for forgiveness and repent for my sins. Anything to keep in His favour, but I am sure this was cut short, as otherwise I would have died of old age by the time I finished recollecting on everything I had to repent. As I went to stand up, after asking for forgiveness there was a pair of scissors lying on the chair beside me. The voice told me to cut the umbilical cord; I did this without question, although there was obviously no real unbiblical cord. It was a symbolic gesture with the scissors.

I must say I did keep thinking I was cracking up. Yet I knew this was entirely different from anything I had previously experienced. There was an order to this which was not there during my previous experiences when I was psychotic and hospitalised. I also did not feel unwell, other than when I was being controlled by this force for not obeying what I was being told to do. That was a lot of the time! As I journeyed through this event I came to a point where I felt as though I was cloaked in love. It was a completely all-consuming feeling, a feeling I should never forget. It was the richest feeling I could ever possibly feel, no money in the world could ever create such a richness. As the week went on, I was 'allowed' to pick up where I left off with the voluntary work I was doing. It was now Wednesday, and I made my way to the Drug and Alcohol unit where I was doing some work every week. The manager, who went on to be head of a local university counselling department said later, "It was as though you were completely transcendental and untouchable, I have never seen anything like it." As the experience continued, it was as though everything in my life had been predetermined. Now I know how strange that may sound, but it was as though there was a complete order to everything in the world. Each bird in the sky, each car on the road, each person I saw, seemed to fit into a complete jigsaw. My mind saw a 'perfectly ordered universe'. Although I am telling you just a few of the major things during this period there were certainly a lot more. I am just telling you enough for you to try to make a semblance of sense out of this experience. If you do manage that let me know, as I would like to as well!

It was now Thursday, and I was ready to leave home to do my voluntary work. I was my usual self and full of energy as I made my way to the front door; suddenly the breath left my body. I actually felt as though I was on the verge of death, I was slowly collapsing. The voice told me to go back and lie on the bed, which I did without a running argument in my head. Aren't I improving? A few months earlier I had been to America and was wearing a very over the top, stylish six-inch-thick belt around my waist, which was adorned with large brass stones of various shapes and sizes. Looking back, it was very garish, God mustn't have liked it either! I had to remove the belt and place my hands over my navel, the right hand on top of the left; I followed the instructions. Again, the voice talked to me for about twenty minutes and slowly my breath began to return. After this ended, I got up and made a beeline for the front door, this time there was no drama and my journey to work was successful.

I called in to see the project manager Maria who had helped me in the past to make sense of some of my previous experiences. She had also been helping me through this difficult period, as she had studied medieval religion, as well as having some knowledge of numerology and symbolism. When I reached her office she said, *"Catherine I would like to meet you after work, as something strange happened to me during my lunch break. I was supposed to be having my lunch and instead I found myself standing in a book shop with a book in my hand which described many of the things you have been going through recently."* I agreed to meet her at five O'clock when she finished work. I did a couple of hours work in the drug and alcohol unit, which was a small snack bar where people with addiction problems could go to chat, get support and counselling. At about three o'clock when the club was closing for an hour, I made my way home.

On my way home, I called in and bought fish and chips at Bimbi's restaurant and took them home. As I walked into the kitchen twelve tiles fell off the kitchen wall onto the floor. I then accidentally knocked an egg off the bench, which cracked open as it landed on the tiles, with the yolk unbroken. Things seemed to settle down a bit as I ate my lunch, but you know when you're eating, and the food feels like a lump in your throat? Well that is how it felt. At about quarter to four the voice in my head said, "Look out of the window." I got up and looked out, there was nothing too much to look at which I had not already seen so I went to sit down again. "No," said the voice, as my feelings went haywire when I attempted to sit back down, I was told to stay at the window. I stood watching the clouds in the sky. My attention focused on what seemed to be two rather dull octagon shaped orbits spinning around in the sky. They were spinning one over the top of the other in different directions from one another. They did this for a while, then stopped and went in the opposite direction. As this was happening the clouds were slowly drifting across the sky on this dull October day. I was beginning to be aware that the time was pressing on and I had to meet Maria at 5pm. A much more pressing engagement than anything God might want me to do!

I was rambling on at God about this in my head and asking if I could go. Not waiting on a direct answer, I attempted to walk away, and guess what. Yes, my legs just started to fold from beneath me. I quickly stepped back to my position, now waiting as patiently as I could. Next, a half-moon shaped hill appeared, something swept in front of it like a blowing bush.

MY PROFOUND MYSTICAL EXPEREINCE

Then three red crosses appeared in the sky to the left of the hill, they slowly glided over the hill and disappeared into the clouds again, as the crosses disappeared a bush once more swept across the sky and everything went back to its normal self. I was stood awe struck at this sight. By this time, I was convinced I was going mad although I knew this was not insanity, I knew I was really experiencing this. The time was getting on, I was worried about missing my friend. I muttered to God in my head, "Is that it?" Speaking as if this is the sort of thing I see every day of the week and He was keeping me late for a more pressing engagement! It clearly was it! I headed straight for the front door to go and see what Maria wanted. I was really curious to know what she had found which was so important.

I dashed down to work, but don't worry I was not going to run in and tell anyone about my experience. Can you imagine it? I have just seen three red crosses floating through the sky! I would not doubt that I would have been taken away to a psychiatric hospital.

Maria took me to the book shop where she had found herself standing during her lunch break. As we walked to the shop, she described how frightened and bewildered she felt when she found herself standing in the bookshop, rather than in the little café where she normally had her lunch. She said, she didn't know how she ended up there with this particular book in her hand but knew while flicking through the pages that it described some of the experiences I had recently been through.

At the bookshop she showed me the book she had held in her hand that afternoon. She went through a number of things in the book which illustrated in writing some of my recent experiences. She also pointed to a sentence which said, '*You will find all the answers within yourself.*' She showed me different section in the book which she felt connected to my recent experiences. The book was called, 'The Elements of Mysticism by R A Gilbert' She pointed to the last paragraph in the book which read:

But although his path ends in union, and his return to the world is with the purpose of bringing that union – both in the world and out of it – to others, the mystic never truly finishes his quest. Arthur Machen "once saw a little glint of the secret, merely a flash of the great radiance', and although he never forgot it, he knew in truth, 'We shall go on seeking it to the end, so long as there are men on the earth. We shall seek it in all manner of strange ways; some of them wise, and some of them unutterably foolish. But the search will never end'.

I asked her if she thought I should buy the book. She shrugged her shoulders as she said, "No, it tells you, 'The search will never end.' Just forget it." Just before she left she asked if I knew anything about numerology. She said, "Today's date is Thursday the 10/10/1991." Because of her background in numerology she explained to me the significance of this date. She said, "It is the tenth of the tenth nineteen ninety-one. Which reduces to the primary numbers; 10/10/10/10 which is the 1st of the 1st of the 1st of the 1st and 0000 which brings you back to the beginning or end of time. The Alpha and Omega." I registered this but did not think much of it at the time, probably because I had never heard of 'The Alpha and Omega'. As she was leaving, she said, "I'll meet you up the Strawberry later if you're going out." I laughed as I replied, "It will depend on what He has on his agenda for this evening."

I went home but knew in my heart that whatever I was experiencing was not yet finished. I had an uneventful evening and the Friday passed away with just a few strange phenomena. On the Saturday morning a friend telephoned to say there was a list of types of abuse which counsellors inflict on their clients, in the national newspaper. She began to read this list, and as she did I added up the numbers she read which totalled 95. Believe me I did not bother to tell her what was going on in my head, as I am sure she would have thought I was crazy. After ending the telephone call, I thought to myself that this was a sign that I now had 5% of this experience to complete. I gave this some thought and reasoned that, as Maria had acted like a mentor throughout my experience that she was a link to finding the 5%. I sat and thought about what I needed to do next, intrinsically I knew I had to go to the shop and buy the book she had shown me. I made my way to the bookshop with a kind of knowing in my heart that I was doing the right thing.

The book was still on the shelf where it had been left. I picked it up, the price on the back was £4.99p, this meant I only had 1% of the story to complete before I knew the answer to whatever had been going on. I opened the book on page 5 and the last paragraph read:

And this is something of which the mystic is fully aware. He is, admittedly, seeking to unite his own soul, the core of his being, with the divine; but this is not a selfish act. Having seen the Divine Vision, or having attained to Divine Union, the mystic does not remain in this exalted state. He comes back, and returns with the burden of duty to his fellow men: the yoke of the Kingdom is upon him."

I knew as soon as I read this paragraph that I had been through some profound mystical experience, although I remain a long way from understanding why. Recently I did research into some of the symbolism of the experience; and most of it indicated a rebirthing or new life. This was quite profound given the way my life was to change. After that experience I had no doubt in my heart about the existence of God and Jesus. I did not have faith I had knowledge, a knowledge which to this day is unshakable and unquestionable. Almost thirty years on it remains by far the most important week in my life.

I am going to add a story to this chapter, as it is about the night the same block of flats, I was living in caught fire. It was about two in the morning, when I was woken up with the sound of a fire alarm. I did not know there was a fire alarm in my flat until that night; so, when I heard it going off, it took me a while to realise what was happening. When I pulled myself together sure enough the bedroom was full of smoke and I could hear a commotion going on from the apartments below me. There were quite a lot of apartments below me as I was on the top floor of a nineteen storey building in the centre of Newcastle on John Dobson Street. I rang 999 and was told to stay in my flat as the emergency services were at the scene and someone would soon be with me to escort me to safety. I was told not to open my front door as the smoke would overwhelm me. I think they meant it would kill me. Apparently, they were evacuating the residents from the ground floor up, this put me last on the list; a daunting prospect I might tell you. They said, "Just put your head out of the window to make sure you can breathe the fresh air."

MY PROFOUND MYSTICAL EXPEREINCE

When I opened my window people below were screaming and throwing things out onto the streets. Someone with a loudspeaker was instructing people to stay calm until help arrived. The idea of staying calm did not seem to be on the agenda for most of the residents as a way of dealing with the threat of being burnt to death. After a while I tried to ring them again to find out what was happening, but my luck was out. The telephone lines had been burned through, so I had no way of contacting anyone; this too was before we had mobile phones. All the electricity was also off, as the cables had burned through. This, along with the smoke made it difficult to see anything. As I waited, I imagined what it would be like if the fire burned through all the floors, and I fell the 19 floors to my death. That is if I wasn't burned to death first. I've had better thoughts I can tell you. Nevertheless, I remained relatively calm under the circumstances, even though I could hear people panicking and screaming all around me. As the hours past, it was getting quieter; the emergency services were working full out to remove people from their flats. I continued to wait patiently for my turn to be escorted to safety. All the noise had stopped, the streets were now deserted, and the fire engines had gone home. They had left me alone with no way of contacting anyone. That is when you know you're out of luck! It was now clear that no one was coming to escort **me** to safety. I started to rant at God, as you do, and must have fallen asleep. This was about all I could do, as anything else would have been futile, the whole area was now deserted.

Fortunately, they must have got the fire under control, as I did wake up the next day. When I ventured outside, I was told that the emergency workers couldn't get up to the 19th floor, nor could they get a helicopter close to the windows because of how the flats were positioned in the city. I don't think an explanation is necessary for why I moved out of the block of flats not too long after that incident!

ME A LOCAL PREACHER

I was now about thirty-eight years old and after my spiritual experiences in 1991, I decided I wanted to go to church to find out more about Jesus and God. I was not searching for more of the mystical experience. No, I'd had my share of that. It was just the experience had evoked in me a curiosity, and keen interest in spirituality, philosophy and religion. I was fascinated with books about healing energies, the chakra system, spiritual phenomena, reincarnation, psychic power, rebirth, miracles, parapsychology, theosophy and numerology. Not to say I still had an addictive personality and did nothing in half measures! During this period, I was introduced to many ideas and experiences which felt like nourishment to my soul. I read avidly, and quite controversially I believed that no religion had all the answers and all religions had something to offer. I loved the meditations practised by Buddhists; and often joined groups and attended weekend retreats just to meditate. However, I knew that what I had experienced was linked to Jesus and I needed to learn more about Him. I did not have time to study religion, as I was already doing a degree in Psychology with the Open University and a Diploma in Counselling. I decided that as a result of my limitations in time that attending church would be the most practical solution.

ME A LOCAL PREACHER

I had never been a regular attender of a church other than the usual christenings, weddings and funerals, of which there were not too many. I made some enquiries with numerous churches and did not like them, or rather did not like the people who I met; the churches themselves were fine. Some of the people I met believed that women were second-class citizens and I'd had my share of that too. Some did not seem interested and did not take the time to respond to my enquiries. I eventually telephoned a diocesan office in the yellow pages and discussed my situation with the man who answered the phone. He was helpful and suggested I get in touch with a female Minister he knew at a local Methodist church.

I telephoned this Minister and after a short discussion she asked if I would like to come to the church and have a talk with her. This was arranged for a few days later; I found the church not too far from where I lived in Newcastle. She welcomed me with a smile and a friendly handshake. She was about five feet eleven inches tall, of medium build, with short dark brown hair. She was dressed in what we might describe as very plain clothes. That is, she paid no attention to fashion, either that or she was completely oblivious to the clothes that were trending in the 20th century. She wore either a flared three-quarter length skirt or a pair of trousers, with a blouse or tee-shirt and short cardigan with flat shoes. Yes, this woman would certainly gain little street cred if she was judged on her dress sense. I was unsure of her at first, as she spoke with her strong, clearly educated voice and seemed very grounded and self-assured. I do seem to have an issue with well-spoken people, don't I? Nevertheless, I was a bit in awe of the ministry, as I had grown up in the days when professional people like those associated with churches or doctors were treated with the utmost of respect.

This Minister did not seem as formal as I imagined she should be, I found this uncomfortable; how dare she have the audacity to talk about things other than God. I found this difficult to tolerate at first, as I held a far from realistic idea of the clergy. I believed they were aloof from the general public, and other than Ministering to them they should not socialise or be engaging in chit chat. This Minister was friendly and interested in me, she enquired about my background and why I wanted to join the church. I tentatively told her about some of my spiritual experiences and she did not freak out; although I did not tell her the whole story, but bits just to test her response. Nevertheless this 'non-aloof' Minister invited me to the coming service the next Sunday morning. I asked if I could wear my Levi jeans adding, "If not I'm not going." She just smiled with a raise of her eyebrows and said, "Wear what you like." By the time I left I felt quite comfortable and pleased. I was looking forward to attending my first service. She'd passed the test!

I suppose I need to put a paragraph in about my perception of church goers at that time. I used to say, "They are sixty-minute-a-week Christians." My impression was of a middle-aged, middle-class group of self-righteous people. They sat an hour a week in church listening to someone telling them how good to be; went home, did a few good deeds so that they could feel they had contributed to the improvement of the human race. I had also come to the conclusion that religion was associated with theology and not God. I hung that believe on the whole of Christianity; believing that they all had no personal experience of God just an intellectual understanding. Not to say that I was arrogant, conceited and felt I had the monopoly on God!

I also had to consider that the majority of my friends from my new sober life were anti-religious. Some were feminists who disagreed with the male power in Christian religion. Others were atheist and agnostics. In fact, no one who I knew was interested in religion; they believed it was for sheep - people who could not think and wanted a set of moral rules handed to them. "Opium for the masses" as Karl Marx said. Others believed that it was a myth, just a made-up story. Some believed the Bible was written just to frighten people into being good! Then others said the Bible had been doctored in the second century by the church elders and did not resemble the original text as a lot of the original material had been removed or altered. Yes, I was well informed about religion by my new friends, but to be fair no one was too bothered.

You might be thinking, well given all that, why in the world would you want to go to church? Although I knew my mystical experience had ended, it had left me with it a deep curiosity. Yes, I knew from all the reading I had done that there were various psychological explanations for my experience, but there was no explanation that came close to describing what I had been through. It was too real, it went beyond all your theorising, psychological and scientific explanations. So, even though I knew that I had experienced a mystical experience far more profound than most people, I was now left with a curiosity which needed to be fed. I needed to learn more, I also wanted to be 'good' and was failing drastically.

Now that I have given a few reflections about my thinking at that time let me return to the Minister. She was broad-minded, very earthy and probably a lot more down to earth than me. This woman was there for me on numerous occasions. I had applied for umpteen jobs with no success, probably because I was rather stupidly telling the truth in my job applications about being an alcoholic. Nevertheless, I did a lot of voluntary work on one of those work schemes, which meant that I was paid a small amount to meet basic needs and still paid my stamp duty. When I could not afford things, such as events organised by the church, she would always push the money my way and say, "When you have it, return it." She turned out to be one the loveliest people I knew.

She would invite me to her home for Sunday dinner and Christmas day, although I felt uncomfortable, I would force myself to go. Yes, anywhere there was food was like a magnet to me, no matter how uncomfortable I felt. Her children were well-behaved and well-spoken; they played the piano along with other musical instruments and sporting activities; tennis and swimming. You know the sort of child who is chauffeur driven by their parents to all their afterschool activities. It used to resonate with my childhood, when we used to jump on the back of the wagons for a free ride, only thing was our chauffeurs were not so willingly accommodating with our afterschool activities! Reminiscence over, back to the Minister and her family. When the children came in from school, they had a routine and had to do homework before watching the TV or playing games. The whole family would play board games after dinner, Joan would use a firm yet fair hand if the children argued, as they do. In other words, she didn't smash them over the head with tins of soup. No, she used voice control without even shouting. I felt absolutely clumsy at the dinner table, but I knew it was not her intentions for me to feel anything other than comfortable. They would say prayers before eating, and then be polite at the table and hand the food around showing consideration for each other. In fact, I thought I'd entered into a parallel universe with the Waltons. There was no fighting over who got the most, or anyone insisting that the males should get more than the females. No, there was always enough food to go around without the need to punch someone to get a bit extra. Can you imagine me punching the Minister as she reached out to get the last scoop of potatoes and saying, 'I'll have those.' as I grab the scoop, well pleased with myself that I had beaten her to it? No matter how altruistic she was I don't think she would be in a hurry to invite me back somehow; do you?

It was around that time when I went out for Sunday dinner with Sarah a posh friend. Yes, I did say 'posh' friend. When the waitress brought the dinner, I noticed immediately that Sarah had seven potatoes and I only had four. As the waitress walked away, I shrieked across the restaurant, "Excuse me!" The waitress returned to the table as I exclaimed in indignation, "She has seven potatoes and I only have four." Standing at the table the waitress slowly and deliberately counted the potatoes on each of our plates and replied, "So she does." She left and returned with another three potatoes to make us the same. I felt mortified. That had to be one of those really cringe worthy moments where the words were out of my mouth before I had time to put my brain into gear.

I was surprised that the Minister often visited my house, even though at the time I was living in a small one bedroomed Tyneside flat. I remember once switching the freezer off to defrost and three days later it was still frozen. Being so bright I worked it out that the temperature in the kitchen was so low the freezer couldn't defrost. My only heating system at the time was a small calor gas heater in the living room. I lost count of the people who sat over that heater in the winter sharing stories and reminiscing about their lives. There were; therapists, university lecturers, project managers and ministers who sat over that heater for hours. In all fairness it was a very happy time in my life. I was lucky to be around a Minister who helped everyone; she helped people when they were moving house, she cleaned people's houses, and contacted authorities for those who were not confident on the phone. If anyone from the Salvation Army or homeless people came to the church, she would invite them to her home for a meal. She even helped to finance people through university.

Nevertheless, I did take issue with the church stewards and members of the congregation when I realised that the elderly members who could no longer make it to church were being forgotten about. I said, *"At least in Newcastle if anyone couldn't get to the bars someone would probably steel a wheelchair from the hospital to take them to their local pub. If they can do this, then surely the church can do the same."* Now don't get me wrong I didn't mean that the minister or church goers should steal the wheelchairs from the General Hospital. Can you just see them all fleeing down the street with a stream of wheelchairs? Nevertheless, I did think they should organise some form of transport for those who could not make it to the church unaided and wanted to attend.

Once a month the Minister put on a tea party with a short service for the children and residents in the local community. Some of the elderly women would moan and try to engage others in their disparaging chitter chatter. "Those kids only come here for the food." No, they are flocking to the tea party to meet all these stimulating, elderly dears! I certainly knew why the kids made their way to the church when there was food on the 'Order of Service'. I would refrain from saying what I really wanted to say. See how much I have changed already! Nevertheless, I would respond as politely as possible with, "So what, if they are hungry just let them eat their fill." I must say though that the women from the church made the most mouth-watering scones and cakes; and in all fairness it was the minority who complained as most of them were absolutely fine and happy to see the children from the local community joining in with the church activities.

The Minister, Joan was kind yet strict with the children. She tolerated no nonsense, and even the worst of the bunch would behave in her presence. After she started putting on the tea parties the children came to the family services where they were always encouraged to participate in the activities. She gave them special things to do, such as lighting the candles at Christmas, decorating the tree, reading parts of the service, doing little plays for the congregation, she made them all feel welcome. She used the opportunity well to plant a seed for these children and show them that there were better things in life.

Now don't get me wrong here, I am not putting her forward for an OBE, I am just telling you how she influenced my life and the regard I held for her. The reality was I had some terrible arguments with her. She was no people-pleaser, and was not looking to be top of the popularity list. She was a very straightforward direct woman with no messing. The good thing was, that I no longer built disagreements up in my head to crescendo level where I wanted to tear her limb from limb.

ME A LOCAL PREACHER

Yes, the therapy was working! I now had some coping skills to address problems with some degree of decorum. Take note I did say, 'some degree of decorum'. On one occasion I read the minutes of the church meeting. Everyone present at the meeting was named as a member of the church. I was stuck on the end of the list as an "adherent". Joan the minister was not at the service that Sunday, but I informed the congregation I would not be returning to the church as I was not prepared to be insulted and called an 'adherent'. I thought it was a disgrace, and she could keep her church and all that belonged with it. I made such a scene. I imagined an adherent meant I was stuck on the end like a piece of glue (adhere) a follower like a sheep. That was it. I went home deeply offended. I took the dictionary down from the shelf, these are books which existed before the coming of Google, which at that time wasn't even science fiction. I read what an adherent meant. Oops how wrong can you be? Far from what I imagined, it actually meant, '*a supporter of a party*'; and given that I was the only one at the meeting that was not a church member I had to be referred to as an adherent. I had to eat humble pie, (again) and ring up to apologise for the misunderstanding and explain why I acted the way I did. Talk about humiliation, people must have really thought I was as thick as two planks. There were many such arguments from both sides, nevertheless we were always able to work through our differences, as fortunately she had a maturity to her personality which made her feel safe to argue with. That is, I did not imagine that she would smash me over the head with the church candle sticks!

I had only been with the church a few weeks and realised that some of the people doing the preaching were not 'preachers'. These preachers were called 'local preachers' I used to listen to their services and admire their biblical knowledge. I would not dare ask if I could become a local preacher. Or would I? The majority of these people had a life history embedded in the church. I imagined that my background would act as an obstacle to becoming a local preacher, a bit like the jobs I applied for. I also asked myself what I would have to offer a congregation of ardent church goers. I gave this question some thought and knew I would feel compelled to study the Bible at a much deeper level if I was delivering services to other people. Thus, killing two birds with one stone - that is meeting my need to learn more and providing a service for church. Couldn't be better!

Reasoning finished I eventually conjured up the courage to approach the minister. "How do people become Local Preachers?" I asked the Minister in a bold, brash voice. She gave me one of her looks, and after a bit of thought said, "First you have to make an application, then you have to say what your calling is, in front of senior church members, then if accepted, you train, prepare and deliver services. Alongside this there are nineteen written assignments to complete. Periodically there are meetings held where your supervisor and other Ministers assess your work. At these meetings your progress is assessed, and a decision made as to whether it is believed you should be allowed to continue with the preaching."

Well I could do that standing on my head! So, I asked, "Can I be a local preacher? Joan looked somewhat dumbfounded as she said in a surprised tone, "You are not even a member of the Church." And continued, "Without being a member you certainly would not be allowed to train as a local preacher." God, I had some nerve, I was not yet even a member of the church nor did I have a church background, yet I wanted to take a leading role in the church. Well how bad does it get? Never mind, I was not going to allow this to be a stumbling block. "Well if I become a member can I train to be a local preacher?" To my utter surprise she said, "Yes," She did have that funny look in her eye as she responded. You know that look that says this is going to be a monumental task. Did I care? Not a bit, I was just so pleased with myself, I felt really excited. In all my dreams I had never imagined me standing up behind a pulpit! I'm sure you couldn't either.

ME A LOCAL PREACHER

I got my church membership and started the training. Joan the Minister was my supervisor. This seldom happens, as it is usually the fully-fledged local preachers who supervised the work of trainee local preachers. I felt great, the crème de la crème. Nevertheless, I knew I would have no easy time with her. She was notorious for getting things done the way she wanted. She would read my sermon and say, "Put it in the bin." Yes, that is what she would say. I would be mortified, as her words swirled around my brain. "It is more like a thesis than a sermon. You need to reach the people in the congregation, they are not all university graduates." Well she wasn't mincing her words that was for sure, but believe me she certainly wasn't at the top of my popularity list when she said this. Why did she just not appreciate my flair for selecting thirteen letter words, along with my talent for impressive articulation? To put it mildly I would feel upset, given I had worked for an average of twenty hours on these sermons, and diligently researched my material. Shakespeare would have been proud of them too, I do not know about anyone else. Joan would go on about the importance of keeping the sermons simple and down to earth.

Given I now had several degrees, I prided myself on using all the jargon from my psychological studies in my sermons. When I look back, I must have sounded like a pretentious, prize prat! Never mind, one lives and learns. I did eventually wise up and make a decision to stop using jargon. To this day I deliberately keep my language plain and simple.

Next on the agenda was my speech. I was oblivious to the way I spoke and how it sounded. That is, until she pointed out that I ran all of my words into one another and missed off the endings. Being born in Northumberland I was blessed with a broad Northumberland accent, and you know when people speak so fast it sounds like another language, well I fitted that category. Joan would spend hours teaching me to improve my speech. She patiently persevered until I could actually string a sentence together which could be understood by anyone in the world who spoke English. Now that was an achievement. She would stand at the back of the church and say she wanted to hear the ending pronounced on each word I enunciated. I found this quite difficult to do but persevered gradually improving. My voice was also often very breathy; this was due to not breathing into my abdomen. It was like taking singing lessons in order produce a richer sound. Then there were my vowel sounds, which also left something to be desired. Often when I went places outside of Northumberland people would say, "Catherine you have a wonderful voice, but I can't understand a word you say." I think that about sums up just a few of the improvements I had to start to make in order to be taken seriously as a local preacher.

I loved doing the local preaching. It usually took hours to prepare a full service, but it was worth every bit of energy when it was delivered. I oozed with pride as I stood at the church exit shaking people's hands as they left the church. I savoured their comments about my service and felt so rich inside my body. I was always on a massive high afterwards. Sometimes the Minister would telephone me and ask how the service went. I would say, "It was excellent." She would respond with her sneering laugh, (a bit like the cartoon dog Muttley) and tell me that I was not supposed to say that. I was supposed to have some humility. I would reply with, "It would be a false humility as I was excellent." She would just laugh again.

When I joined the church, I refused to get involved with any of the cliques; I made it clear that I would not gossip. If anyone did try to say anything about anyone else, which was in anyway uncomplimentary I always said, "Why don't you say that to their face rather than behind their back?" Everyone knew that I was not party to any gossip which evoked a sense of trust. I promised myself that I would practice in my life all the skills I had learned in the rehab; these skills reflected for me a very moral, ethical and straightforward way to live. As a result of this I think the members of the church trusted me and often left messages on my answerphone to pray for them if they were going through a difficult time with anything. They certainly had faith that my prayers would work.

If I was preaching in the other local churches most of the congregation from my church would come along to my services to give their support. The Minister used to say, "Your 'groupies' will be there in their droves on their Zimmer frames." I did feel chuffed with my groupies I must say.

When preparing the services, I used to think to myself, I must really touch the souls of the congregation. I went to great lengths to prepare tear-jerkers. I was never happier than when the whole congregation had tears in their eyes, as I stood in the pulpit delivering my sermon. Some of my stories were so sad I had to struggle to refrain from crying myself. I used to hunt through magazines and healing books to find the most moving stories; I often told stories of people who had terrible lives. I once told them about a good friend of mine Angela who had been in jail; she was a drug addict and I likened her to the Good Samaritan. She often helped people in trouble, and on several occasions put her own life in jeopardy to help others. She was certainly one of life's characters; the only one she really hurt was herself. Although I lost touch with Angela, not long before her death we got back in touch. I was by her bedside the night she died, along with half the drug scene in Newcastle. Actually, I will never forget that night; she had been given the 'last rites' and was dying as I walked into the ward. As I did, her daughter got up and said, "Hi Catherine, I'll move and let you sit by me mam's side." Everyone in the room stepped back to allow me through as Angela lay lifeless on the bed. I sat down and took hold of her hand, as I did, I felt a surge of electricity and Angela jolted up the bed. She sat up, smiled and started to talk, just rambling I hasten to add. I was shocked, as everyone in the room looked bewildered, they soon started to laugh and said, "What on earth happened there? Things settled down again, I moved to allow someone else the bedside chair. I was leaving for Portugal the next day, so said I would have to go. Angela's daughter beckoned to the person now sitting by her mam's bedside holding her hand to allow me to say my goodbyes. I once again took her hand, and once again she jolted up the bed and started talking. Everyone in the room was taken aback. They said, "It looks like she wants to come to Portugal with you." I laughed, although it was clear that I was getting some peculiar looks. One of the guys who I knew quite well from the drug scene walked me to my car. He said, "Catherine I have never seen anything like that in my life, it was as though your energy was going right through her." I could only agree, given on both occasions she was just lying there dying until I held her hand. Angela died later that night,

I've no doubt she would be greatly missed by the many lives she touched, but mostly by her daughter who idolised her mam.

That story reminds me of the time I was robbed by a group of drug addicts who lived next door to me. I went home one day to find all my personal belongings gone. They had stolen all my clothes, as well as anything which would sell; my Amstrad computer, books, ornaments, jewellery; you name it and they'd taken it. I was gutted. Prior to this I had been putting food at their door to help them out. Well believe me, religion and spirituality went out the window that day. I kicked their door, which swung open as it wasn't locked. Three of them came running out at me. I think because I had been so kind to them that they thought I was a soft touch. Well they were just about to get an education. I made it clear that I would find out for definite if it was them, and they would live to regret the day they thought fit to step over my threshold without an invite. I caught one of them in the lift and physically smashed him into the lift wall by the lapels on his coat. This was followed by a string of threats which would have made my mother turn in her grave. I caught another one as he passed on the street, I also whispered in his ear the consequences of crossing me. You know when someone's legs go? Well, I could physically feel his legs going beneath him. I was proud of myself. Love and forgiveness were not on my agenda that day. I did now have it on good authority that it was this motley bunch of low life who had robbed me. Angela (from the above paragraph) put the word out on the grapevine and confirmed it was them. She said, "It wouldn't matter if you were eight or eighty that shower would rob their own mother" Also the caretaker had seen them leaving the building with black bags full of my stuff. One outcome from my solo crusade was, that whenever I saw the gang of them, of which there were normally about eight, they dispersed rapidly like a brood of frightened chickens. I never understood why!

Back to the local preaching, I was doing the church service at my local church with a worship group. This is a service where different people in the worship group do different parts of the service. When I arrived one of the elderly women asked me to stand with her, instead of the worship group. In the middle of the service there was a silence, as no one was at the pulpit. That is a definite disaster; the pulpit should never be left empty. The other members of the worship group were bobbing up and down the aisles desperately look for something. I wouldn't could guess what! I sniggered to myself, as I wondered what the panic was. Oops silly me! Should I not be up there conducting the next part of the service? I gathered as much grace as I could muster, took my place at the pulpit and continued the service as if nothing was a bother.

When the service was finished one of the elderly church stewards said to the leader of the worship group, "Wasn't she great." In a voice which oozed pride, referring to me. This fell like a lead weight on the ears of the worship group leader, who looked at me and grimaced. She did not need to say another word; it was clear she was thinking, 'She was anything but great she ruined the service.'

On another occasion there was a prayer meeting before the evening service which I was delivering. All the heads of the other local churches attended the prayer meetings and stayed for the service too. As a result, this particular evening there were lots of clergy from other churches including: priests, ministers, vicars and lay preachers. On this occasion my service was also being assessed by a Minister from another church. A few days before I had an argument with him, surprise! I had a lot to learn about tact and wisdom. Never mind, he had taken his place near the rear of the church and was sitting comfortably in the pew. Everything was going well, I was at the backend of the sermon when I turned to the final pages, and they were not there. My heart sank, I had prepared so well for my assessment. As I stood looking dumb, the best that would roll out of my mouth was, "Oh God the pages are missing". That woke them up!

It took me seconds to regain my composure and decide my next move. So, I stepped out from behind the pulpit, and introduced new thinking to bring the sermon to a brilliant ending. The new material was actually better than the original written material. When I finished everyone thought I had planned to deliberately lose the last pages for effect. The feedback I received was brilliant; I was well pleased with myself. Yes, I do now spend a lot of time being well pleased with myself!

Although I preached on all sorts of issues, my favourites were the ones which followed themes of love or pain. These sermons really captured the congregation. I would like to share with you a piece of sermon I particularly liked and hope you do too:

What is this thing that poets write about, literature is full of, story after story is told about it? We all search for it, we long for it, we need it for our souls as much as we need food for our bodies and knowledge for our minds. It is love.

Love is the most sought after experience in the world. People have died and killed for love. We feel our greatest pain when we lose our loved ones. Yet, we keep on loving. Why? Because without love our life would be empty and impoverished. Yet millions of people are starving for this thing called love.

A friend of mine Tracy, who was a recovering alcoholic, told me, *"Catherine, you know when I was a child I had everything, two wealthy parents, a big house, plenty of food, toys, money, you name it and I had it. I had everything in the world materially. Yet I jumped from a fairground ride on Newcastle town moor so that someone would touch me. No one ever touched or cuddled me. I longed for someone just to put their arms around me and love me."* She felt deprived of the most important thing in the world - love. Tracy was an alcoholic from a young age, as she could not bear the pain she felt living in a house without love. On numerous occasions she almost lost her life before finally finding Alcoholics Anonymous. There she finally found recovery from years of addiction. Why? Because, in AA, it is customary to give each other a hug, to touch each other, support one another and encourage one another. She is now a productive member of society who continues to help recovering alcoholics.

Sadly, I think you will find this next story lacking love, but rather reflecting a sign of our times. It was after I had stopped doing the local preaching and moved to a new house. There was a boy about eleven years old who had plagued me to death for months; I felt as though I was being stalked by an eleven-year-old. Every time I went home, he was sitting at my door looking for attention. I was beginning to dread going home, as he would be there waiting on my return, with some excuse to be there. This particular Sunday morning I was returning from church, and yes, he was there waiting. Once more he had thrown his ball into my yard and broken my plant pots. I'd had enough. "Son I am taking you around to see your parents," He picked up his jacket and started to walk with me just as a car came around the corner. A loud mouthed, gormless looking woman shouted at us, "What the hell are you doing?" She was obviously some relative of his. The boy said his ball was in my yard and I was taking him home to see his parents. She shouted to the poor little soul. "Git in tha f...... yard an git yu bal back." I said, "He is not getting in my yard, I am taking him home to speak to his parents." She got out of the car with her partner and walked up to me with a fist. "He'll git his f....... bal oot yu yard" she yelled with her big ignorant mouth. As she went to throw a punch I grabbed her arm and said, "I will make one f......mess of you if you bother me." Fortunately, my past held me in good stead; I went into mode automatically even though I had just been to church! Her partner jumped back in the car as quick as a flash, she was not too far behind him. The boy and I went on our way to speak to his parents. I knocked on the door and was met by several youths with pit bull terriers; his mother was there too. I was invited in, negotiating my way past the dogs which looked somewhat menacing. After overcoming my terror of the dogs, I explained the situation. She promised it wouldn't happen again. I stressed I was not there to get the boy into trouble; I just wanted him to stop sitting at my door night and day. It did the trick, as he stopped hanging around my house; I only prayed that he did not get a hiding from his mam.

Although this phase in my life was extremely rewarding and memorable, I chose to stop doing the Local Preaching when I was doing my Masters in Psychotherapy, as the work load was too much. The training was not in vain, I went on to use what I had learned to help others. That is, the wisdom gleaned from the biblical writings and stories I researched came into good use. I also achieved during that time what I set out to achieve, which was a better understanding of the 'Christian' understanding of Jesus and God.

THIS IS PSYCHOANALYSIS!

In this chapter more than any, I have written about some of the techniques I used along with the therapy to improve my own life. If you glean some gems of wisdom and insights from reading this, I will be very happy. Nevertheless, it is not my intention to suggest that any reader follow my examples, as I would not be held responsible for the outcome. Now that I have provided my disclaimer read on.

Although I could see a huge improvement in my behaviour and my ability to deal with situations I also knew I still had a long way to go. I was continuing to struggle with an understanding of my feelings and was limited in my repertoire of coping strategies. As a result, I was referred for psychoanalytic psychotherapy. On receiving my first letter to attend an assessment interview I felt quite anxious. I had read so much about the criteria needed to be accepted as a client. I was concerned that I would not be considered, as my psychology books described the 'YAVIS Syndrome'. This is an acronym that stands for: Young, Attractive, Verbal, Intelligent, and Successful. Yes, that was the criteria I thought I was expected to fit. And yes, you have guessed, I would have had more chance of finding a one ended stick than fitting that description. I found out later that clients are no longer assessed on that criteria; just as well or this chapter would be missing.

THIS IS PSYCHOANALYSIS!

Prior to the assessment I had to fill out some extremely personal questionnaires, which were as sensitive as washing your face with a scrubbing brush. There were a lot of intrusive, probing questions regarding all sorts of abuse. Given these were to be completed in potential clients' own homes without professional support I felt they were extremely thoughtless and inappropriate. Without a doubt they could have caused problems for anyone who was vulnerable. I did make a comment at the end of the questionnaire, as to how inappropriate I thought the questions were. I said that anyone answering these questions without support could be left traumatised. I am aware that there were so many complaints that they were eventually changed. Well done us!

A couple of months later I was given an appointment to see a therapist in the unit. He asked if I would mind being watched through a one-way mirror and listened to through a microphone, which came down through the ceiling. Well yes, I would mind, but could I tell them that? I thought if I said 'No' that they would say I was an unsuitable candidate for the therapy. Listen to the fear of retribution in my response. I just projected my experience of previous relationships straight onto the therapist with no evaluation of reality. I was asked to attend a total of three assessment interviews which were spread over five months. They told me months later that I had been accepted, and my name would be placed on a waiting list. I could expect to hear from them in about a year and a half, in all I waited just under four years. They obviously weren't in a hurry to see me, probably hoping I would get better or die so that they could strike me off their waiting list.

I arrived for my first session about ten minutes early to give myself time to feel comfortable. Who was I kidding? A woman came down the stairs and called my name. I walked forward, put my hand out, and introduced myself. That went down like a ton of bricks. She gave me a look that said, 'Who do you think you are shaking hands with me? I'm the therapist.' We made fleeting eye contact, before she led the way upstairs to her room. It was a square room, not very tastefully decorated. A picture of a bridge hung on the wall, which obviously was meant to reassure the client of the therapeutic process of crossing over to the other side and feeling better. Of course, unless you had some knowledge of the symbolism of the bridge there was little chance of knowing the therapeutic implications of the picture. It would just look like a meaningless picture, making the observer wonder why someone would choose such a hideous piece of artwork. The room was furnished with three chairs, a desk, filing cabinet, and large green plant. Behind her seat was some shelving which supported her book collection; of course, each book was clearly related to her work. It would have been far too revealing to have a collection of books which represented her real taste in literature. Her desk was usually littered with paperwork and her briefcase was always placed down by her chair.

At the beginning of the session she did not speak to me, she just sat and looked at me. I can remember feeling the fear of God rising up in my chest area. I started to babble and continued to babble until the end of the session. It was a daunting experience being left in a room alone with her. I began describing my life in some detail, as I understood it at that point. Just prior to the end of the session I made a remark about the chair she had chosen to sit on which was higher than the one for the clients. I asked her if she had an issue with power and needed to represent this in her chair, rather than any 'real' power. That was brave of me wasn't it? At the end of the session I felt as if she had started an operation and cut the centre of my chest open. The second session followed a similar scene. However, I did notice that she was sitting on a chair the same height as my own. I did not dare think that she had made this change because of my remark the previous week. I did find out near the end of my therapy almost six years later that this was the case. At the end of the second session I felt as if she had opened the top of my head up and started to pull out all the stuff I had buried for years. In the third session I felt as though I walked out with no clothes on. At the beginning of the fourth session I said to her, *"In the first session I felt as though you started an operation and cut my chest open. With the second session I felt as though you had opened the top of my head up and started to pull out all the stuff I had buried. The third session made me feel as if I had walked out with no clothes on. When I work with people I try to put them together before they leave the session, not tear them apart. You are sending me out feeling worse than when I come in."* With her expressionless face she responded with, "This is psychoanalysis." What could I say? If I wanted to continue, I had to take what she offered, which was clearly not quite what I imagined. I had imagined a wonderful, kind, caring therapist who was going to make all my psychological problems disappear. Not a steely eyed bleached blond-haired woman who was making me feel as if I had more problems than I started with.

Nevertheless, I persevered, as I had read so much about the potency of psychoanalysis, I was going to give it my best shot. The first months of therapy were spent with me urgently trying to build a picture in her head of my life. I was terrified of this woman, I would arrive at the session and not be able to breathe for the first five minutes. This was not because I was out of condition and found the stairs too much, but rather that I was having an anxiety attack being in the same room as her. I spent most of my time talking while looking at the ceiling. I was more frightened of her than I was of all the criminals I came across in Newcastle. Every week I would suffer from anxiety at the thought of going to see her. If I felt as though I had upset her during a session I would be in a state of terror for the whole week. I'd expect her to be really nasty when I returned the following week. I would walk into the therapy room and bring the matter back to her attention. I would tentatively explore how she felt, (making her the client hee hee) she just sat with her expressionless, steely eyed face and turned everything I said back on me. She would interpret my feelings towards her as how I felt towards my mother as a child. At first I really didn't understand this. Eventually I could see what was happening, and as the months passed, I began to get in touch with the reality of my childhood feelings. This took a long time, given that I had spent the last thirty odd years from the age of seven repressing them.

I will explain the difference between repressing emotions and suppressing emotions, as I think you might find this helpful. We suppress memories when they are uncomfortable, painful, or we are just unable to face up to or deal with a particular memory. That is, we make a conscious decision to stop thinking about whatever it may be, nevertheless the memories are still held in the conscious mind. Repression on the other hand, is usually the result of very painful, traumatic or distressing emotions or thoughts. When we repress memories, they are put into the subconscious mind and we have no knowledge of their existence. These memories are more difficult to deal with in therapy, as they are extremely difficult to access. However, they will hugely affect a person's life, their thoughts, feelings and influence all their decisions in an unhealthy way. The person will have no awareness of why this is happening. At some level they will know there is something wrong, but they will not know what it is. For instance, if someone has been beaten with a belt by a teacher as a young child, they may not be able to remember the beatings, but could go into a state of terror when meeting anyone who resembles that particular teacher or anyone holding a belt in their hand.

The brain is a lot more complex and cleverer than we give it credit for, and will use various methods to protect us from trauma. Only thing is, it will usually bring the trauma into our conscious awareness later in life when it feels we are more able to deal with the situation. That is, if we live in an abusive environment our energy is focused on surviving that environment rather than dealing with the abuse. If we are eventually lucky enough to end up in an environment that is loving and supportive the brain begins to feel safe enough to allow the past into the conscious mind. This is in order to deal with what was previously buried in the unconscious. Bit of a bummer that, is it not?

A lot of my early therapy was spent dealing with my completely neurotic thoughts; everything was out of all proportion. If I'd said something to someone, I would play it over and over in my mind, and wonder what the other person would think. Or more to the point, I would imagine there would be repercussions for what I'd said. When I was drinking, I had none of these problems. Yes, that is right, being sober brought a lot more psychological problems than being drunk, that was for sure. When I was drunk, I didn't care what anyone thought about me, as it really didn't matter. Nevertheless, I found I constantly struggled with my emotional and mental health during the first few years of my sobriety.

It took a long time to stop the overreactions I was having to various situations. For instance, I would find I was really distressed about something which had happened. Then in the therapy sessions I would be able to explain what was going on in my mind and eventually access the root cause of the problem. Your right in thinking it would normally be traced to some childhood event which I had not dealt with. It would then be dealt with on the emotional and intellectual level, after which the neurosis would disappear. That sounds simple, believe me it was far from simple. It often took months to deal with the repressed emotions of a particular situation.

One day during the therapy I accessed a particularly traumatic memory which left me unable to speak. At the time I was doing a degree in Psychology with the Open University and ran the self-help sessions for our group. When the other students were ringing me up, I could only stutter. The beginning of words would repeat rapidly before I could complete the whole word. Trying to complete a full sentence was out of the question. This was a tough time; I felt so vulnerable and avoided speaking on the telephone or having conversations. That was a first! In all fairness I was very worried, as I did not know if I was ever going to be able to speak properly again. That would have ruined my public speaking career!

I think the therapist was also scared; I could see the fear in her face when I arrived at the sessions. Of course, psychoanalysts don't take any responsibility for problems which might arise during the therapy. No, that would be my mother's fault. Nevertheless, weeks later my stuttering stopped as quickly as it started, much to my delight.

THIS IS PSYCHOANALYSIS!

Given I was experiencing so many problems with the psychotherapy itself, you might be wondering why I kept going to the sessions. It was a bit odd, but I knew at some level that this woman was triggering issues from my past that really needed to be dealt with if I was to be free of my baggage from the past. During our encounters I was being pivoted back through time, to those childhood experiences with my mother. Now that is what they call transference in the world of counselling and psychotherapy. We all experience transference in different relationships, but just for those who are unsure of the meaning of this word I will provide a simple explanation. Transference is the transferring of feeling from an earlier relationship of an important person, such as a mother, onto a new relationship. Now my therapist provided the ideal environment for transference, as she acted as a blank slate. That is, she would just sit and allow me to project all my feelings, fears and fantasies onto her. This gave me the space I needed to deal with my past.

After starting the therapy, I began to realise that my thoughts about myself were very negative. That is, my internal dialogue would go something like: You are useless, stupid, worthless and on it went. I had clearly internalized all the negativity from my childhood and relationships to date. That is, their way of thinking about me had become mine. I read a book about *The*

THIS IS PSYCHOANALYSIS!

Power of Positive Thinking by *Norman Vincent Peale.* After reading the book I decided I was never going to say a bad word about myself again. You know what happens when I decide to do something. I do it! I started to monitor my thoughts; and every time I thought something negative about myself, I changed it to something positive. It was a bit like learning how to drive a car - at first, I had to think about what I was doing and eventually it just became automatic.

This really helped when people came to me and said they had low self-esteem; I would ask them what their self-talk was like in their heads. Inevitably they would say things like, I tell myself I am stupid, ugly, fat, useless, a failure and so on. I would ask how they would feel if someone else called them these names. The answer would usually be, "I would feel devastated, angry or hurt." I would go on to point out that it did not matter whether we said these things to ourselves, or other people said them, it would have the same impact. That is, this destructive way of talking to ourselves would destroy our self-esteem and confidence. I would ask, "If you had a child and you wanted it to grow up confident and self-assured how would you treat it?" Most people would know the formula required to produce such a wonderful human being. They would reply, "I would love, praise and encourage my child. I would not criticise, berate or put my child down." Exactly, well why don't you treat yourself as though you are the most precious child in the world? That is, you do a reparenting job on yourself and this time give yourself all the love, gentleness, encouragement and praise to build your own self-esteem. Believe me this way of thinking actually works wonders.

As trust was developing in the therapy I was ending up in full-blown regressions on a weekly basis. It was as though my adult self was taking my inner child to the sessions, and when I got there, there was no adult self to talk to the therapist. During the regressions I would have the intellect of whatever age I had regressed to. In hindsight I found this whole process fascinating. For example, if I regressed to the age of a three-year-old, I would also have the intellectual understanding, the language and voice of a three-year-old. The dialogue of a three-year-old is quite distinctive, for instance they might say, 'Me frightened.' rather than, 'I'm frightened.' I was becoming quite a master at recognising the age I had regressed to, by identifying the grammatical structure of the language I used during the regressions. What I found amazing about the regressions was that the time was not experienced as the actual time in the session. That is, when the therapist called time, (a bit like the bar staff when I was drinking), I would argue that it couldn't possibly be time; I had only been in the session for a few minutes. I found it fascinating that the regressed state I was experiencing not only took me back to a reliving of a particular event, but that it also took me from the 'real' time I was experiencing during the session.

As I journeyed through my therapy, I started to understand why I was so emotionally stunted. Although saying that, I had no concept of ever being emotionally stunted until I started therapy, I just thought I was perfectly normal, as you do! I was soon to learn that with an addictive personality where the attention is focused on the object of the addiction, it was not possible to invest in my own emotional growth. Now I am going to explain this further, not that I think you want to train as a psychotherapist, but because I hope you will find all this very interesting. If we take any form of addictive behaviour, of which there are too many to mention here, but whether it be: eating disorders, drug or alcohol addiction, workaholic, co-dependent relationships, social media, gambling, exercise or religion the person's thoughts are constantly focused on the object of their addiction. The energy is seldom used to look inward. We can only grow and learn about ourselves if we take the time to get to know ourselves, and how the world is impacting us. If we look at all the great spiritual gurus who ever lived, one of the main things they all had in common would be that they spent time alone meditating and reflecting on life. That is, they understood themselves and their emotions. I have met many highly intelligent professional people who are geniuses in their field of work, yet they lack self-awareness. This is often a result of all their energy being focused obsessively on their work, rather than their own emotional growth.

I am not suggesting that everyone should take a course in meditation or sit in the desert for 40 days fasting to get to know themselves. In fact, a friend of mine joined a Buddhist Monastery and started to meditate three times a day for two hours each time. No one told her how dangerous this could be. Meditation can and usually will have the same results as psychotherapy, in that all the repressed memories will begin to surface during the meditation. She was on the verge of a complete breakdown and could not cope with the memories which were now surfacing. So, we see that even though meditation, just like psychotherapy can be useful, it also has to be treated with respect. That is, it has to be done sensibly with experienced, knowledgeable guides.

Over the years I watched thousands of my clients change their lives through counselling and psychotherapy; it provided them with the space and the tools to make the changes. It also never failed to surprise me when people came through my door and said. "I've been good all my life; I'm a good person or a good Christian." What they meant by this was - they were a doormat for other people to abuse and misuse because they put everyone before themselves. They deviated from any form of honest straight forward communication, as this would upset the other person. If they mentioned being a Christian, which they often did, I would ask, "Is Jesus good?" After a few seconds thought the response would be, "Oh yes, Jesus is good." I would follow through with, "Did you know that Jesus was one of the most straight forward, straight talking people who ever lived? He didn't pull his punches and said it how it was. In other words, he was honest and never put up with inappropriate behavior." For some reason we are conditioned to keep putting the feelings of others before our own, at a great cost to our own psychological wellbeing. People often muddle up being good with putting up with insults and abuse. They would say, "I don't want to hurt their feelings if I tell them what I think." I'd say, "In other words, let them get away with upsetting you and hurting your feelings while you continue with your dishonest relationship allowing yourself to be abused." Well this was certainly something I'd stopped doing, and fortunately many of the people I came into contact with followed suit. That is, once they started to understand the importance of attending to their own needs before succumbing to everyone else's. As a result they developed a far more honest way of communicating.

THIS IS PSYCHOANALYSIS!

Better get back to telling you about my own therapy. Not long after starting I felt as though I had a huge black pool of mud in my chest, it was like a constant dull ache. I mentioned earlier that my head felt like a pressure cooker, steaming away. Both these feelings went on for years while I was having therapy before eventually disappearing. Now I have no real psychological explanation for the constant discomfort I felt in my body during this period, but would go so far as to say I believe it was a result of the undealt with emotions. I drew this conclusion because, as I worked through the baggage I was carrying, it was like a massive weight being lifted. I felt so much better and free from the torment that had gone on for so long.

Now no chapter on psychoanalysis would be complete without the mention of love. Yes, after getting sober I kept falling in love. I didn't know I hadn't been in love until I fell in love properly. I say properly, but it really wasn't, it was what many of us experience as falling in love, but it is a very unhealthy, immature falling in love. That is, it was the experience of thinking constantly about the other person, where the relationship was more in my head than reality. This is the same as the addictive behaviour I mentioned earlier. It takes the persons thoughts away from themselves to focus their energy on the object of wherever their love is directed. Before this I thought that love was 'in my eye' and that is just how it was. I must say that my eyesight must have been terribly poor given the 'clips' I chose for partners. I should have gone to Specsavers. I was now falling "in love" with people who I perceived as intellectually superior, although I did not realise this at the time. I did not think, 'Oh there's a bright spark I will just fall in love with them.' No, there just seemed no rhyme nor reason for what I was experiencing. I had no idea why I fell in love at that time nor why I chose the person I did to fall in love with.

I certainly had a lot to learn; you know when everything the other person does is a sign of their love for you and you tell your friends, 'I saw him wink at me.' Not that he had a piece of dust in his eye. 'He was smiling at me, when I was in the audience at the conference.' Yes, and another two hundred people. The whole world could be falling apart, and it wouldn't matter; the only thing that mattered was the object of my love. This was an education, a very painful education I may add and certainly one I would have been happy to do without. I went through this state of affairs several times, and I must say the emotional pain I felt was excruciating. There was also the other side of this coin, as the process of falling in love is the highest high a person can experience; apparently it is even higher than taking ecstasy. I think for a while I was getting addicted to the highs created by falling in love. Does that make sense as it did to me at the time? After a while I started to realise that I was being taken to new heights, as I was going through these experiences. It took several years, but I eventually got to a place where I stopped 'falling in love'. And no, this was not a result of becoming bitter, twisted and hating the human race. It was a result of reaching a level of psychological maturity with the combination of my spiritual experience and therapy that made me a lot more comfortable in myself.

The therapy really helped me to move forward intellectually too, which was a phenomenon I least expected. Before you begin to wonder how I could possibly become more intelligent, given intelligence is often considered reasonably stable from the cradle to the grave, I will explain this. Most people do not realise that the brain uses more energy than any other organ in the body. A massive amounts of my energy was being used to keep my repressed memories out of my conscious awareness. As the repressed memories were being released with the therapy, my energy was no longer needed to keep them in my unconscious mind. I could actually feel my brain taking quantum leaps, this was an amazing bonus from the therapy. I could feel my ability to think clearer and solve problems improve. I was free to use my energy now, not only to improve my life, but I also felt as though I was academically more able than I'd ever been. For the first time in my life I was becoming free from the shackles of my past. I was also beginning to stop repeating the constant steam of chaos from the past.

Therapy was now providing me with the opportunity to tell someone what I felt and workout why I felt it. That certainly put my brain into overdrive. I did feel self-indulgent; a whole hour a week just for me from someone who gave me their undivided attention, with the whole purpose of helping me to improve my life. I did not only spend one hour a week in the therapy, I made sure that almost every night I put at least an hour aside to work through the material I had brought up during the sessions. This hour was probably the most productive hour of the day, given the amount of pain, hurt, anger and rage I was able to deal with outside of the therapy. I had no idea I'd buried so many feelings over the years.

Although after getting sober I had started to slowly become aware of many feelings, during the therapy even more feelings were evolving. My brain seemed to be going through a slow defrosting, I know that might sound a bit crazy, but it is how it felt. As my feelings were coming into being I was beginning to be able to identify and make sense of them. I found this a really peculiar experience, as I was so disconnected from myself.

As I was getting stronger, and my confidence was growing I stopped tolerating people who I found abusive or inappropriate. If I felt someone was being inappropriate, I would say, "I find you insulting, abusive or whatever." But one thing was for sure I would no longer put up with anyone who I felt would damage me in any way. I once told a friend who was complaining about some of the friends she had around her. "Why don't you score people on a scale of 1 to 10 and if they fall below 5, three times, knock them off your party list." Now I know that might sound harsh, and completely understand that when our friends hit difficult times they need a lot more support from those around them. In those circumstances doing this would not be justified. However, many people foster friendships with people who are pulling them down and needy all the time. In cases like this I think the method I described works wonders. I am also aware that some people like to have this sort of friend, as it makes them feel needed. If that is the case continue as you are, but at least be aware that you are choosing to have friends who are full of doom and gloom and will drag you down. Occasionally I meet someone who wants to play the martyr and tell me, or rather bore the pants of me, telling me all the woes of their other friends. I usually just make it clear that I am not the slightest bit interested and would rather go home and watch a good film than listen to a load of doom and gloom about someone I don't even know. I imagine most of us feel this way, when someone is going on about someone's problems who we have never met, but think most people are too polite to ask them to change the subject. I've wasted enough of my precious time in this life time and believe by telling the person what I think helps to improve their social skills! A bit of tact does come in useful here.

One thing is for sure I no longer chose to have a load of negative people in my life. I am now very selective of the calibre of friends I spend my time with. I was now also improving my ability to assess a person's personality quite early in the relationship. If I found they started with the off handed put downs, negative remarks, or calling people names, I quickly put a stop to the relationship. This would be best understood with a story about a friend who told me she was being bullied at work. We discussed how she could handle these situations in the immediacy of them happening. She came back and said things had improved, but would it be all right if she allowed them to go so far before tackling the situation. My response was a resounding, "No, if you do that where do you draw the line?" If someone is being inappropriate or abusive it is important to address it in the here and now, or as soon as possible afterwards. I found that if I did not deal with inappropriate behaviour in a healthy manner I would become resentful. I also believed that if I did not respect myself then no one else would. When I was in the rehab this is a skill, I really did master. We were encouraged to say if there was anything which we were uncomfortable with. If there was anything going on in my head that did not feel right, I learned to address it. Sometimes it would amount to something, other times it would be a misunderstanding. One thing was certain, once it was addressed, it no longer messed with my mind. When issues aren't addressed, they will always fester. We have probably all experienced that internal dialogue going; I should have said this or that. It is not worth the hassle; when all this can be prevented by just asking the other person what they meant by what they said or did. At least that way they will either say, "Yes I meant that" or "No there is a misunderstanding." Whenever I checked out my understanding if I felt uncomfortable or confused, I certainly left the situation a lot happier than if I had not checked it out.

Another technique which I used, and if appropriate went on to show numerous other people how to use, was 'The Page in my Diary'. I would ask if they wanted to know about the page in my diary and without fail they would say, "Yes." So, I would tell them, "Every diary has a 'notes page', so every January I would write a list of the things I wanted to change down the side of the page. Along the top of the same page I would write the numbers between 1 and 10. For each issue down the side I would score it where I felt I was, and where I wanted to be. So, for instance, 'being more patient' I might have scored it a four and the goal was to make it an eight. I'd hate to be too patient! It would therefore be scored under the number four and under the number eight.

I would do this right down the list, and for the first few years my page was full of things I wanted to change. That is because I had such a lot of things I felt I had to work on to get to where I wanted to be. Also, the further apart the numbers the lower the self-esteem. I can assure you mine was very low when I first started to do this. I would put all sorts of things on this page like; improve my speaking, confidence, remember birthdays, learn something every day, stop swearing and so on. During the year I would frequently look at the list to check how I was doing. Each January I would write a new list; some things stayed from the previous year, and some dropped off if I had reached my goal. The new list also gave me the opportunity to add new things. As the years continued, I found my list was gradually getting smaller, and eventually I had nothing to put on the list. This was because I was absolutely perfect! This never failed to get a laugh, but it certainly was a brilliant way to have an image of the sort of person I wanted to be and keep track of how I was working towards the image. A lot of people who I know used this method and had great results.

Just in case you hadn't realised I was finding the therapy really helpful. I now had coping skills to deal with difficult situations and could work out the possible consequences of my actions more accurately. I had gained insight into why I kept going into more and more chaos. That did not stop me at that point, however, at least I knew why I kept repeating the behaviour. I was making sense of how my adult life was replicating my childhood. It was as though I was a massive jigsaw and I was beginning to put the pieces into place. Or metaphorically I was slowly making my way up a mountain and the view was growing as I climbed. There was not a therapy available which I did not try over the years after getting sober. Between counselling, thought field, tapping, spiritual healing, voice movement, shen, body massage, Chinese medicine, hypnotherapy, acupuncture, reiki, cupping, you name it and I'd tried it. Most of these therapies played a part in my journey of recovery, as did quite a lot of the people who I met during that period.

THIS IS PSYCHOANALYSIS!

Another very powerful technique I started to use was visulisation. Yes, given I now had an idea of the sort of life I wanted to create for my future, I started to visulise this new life. That is, if I had thoughts about how things might go wrong I immediately stopped them before they could take hold. If you imagine a small spark and that flares up into a flame then a fire, well our thoughts are the same. I had to stop them before they flared up and this was best done when they were just a spark. As you might imagine I did get extremely good at doing this! I do like the two quotes; "99% of worry doesn't happen" and "All anxiety is caused by a protection into the future".

Just to give you an example of this I was sitting in my friend's house and we talked about the house I would like. She took out a magazine and as we browsed through it, there was a picture of the exact house I thought I would like at that particular time in my life. I say that, because as I get older and circumstances change I have different ideas of my ideal house, flat or accommodation; but that is how it was at that time. I cut out the picture of the 4/5 bedroomed house with a large garden and conservatory, a driveway and big bay windows. I put the picture where I could see it and kept imagining living there. Yes I had the house within two years with all that I wanted. I must add that after using this way of thinking now for many years, one of the most important things I have learned is that you can't do this halfheartedly for it to work. The thoughts have to go right into your subconscious mind, it is no good thinking, this is what I want, but there is not a hope in hells chance of it happening. Afraid to tell you, this will not work. You have to believe it will happen, you have to see it happen and put your energy into it. Use concrete images in your mind see in images exactly what you want, your energy will follow your thoughts and come into being.

I used this method when I studied for my degrees and also when I saw myself travelling the world. I continue to use this technique constantly and never fail to be impressed with the results it provides. Wouldn't doubt also that God played a helping hand, but I suppose even he needs to have some knowledge of what it is I want from life! I do know that before all this I seemed to know it was inevitable that bad things were going to happen, and they did! So yes, I am now very careful of what I wish for or think about and try always to make it as positive as possible. Don't get me wrong, obviously this does not mean that bad things don't continue to happen as this would be delusional thinking. I can assure you that the changes I made and continue to make were and are certainly helping my dreams to come to fruition. In short, see the life you want and not the life you don't want.

THIS IS PSYCHOANALYSIS!

I stopped catastrophizing and thinking something would go wrong and replaced this with visions of my successful, prosperous future. I also need to tell you that this way of thinking really improved my mental health. When the brain is in a positive place it is very near impossible to feel negative, depressed, anxious or sad at the same time.

I used to often do this experiment with people I met. I would ask them to sit for a few minutes and think of something negative or upsetting. After a couple of minutes I'd ask them what they felt. The response would be. "I felt depressed, sad, angry, anxious or whatever." I would then ask them to think of something positive for a couple of minutes. After a couple of minutes were up I'd ask them what they felt. The response was always. I feel happy, content, joyous, warm or loving. So within five minutes people had gone from having uncomfortable negative feelings to feeling good in themselves.

Now I know life is not that simple and it is normal to feel negative feelings depending what is going on in life, so don't give yourself a hard time if you fail to stay positive around the clock. Just be realistic and practice changing your thoughts to affect your feelings.

I worked on lots of issues during this period of psychoanalysis, as although my therapist would have benefitted from a lesson in social skills, she was what I needed. She was predictable, strong, gentle and had clear boundaries. She didn't flinch when I got angry. I once said to her, "When I die you will put my therapy notes into that filing cabinet and forget that I existed." She responded with, "And what would that feel like?" I just wanted her to say that she cared a dot. This was never to happen, as psychoanalysts would never allow themselves to tell you what they felt. That would be a cardinal sin and worthy of immediate termination of employment. On a few occasions I wanted to discuss what I felt were problems with the venue, dates or times of sessions. There was no way that this woman would engage in a conversation; she would analyse my questions. I can't begin to explain how frustrating this was. I would ask in a very forceful voice. "Will you just respond to the question?" She would respond with, "You sound angry." That is Psychoanalysis!

THE ROAD TO RECOVERY

This chapter looks at some of the changes I was making on my road to recovery; before and after my spiritual experience. While in the rehab I began doing voluntary work for a drug and alcohol unit in Newcastle. This is where I started my academic career, at first doing a few 'in-house' courses. I was very nervous because my spelling was atrocious, grammar - well it didn't exist, and a full page of text would describe my thoughts without any punctuation. That's as good as it got. As my friend said, "You missed the English classes at school." Those must have been the lessons where I was happier running wild on the moors or sorting out my mother. Now, at this stage in my life I had little faith in myself; I also had no confidence that I could achieve anything academically. This had something to do with being told on several occasions that, "Someone like you would never have the academic ability to complete a degree." Yes, me from a council housing estate, with a broad Northumbrian accent, who did I think I was? Nevertheless, I did well on the smaller courses, probably because they entailed a lot of experiential work. That is, the courses focused more on practical activities than written work, for instance, role-play, or managing difficult situations. Yes, I was now learning the polite way to do this; they would not take too kindly to anyone banging the course participants off the classroom walls.

I was also now surrounded by a very different calibre of people; the residents in the rehab and the people I was working with believed in me. They encouraged me all the way, saying "Yu'll mak a brilliant coonsellor." Or, "Yu're as intelligint as anyone else." They pushed me to keep going and aim for better things. They had the belief in me which I needed for myself. As a result of all the praise, support and encouragement I was receiving, I was beginning to also believe I could go further. The bombardment of praise was also doing great things for my confidence and self-esteem.

It was with great pride I began to collect umpteen certificates. Nevertheless, although no longer drinking or using drugs I was still hanging out on every 'scene' in Newcastle. For a while I spent time on the drug scene. It was rare when anyone was allowed on this scene who was not taking drugs, but I was made welcome and trusted. A funny expression for a group of people who by the very nature of what they do often develop very devious behaviour. I was oblivious to this, and just keen to begin building my new life. I enjoyed myself on this scene; the people I hung out with were intelligent, interesting and fun. I would go back to my friend's house. (This was Angela's house the woman who's bedside I sat by the night she died).

THE ROAD TO RECOVERY

There would normally be about another dozen people sitting around smoking dope, listening to good music while engaged in riveting conversations! We would rock away to Chris Rea, Led Zeppelin, Bob Dylan, Queen and many more of the musical geniuses of the time. I would drive home in the early hours of the morning giggling and laughing. I would walk into the rehab and wake up all the residents with my jollity. What I did not realise was that I was getting high on the fumes from the dope. Silly me!

Nevertheless, this was unlike my experience in the East End of Newcastle; since there was none of the violence I had previously experienced. Although things could get tricky, if my friend had spent the money she was supposed to collect to pay the dealers. This would invariably lead to a speedy exit from the bars. One night we were sitting in a bar in the Haymarket, when in walked two huge men, you know the sort, not to be tangled with men! Yes, the odds would certainly be against us if we hung around for the party! I felt a tug on my sleeve as my friend gestured to me to make a quick getaway before they noticed her. How quickly can two people do a disappearing act? We laughed with nerves as we weaved our way through the drunken clientele and out into the main street. Those times were both anxiety provoking and exciting. So, although I was now sober, and my life had improved in many ways, I still could not imagine my life without bars and night life. That is, I was out every weekend until all hours of the morning dancing; and was certainly familiar with the gay scene in Newcastle as they have some of the best night clubs in the country.

This was also the time when I picked up lots of parking tickets. Not to be fazed by this, I would walk into the reception where I was doing my voluntary work and dictate a letter to the courts to explain why the traffic warden had quite 'wrongly' put a parking ticket on my car. I would also dictate letters to Durham jail, and other organisations in relation to some of the prisoners who were my clients. I would then take the letters to get them signed by the project managers. I was ever so efficient and conscientious! I quite enjoyed myself and the power I had, as everyone just seemed to do what I said without question. I was 'surprised' when I was sent for by the executive committee at work. The chief executive officer Ms Richardson had found all my messages on her secretary's computer. She seemed to think her secretary was doing more work for me than she was doing for her. I ask you! I felt as though I had walked into the Spanish Inquisition; the whole committee sat there looking at me. You know that look I'm talking about, with the brows furrowed and tightly closed downturned lips. Yes, it was blatantly obvious, these people were giving me that look of disapproving shock at my behaviour. How bad was I dictating numerous official letters for months without anyone questioning anything I did? A volunteer too, not even on the staff. I was even appearing in the courts to support prisoners with the charges against them. I felt so important it did enhance my self-esteem. I'll never forget Ms Richardson's face as she said, "You seem to have more power in here than all of us put together." I was so proud and thought I was in for a promotion! She was clearly not on my wave length, as she said in a tone filled with accusation, "The receptionist has written more letters for you than she has for me. I'm going to have to write to the courts and tell them what has happened." I looked at her and said in a very sincere, serious voice, intrinsically mirroring the atmosphere in the room. You can just see it as I practiced my newfound counselling skills like an expert. "I hope you are not derogatory about me in any way whatsoever." Her mouth just dropped open as she looked at me with utter disbelieve at what I had said. I just didn't get it. I really didn't realise I had said or done anything wrong. Oops still not reflecting very well. Would you be surprised if I told you she never did write to anyone? I can only speculate on why that was. Perhaps she thought I had the cheek of the devil, or she was secretly impressed! I like to imagine she was secretly impressed, that keeps my image intact!

THE ROAD TO RECOVERY

As my confidence was growing, I eventually conjured up the courage to think about doing a degree with the Open University. When I first applied to do the degree, I believed that I would not get beyond the first assignment. I can still remember my first piece of work. It was a social science assignment about how the sugar industry affected people in third world countries. I showed it to my friend, who remembered this piece of work as the start of my academic career. I waited patiently for my results coming in from my tutor and was as pleased as Punch when I was given a mark of 67, which meant I could continue with the degree, although I was still struggling with my ability to write. My assignments would be returned with comments like, "Thirteen lines are far too long for a sentence." This tutor failed to appreciate that this was a massive improvement from a complete essay without punctuation! I eventually decided to go along to the 'adult basic literacy classes' at the local high school. I did feel a bit embarrassed going to learn how to write when I was doing a degree. I must add, that I still have a few problems with my writing, as I am dyslexic and muddle some words up, but this book is evidence that I have greatly improved. If it was perfect you would think quite erroneously that I had paid a professional to write my work. So, I ask you to excuse any grammatical or punctuation problems you encounter throughout the reading of my book.

THE ROAD TO RECOVERY

Now you could be thinking I should have sent it to an editor before publishing. I did and the editing suggestions filled me with horror. They were using a language that was completely alien to me and saying things like, "I was tickled pink" The editing process was going to remove my personality from the book. Now that would be a tragedy and leave any reader bereft of what puts the heart and soul into this book; the fact that I write it as if I was talking to the person reading it. They were changing the style completely. Well a resounding No to that, or it would just be like anyone else's book.

Back to my story, fortunately, I passed all the assignments for the first year with good grades and was beginning to feel a sense of achievement. Four years later I completed the exam for the final year. After the exam I went to a bar with the other students to celebrate, although I obviously was not drinking alcohol, or there wouldn't have been a degree. In fact, there would not even have been a book! I probably would have been dead, and if not can you imagine how a book might have sounded written by an alcoholic still drinking? I'll leave that image with you, as I get to the point with this story. As I walked into the bar there was a two pence piece on the floor which I picked up. I walked another step and there was a penny lying on the floor, again I picked it up. I said to the other students laughing, "That's great I am going to get a 2:1

degree, I've just had a message from my direct line Him upstairs." Well we all laughed as we made our way to the bar.

I waited impatiently for my results coming through the post. You know when nothing means anything to you other than the letter you're waiting for? I would search eagerly through the mail looking for that only too familiar OU logo. Eventually it arrived. I tore open the envelope with real gusto and opened my letter. My heart sank to the floor as I read the results. My grade was a 2:2. That couldn't be right, I knew I had a 2:1, because of that two pence plus a penny I had picked up. But the letter clearly gave me a 2:2. I rang my course tutor who said, *"Catherine I have worked for the Open University for 25 years. They do not make mistakes with their results. An exam committee sits when the grades are issued, and in the 25 years I have been with them they have not altered a student's grades."* I insisted a mistake had been made, and said I needed to write a letter, but obviously could not say why. Can you just imagine it? 'Well I picked up tuppence and a penny and this is how I know I have a 2:1.' I thought it would be wise to keep that bit of information to myself. They would definitely have sent for the men in white coats to take me away. After a lengthy conversation, he eventually said, "If you do go ahead and write to the OU so be it, but do not expect them to have made a mistake or change your grade as that will certainly not happen."

I started my letter by saying, '*Dear Sir/Madam, I could not believe my eyes when I opened my results letter and the grade said I had a 2:2. I would like you to look into this as I know I should have a 2:1 degree*'. I think it will be clear to you that at this stage in my life I really had not yet mastered the art of writing letters very well. After a few weeks, I received a letter to say they were looking into this matter. A couple of months later I received a letter to say, *I sincerely apologise, it is very rare when we make an error however in your case we have had to access your original exam paper and it has been found that someone added the score up wrong on your final paper.* Now that is faith in abundance; I did not for a minute question God's integrity. I knew I could trust that He would not give me such a clear sign and not deliver the goods. I was ever so pleased with myself and Him! By the way, if I had not had that experience in the bar, I would never have questioned my results!

During this period, I spent a lot of time studying, probably my way of making an attempt to be on a par with the rest of the human race. As always, I went into it with everything I had; my addictive personality certainly didn't change. I was also doing several part time courses along with the degree. I completed a Diploma in Clinical and Pastoral Counselling and came out with eight straight 'A' grades. I started a Teacher Training course and again passed all the assignments with flying colours. I eventually decided to go for postgraduate study. I was accepted onto a counselling course at the local university. This course brought a number of problems for me, as I held different views from the other students in terms of what a counsellor needed to do in order to be good at their job. On this rare occasion I failed drastically at being top of the popularity list, yet neither was I prepared to compromise my integrity to fit in with the others. I hated this training, you know when you have that feeling of dread every time you are going somewhere? Well that is how I felt. The main difference of opinion related to students undergoing their own personal therapy, which I believed was essential for therapists to deal with their own baggage, to understand the journey a client makes. The majority of the students thought they were too superior to need their own therapy. It was their job to help the 'sick' client on a journey they did not know themselves. I had little respect for both the staff and students on this course. I knew also that I wanted to be excellent, and this course did not have the capacity to assist me to reach that goal. I needed to move on, although I stayed long enough to get my Postgraduate Diploma; I was pleased to see the back of this training, skipping with delight as I made my way out the door.

THE ROAD TO RECOVERY

It was also as I was progressing with a higher level of academic study that I stopped frequenting the bars so often. I now felt empty as I chatted, engaging in a completely meaningless, non-riveting conversation, trying to sound impressive and intelligent. I would get home and wonder what it was all about, standing like a poser in a bar and not drinking. I started to really question what I was doing and began to prioritise my time. I was now taking control of my life and could think about what I wanted, and how to get to where I wanted to be. This no longer included hanging out in the bars; my time was better spent studying, which now felt like nourishment to my soul. I was thirsty to learn.

In 1995 I saw an advert for training as a Psychotherapist. Yes, I thought, this will take me to where I want to be. I had very little money as I was doing a lot of voluntary work. Nevertheless, I was also determined to make sure I did not get on the wrong track again to land back in the same position I had just escaped from. The course fees to train as a psychotherapist were really high; however, I made an application telling them why I thought this course was for me. I was invited for an interview; I arrived at the large terraced house where I was taken to the interview room and met by a tall, blonde haired woman who asked most of the questions throughout the interview, while someone else took notes. The interview went well, and I was accepted on to the course.

Where was I going to get the thousands of pounds for the training? No, I am not going to collect scrap metal from the river banks or sell fruit and veg around the streets. I got a job doing community care work for about £4 an hour. At first, I had no transport, so was limited in the number of clients I was able to see. With my first wage I bought a bike at Miller's auctions for £5. Well not quite the Porsche I was dreaming about, but it got me from A to B, and I was now able to take on more clients. I loved that bike, it was so spiritual gliding down hills, and so far from spiritual struggling to go up the hills. I used to play on it more than ride it. I could still ride with no hands, nevertheless I lost count of the times I went over the handle bars or fell off while trying to ride it wearing high heels. Now for those who have never been stupid enough to try to ride a bike with high heels I am going to tell you what happens. You know the peddle has gaps in, for some strange reason. Well my high heel would jam in the gap, and as I struggled to remove it, which was not possible, I could do nothing other than fall over. Now I know you are thinking well you could have put the other leg down. Well this is also not possible when your foot is jammed in the other peddle, believe me I know. Nevertheless, I used my bike for a number of months while I saved the money up to buy a car. Things were really looking up, I could see a lot more clients and soon have enough money to start my psychotherapy training.

On one occasion, when I was due to go to Stockton for my first supervision session my small car needed a repair and could not be driven. The Minister from the church said I could borrow her new Volvo. I was on my way back to Newcastle on an ordinary road when a huge wagon was hurtling towards me. Yes, I did say a 'huge wagon' was hurtling towards me. I was in the outside lane doing about seventy miles an hour. I remember thinking, 'Oh God I'm dead.' In a split second I assessed the situation. I had to ram the brakes on as hard as I could and swerve the car through the traffic in the inside lane, which was very busy. Now because I'd tried to get out of the path of the truck, as you would! I swerved in at such a speed I went straight through the grass verge and the roadside fence. The car span out of control; I could see the tree tops through the windscreen as it spun around smashing into one tree after another. I eventually stopped, and checked that I was still alive, as you do! I just sat there stunned for a couple of seconds, then two men appeared looking through the windscreen, and asked if I was all right. They said, "It is a miracle that you are not dead, we were behind you and saw the whole incident." I assured them I was fine. God was certainly with me that day, He'd sent 'two road vehicle maintenance men in their fully equipped repair van'. How good does it get? They put a temporary tyre on my car, as the front tyre was ripped clean off. They kindly sorted the car out and stood it back on its wheels ready for me to drive home; with a caution to go very slowly as the new tyre should only be driven at 30 miles an hour. I drove straight back to the doctor's surgery, washed my hands and face as there were black marks all over my face, although I haven't got a clue how they got there. I told no one what had happened until I finished my work. I took the car to a garage; it had taken the crash a lot harder than me. The two men had put the back bumper, which was completely torn off, in the boot, the petrol tank cap was ripped off, and the car was seriously dented and scratched. I did not relish calling the minister to inform her of the situation. You know what? When I told her, the first thing she asked was, "Are you all right?" I was blown away, she was not bothered about the condition of the car and more bothered about my welfare. Now that is a good person.

I know this chapter has the title, 'Road to Recovery' and as I read it I'm thinking, there does not seem to be a lot of recovery as I continue to get into some amazing scrapes. Remember it is early days, and I certainly did see this time in my life as a huge improvement. I'd now 'turned a corner' having completed several degrees successfully with good grades and was really making changes for the better. Although my training as a psychotherapist put a lot of emotional, mental, intellectual and financial stress on me, thus pushing me to my limits, I loved every minute of the journey. I devoured the training material and spent every spare minute I had reading and learning. I thrived and excelled academically. I was also now feeling a great deal better emotionally. I'd had the time to begin to get to know myself, strengths, weaknesses and everything in-between. Fortunately, I was now surrounded by loving, supportive people who believed in me. Along with this I was also working in a doctor's surgery and seeing private clients while making money. How good does it get? It certainly was the 'Road to Recovery' the destination a long yet colourful road ahead, as you will see in the next chapters.

ESCAPADES AROUND THE WORLD

Now it is difficult to fit this chapter in chronologically as my travels lasted a number of years and are still ongoing. It would therefore be ridiculous to talk about all the countries I have visited, but because I am so pleased with the changes I have made to my life since getting sober, I am going to list them to give you an idea of the magnitude of my travels. I will go on to write about the ones where there is an interesting story to tell, or a story which just helps you to understand how my life was changing.

Prior to getting sober, the only country I had been to was France and I am sure you will remember that was a catastrophe. Next on my itinerary of travels was the USA and Mexico, after which I went to: Italy, Canada, Egypt, Cyprus, Spain, Greece, Iceland, Gibraltar, Austria, Israel, Czech Republic, Ireland, Netherlands, Russia, Cyprus, Switzerland, Norway, Portugal, Germany, India, Kenya, Alaska, Poland, Nigeria, Thailand, Hong Kong, Malaysia, Cambodia, Dubai, Vienna, China, Cuba, Canary Islands: Tenerife, Gran Canary, Fuerteventura, La Palma, Madeira, Lanzarote, Australia and New Zealand. This is in no specific order, it just gives you an idea of how my life began to change for the better as I was beginning to take more control and make a good living. As I made more money, I could afford to go on luxury cruises and visit more exotic places. Mind, I must point out that this was during the latter years of my travels and not the first few stories I tell.

The USA

It was now February 1991 and I had been sober for a couple of years, left the rehab and sold my flat, after which I decided to go to the USA. This was for no other reason than as a teenager when I walked down the street, people would shout, "Where yu ganin Catherine?" I would shout back, "A'm ganin tu America." Thinking, 'Yes in my dreams'. This was nothing other than fantasy; I never expected to go there, but as I had always said it, I thought now would be a good time to do it. Amazing rational I used to make the decisions to inform my life! The good thing was that I was wise enough to decide that I would not wait around for the right person to go along with me, as I'd concluded that the probability was there would never be a right person or a right time. Just do it.

I walked into a travel agent, asked about flights and was told there was a flight leaving in four days' time from Glasgow to New York. "Yes" I said, "I'll take it, and a return ticket for five weeks later." I bought my Greyhound bus ticket at the same time so that I could travel anywhere and not worry about where I ended up. Had I learned anything from my trip to France? Learning from my experiences didn't seem to be a

2.   250

strong point of mine. Well I landed in New York on a snowy winter's day. The roads along the sidewalks were covered in slush. As I plodded through the slush I must have looked like a typical British tourist, people seemed to spot me from a distance. It was like bees to a honey pot everywhere I went, "You got a dollar man?" I was not going to start dishing dollars out, as I did not have a lot of money. I had just taken what I thought would get me through the five weeks. Nevertheless, I was never too far from a grocery shop and very happy to buy bread to make sandwiches. I lost count of the people who ate my sandwiches on my journey through the States. 'Stranger danger' was not in my vocabulary. After a couple of days in New York I continued on my journey to Florida, Disney World, and in Memphis I visited Elvis Presley's birthplace and Graceland. I bet you're wondering when the trouble starts. Well, it was not long before I was approached by a woman with a man in the Greyhound bus station. She was well dressed in nice clothes and beautifully polished nails. She had been robbed and was destitute as she waited on her rich family sending money which had not yet arrived. In the meantime, she was struggling to survive with her male counterpart on the streets. Well how stupid was I? I helped them out, which meant I was keeping them in a life of luxury until her money arrived.

ESCAPADES AROUND THE WORLD

I did not know until a hotel receptionist asked me what I was doing with this woman, and when I explained the story, she told me, this is a con job carried out all over the USA. Often families travelling with sick children or relatives with cancer are targeted by these vultures and end up falling for the same con. This costs lives, I had a lot to be grateful for. The receptionist did say that since we were in Louisiana the gun laws permitted use of a gun without a permit; and I was allowed to shoot anyone who had robbed me. She offered me a gun which she kept in her desk at the hotel. I think that was the first real gun I ever held in my hand, probably just as well or I might be writing this from a life sentence. Nevertheless, in my ever so wise head I said, "I think I will give it a miss." I did, however, knock on the woman's hotel door. She knew that they'd been rumbled and did a quick disappearing act. That was the last I saw of those two, but without a doubt I was left all the poorer and wiser for the experience!

Because this woman had so deviously swindled most of my money, I was now running quite low on funds. I was left with very little money for the rest of my journey. The hotel receptionist, who invited me back to her home, asked if I would like to stay until my flight left to return to England. No, I was happy to continue with my journey on a shoe string.

There was just so much I wanted to see and was going to make sure nothing held me back.

It shames me to say, but I also realised with hindsight that these people get away with the con because the recipient (me in this case) is motivated by greed. The con works because there is always a promise of a big pay out from a wealthy family. Oddly enough, when I was back in the UK, two colleagues of mine were talking and I realised they had fallen for a very similar con job. This time the man's estranged family had been killed in a car crash and he was to be the recipient of a very healthy sum of money, given there were no other relatives. My colleagues had given him quite a lot of money on the assumption they were going to get a good return. I brought it to their attention what I thought was happening, as it was clear they were going to continue to keep feeding him money.

When you fall for a con like this it is hard to let go just in case someone is going to turn up with the goods. Believe me, it is better to count your losses than continue on a hiding to nowhere. I asked their permission to set this man up, which they agreed to, and sure enough there were no dead relatives. I really called the bluff with him, and he fell for it. But of course, in these situations there is nothing you can do, as you have handed the money over willingly.

ESCAPADES AROUND THE WORLD

Now I know this is going to be hard to believe, but in a strange sort of way it was better after I was robbed. I had so many unusual experiences which I would not otherwise have had if I had been travelling with money and staying in hotels. Before leaving Newcastle, I had discussed with the drug and alcohol unit where I did the voluntary work about doing some research into drug and alcohol problems while I was away. I was now in an ideal position to find out a lot more about the drug and alcohol recovery scene in the US. Since I no longer had the money for hotel accommodation I stayed in shelters. Some of which were dire, you had to strip off and shower before being allowed to enter the dorms. In most, you had to be out by five or six am; so, in other words I had just fallen asleep when I was being woken up again and turfed out onto the streets. (They usually didn't even serve breakfast!) It was also sinful, the number of women with babies and young children who lived their lives going from one shelter to the next with no food and nowhere to go until the shelters opened again in the evening.

As I travelled through the USA, in the early hours of the morning, the streets in most cities were lined with people living in cardboard boxes. When I went to Hollywood, I was told by one man that, "If the 'down and outs' try to go into the richer areas of the city they are beaten back with truncheons."

2.   254

ESCAPADES AROUND THE WORLD

Sometimes people sitting on the streets were so thin it was hard to believe they were going to make it through the day. I did several times find some food to take out to them or keep any breakfast from where I was staying to give to some of the people on the streets. Sometimes their ankles were so swollen they looked bigger than my thighs. My heart went out to these people, as there was no system to support those with failing health if they had no insurance. Britain needs to be careful, as it is not far behind the way we are going with the selling and privatisation of our NHS.

The AA meetings in the US were quite different from the UK, as in almost every city there were meetings running 24/7. They had meetings for teachers, professionals, executives, down and outs, you name it and there was a meeting for it. I was not sure which category I fitted but thought I would try whichever meeting was closest to where I was staying. Most of the meetings had an area where people could rest or sleep; this was so useful, especially since my financial situation left me somewhat destitute. I could now get my head down with the echoes of "Hello my name is .... and I'm an alcoholic." The serenity prayer went into my subconscious like one of those subliminal messages we hear on hypnotic recordings. I also lost count of the people who invited me back to stay with them in their homes. It was as though they felt it was a great honour to host someone from England. It was amazing the amount of people I stayed with as I travelled. Most of the Americans I met also wanted to know how we live in the UK. The Americans, like the people in other countries often imagined that the English live in homes similar to those in Downton Abbey, have servants and a personal relationship with the Royal Family. I did enlighten them.

I also learned an important difference between the UK and the US in terms of the treatment of drug and alcohol problems. People who had committed less serious criminal offences were sent to AA meetings instead of jail as part of their sentence. If they failed to attend and get their card stamped their probation officer had to bring them in for a custodial sentence.

When I arrived in Los Angeles, I told people I was going to the midnight Mission. The response was, "You can't go there," as they gave me peculiar looks, without explaining why. So, I set off on my journey through LA to the Midnight Mission in Skid Row. Me being the enlightened one! Did you know that Skid Row has the largest population of homeless people in the United States and the expectation is that any stranger stupid enough to venture in the area might be raped or murdered? Well I didn't know either. I survived the journey incident free, as I marched around Skid Row looking invincible in my trendy white leather jacket, 501 Levis and high heels. You know that look, the one where people look at you and think, is she for real. Well, that is the look I exuberated as I marched along the street completely oblivious to anyone or anything. On reaching the Mission I was invited by Clancy Imislund, who is known worldwide for his work with recovering alcoholics, to attend the biggest AA meeting in the world. That was after he gave me a good talking to about walking through this area alone and insisted someone take me back to my accommodation.

That evening a car arrived to take me to the AA meeting where there were over 1,500 people. I was chuffed when Clancy announced that there was a woman called Catherine in the meeting who had come all the way from Newcastle upon Tyne. Announcing also that, this is where they mine the coal and support the footballers. He also insisted I stand up and address the meeting, which was a daunting prospect in those days, but I did it anyway, although I was very brief.

After the meeting I was making my way to San Francisco; Clancy told me someone from the meeting would take me to the Greyhound bus station. It was late in the evening when the car, with a driver and another passenger, pulled up to the bus station. Within seconds it was surrounded by men, who looked of African origins, but I did not bother to ask. The man who got out of the car with me to carry my rucksack looked terrified. We were followed up the ramp surrounded by the men asking for money. The armed police stood at the top of the ramp about two hundred yards away. I took my rucksack and indicated he could go back to the car, as we were now completely surrounded. It is a rare occasion when my legs go, but I could really feel them going, as I made my way to the top of the ramp to safety. When I got home I was telling a man in the Strawberry pub in Newcastle the tale. He said he had been there and was so frightened that he had to get a taxi out of town. His story made me feel much better, proving I wasn't the only wimp.

Nevertheless, now on a restricted budget my visit still took me to all the states I wanted to visit, including Mexico, Los Angeles, San Francisco, the Grand Canyon and back to New York. I was pleased when I reached New York again and some of the people I had made sandwiches for, five weeks earlier remembered me. Did I feel important?

Kenya

By the time I went to Kenya in 2002 I had already done a few cheap package holidays. I began to think I needed to broaden my horizons; I was now ready to venture out and do something more adventurous. An aunty of mine had always wanted to go to Kenya and was unable to find anyone else who was interested in going along with her. "I will go!" We landed in Kenya, and as we made our way in the transfer bus from the airport to where we were staying, I started to worry, we were driving passed broken down old buildings with hotel signs hanging crookedly from above the doors. Time to worry more, they were the most dilapidated buildings I'd ever seen, they were nothing more than old shacks. I could feel my blood pressure rising at the thought of spending two weeks in these less than desirable hovels. My imagination was running wild as I visualised the rickety old broken-down beds, with worn out grey bedding, a very old lumpy mattress with a grey stripy pillow. The image was enhanced with creaky, rotten old floorboards infested with vermin. No, I did not have the guts to share my images with my aunty, I spared her the ordeal. Eventually we reached the hotel we were staying in; my heart danced with delight it was absolutely beautiful, far superior to anything I had expected and definitely the best hotel I had ever had the good fortune to stay in.

A huge section of the hotel was made with coral reef, it was stunning. A bar was positioned right in the centre of the swimming pool. To top the lot, we were on a fully inclusive contract, so we had access to all the food and drink we could consume. We each had our own one bedroomed apartments, which were richly decorated with a massive living room area. The hotel was superb.

ESCAPADES AROUND THE WORLD

It was clear from the first few days that few of the tourists would venture out of the hotel. "Gosh! How could we? There are black people out there." It was the same in India, I remember one woman saying, "Oh there are Indians on this carriage, can we find one without Indians?" Do people realise how ignorant they are when visiting another country and actually want nothing to do with the native people of that country? I was told by one woman, "Whatever you do if a child offers their hand to shake hands don't, as they are filthy." It did not seem to matter how offensive they were to the children who often ran for miles in their bare feet to see the tourists.

We quickly learned in Kenya that the children placed more value on writing material than sweets. So, whenever we went anywhere, we took pens, pencils and books which were graciously received with shrieks of delight. The delight in the faces of the children certainly made me feel rich. I do love the saying, 'When you give you receive'.

Because we actually ventured out of the hotel grounds the local people organised many special treats. We went scuba diving in the sea, and swam with tropical fish in countless shapes, colours and sizes; a truly mesmerising experience of awesome beauty. I felt like David Attenborough. The locals spent time showing us the different sea creatures which lived on the sea floor and the rocks. I was humbled by their gentleness with nature. They were so careful as they gently picked up the creatures from their resting place, held them with reverence, and always placed them back where they found them.

I must say I was lucky to have my auntie as my companion on this holiday; she really was game for whatever was thrown at us. This was an auntie who knew how to live, without fearing all those things that can go wrong in life. In fact, she was very like myself. We hired two horses, her being an accomplished horse rider, and me having never been on a real horse in my life. Although when I was four, I galloped right through the town where I lived on a sweeping brush; when my mother caught me, she swept the floor with me too. I also believed the back of the settee was a huge black stallion; I would run charging into the house and vault straight onto my horse like Zoro or the Lone Ranger. I'd often be swept off by my mother's arm just as quickly, as she didn't appreciate my amazing world of fantasy. If not, I would gallop away through the fields, jumping fences and capture all the baddies as I went.

I was now sat astride this magnificent creature cantering along the beach and through the countryside. I was overcome with a feeling of grandeur, as I mastered this task with great confidence. My auntie went on to insist that I learn how to dive from a springboard. I did not master this so well, and more than often managed a belly flop rather than emulating the graceful diving technique she was demonstrating. Because we ventured out and spoke to the locals we were invited into the local village; when we arrived every resident in the village came out to meet us. They held a party to celebrate our visit singing and dancing in the street. We were asked to join in as they sang and danced but failed drastically at rocking to the beat. We did manage to laugh at ourselves and had a great time.

The villagers lived in mud or cow dung huts which had a sleeping area, a cooking area and very little else. Now when I say a sleeping area, if you have an image of a nice cosy bed with warm blankets, I'm afraid your image is just about to be shattered. The sleeping area was an animal skin on the floor, there was also no running water or electricity. Yes, I'm afraid there was nowhere to charge my mobile phone and wash my hands before lunch! Most of the children in the village were scantily clad without shoes, the women wore their very colourful native dress and the men wore trousers and tee-shirts or shirts. We were treated like royalty as everyone celebrated our visit to the village. Most tourists never see these areas, so we were the enlightened ones, the privileged two!

ESCAPADES AROUND THE WORLD

One day we decided to take a bus to Mombasa; now this really was one of those lives' experiences. The journey started as we fought our way onto the local bus. At every stop along the way more and more people piled on, just taking their seat on top of another passenger! My aunty was squashed between two people as I hung on to a pole for grim death. People were hanging onto the side of the bus, others were swinging off the roof as if their lives depended on it. Their lives did depend on it. Rap music was blasting from the radio, with the majority of passengers trying to rap along with the racket, producing a sound totally unfit for the human ear. The bus sped through the suburbs with not a care in the world, seemingly oblivious to the array of massive potholes filled with rubble. This added to the totally discombobulating experience, as the bus swerved and swayed from one side of the road to the other while honking and tooting as it went. I bet you have guessed that we were ever so pleased when we reached Mombasa, but I must say, it was a laugh too!

After a few days we booked a safari and went out to the Kenyan jungle for five days. I can only say this was one of my most memorable, scary and exciting experiences to date. To think I might be the evening meal for a lion went beyond exciting. The only way to describe the safari would be to say it was like watching one of the world's most amazing wildlife spectacles. There were herds of giraffes ambling gracefully through the jungle, zebra cantered playfully or grazed on the lush green grass, elephants took their turn for a shaded place under the rare tree, or played in the waterholes, leopards and cheetahs moved like lightening across the plains chasing their prey and lions roamed majestically looking for their next meal. The buffalo just stood there staring out from behind their upturned horns, seemingly contemplating their next move under a deep thoughtful frown. The buffalo actually had a look of grandeur about them. I thought the hippopotamus were just huge rocks as they stood stationary in the rivers that is until they moved and crocodiles lay along the river banks. I'd never seen gigantic anthills before, these just popped out of the ground like miniature skyscrapers.

Now I hope I have painted an image of what it was like driving through the safari park as we travelled for miles, watching the wildlife, in an open top safari truck with canvas sides. We reached our accommodation for the night; this consisted of a canvas tent with two single four poster beds adorned with mosquito nets. The en-suite bathroom was complete with a fully flushing toilet and shower with hot water. How good was this? The lions, elephants and numerous other wild animals roamed around outside. After our evening meal we walked back to our tents and sat outside for fifteen minutes on the balcony listening to the sounds and watching the animals as they roamed freely below where our tents were positioned. We darted quickly into the tent when we felt threatened by a lion strolling through the short grass not far from our feet. I could just see us limping away while the lion licked his lips with that look of sheer contentment. Not an image I wanted to bring to fruition. When we entered the tent, I pushed my auntie into the bed beside the entrance and said, "You're sleeping there." We giggled and laughed with fear; as she lay in bed, she spluttered through her giggles, "I feel as though I'm lying here like a lump of meat." I told her that I would inform the family of her demise and tell them that up to that point she had been really good company. Adding that I was sure that would make them feel better. We couldn't get to sleep for laughing.

The next day as we continued on our safari we watched as a lion killed a deer and after having lunch, sat overlooking his remains with that "Hamlet cigar" look on his face. Watching all the wildlife roaming the African plains was a wonderful experience; there is nothing on TV that could come close to the real experience of being there watching and hearing the sounds of such a fantastic place. We also spent time in the Masai Mara National Reserve. It is regarded as the jewel of Kenya's wildlife there have been 95 species of mammals, amphibians and reptiles and over 400 bird's species recorded on the reserve. As we travelled in Kenya, we also had the good fortune of seeing Kilimanjaro, although not too close it was still a spectacular sight sitting on the horizon.

The day before we left our hotel, we encouraged another few holiday makers to collect bags of food and drink for the young local people on the beach, to give them a party. Now given we were all inclusive, there was a brilliant selection of succulent meats and all that you could dream of by way of food and drink. This was a party the locals said they would never forget; they'd never before tasted food as rich and delicious as what we gave them. I felt like a million dollars at the gratitude and praise which was showered onto us. No words could explain the appreciation that these young people felt for our small act of kindness. Dozens of us danced the Hokey Cokey and the Conga up and down the beach. We had a whale of a time. During the week we had collected clothes, toiletries and shoes to leave behind. Again, the appreciation was remarkable. One young man said, "My sister has never had a pair of shoes before." He took the sandals as I handed them to him and stroked them. This was the best holiday I had been on until I went to Alaska which topped it only because of the awesome scenery.

ESCAPADES AROUND THE WORLD

Russia

This is a story connected to my psychotherapy training. In 2004 I was sitting in one of my 'professional development' group meetings, when the facilitator Marion said she was going to Russia. I piped up with, "Can I come?" "Yes, Catherine you can." I was chuffed to bits, she had loads more faith in me than I had; I was convinced she would have had an excuse to not to let me go. Marion was behind setting up the psychotherapy training in Russia and had been visiting the country several times a year for the last 10 years. She normally took a group of students and qualified psychotherapists with her. This time it was only the two of us going. It was not too long before we were flying through the air. When we arrived the sun was shining, and there was not a cloud in the sky. I walked outside the airport to be hit by the coldest weather I had ever experienced; it was about 15 degrees below freezing. By God my legs and face knew it, as they instantly froze when the icy weather wrapped itself around me within seconds of stepping outside.

We were picked up by a professor called Bronisla, who we were going to be staying with, and his friend who was driving the car. They lived a hundred miles outside of Moscow. Can you imagine travelling this distance through a freezing cold, snow covered terrain in a car with holes in the floor? Bit like the Flintstones. Again, all we could do was laugh as Marion fluctuated from hot to cold. One-minute saying, "Will you close the window I'm freezing?" Five minutes later she was roasting and wanted the window open. I think the menopause might have had something to do with the rapid temperature changes she was experiencing in the car. The holes in the car floor didn't help the matter either.

When we eventually arrived at Bronisla's house his wife had prepared dinner ready for our arrival. How anyone ever got time to eat anything was beyond me, as every few seconds a toast would be made. I wondered how they did not run out of things to toast, but believe me they didn't. I can certainly understand how there is a huge drink problem in Russia, it appeared compulsory to sit around making toasts. Every few minutes a glass of alcohol would be waved in the air preparing everyone to make ready for the next toast. All this was happening while trying to look intelligent, rather than inebriated! I didn't know until I arrived that everyone's apartment was the same regardless of the person's status or profession. The professor's home was the same as the road sweepers, it was so different from our hierarchal society. Yes, I had a lot to learn about communist countries; although this was just a few years after the dissolution of the Soviet Union there remained a lot of the old regime in place.

ESCAPADES AROUND THE WORLD

The following day we made our way back to Moscow, as Marion was teaching and supervising some of the students at Moscow University who were training as psychotherapist. They gave us beetroot soup for lunch; I am sure they had just dipped some beetroot in hot water and made it pink. "Oh, that was lovely," I said in my best unconvincing voice. Did I long for a good old home-made diner, as my stomach thought my throat was cut?

The next morning when we went down for the training, I was surprised to see a lot of young trendy women. For some reason I had an image of older women in Russia who wore huge coats and big fur hats. I suppose they had to start somewhere! While I was in Russia, I completed the '101 in Transactional Analyses' I think that meant I was the only English person to have a Russian 101 certificate. My claim to fame! You might wonder how I managed that. Well, we had an interpreter translating the training from Russian to English, so that Marion could assess the work of the professor. It must have been quite a task trying to capture the emotional content of the participants as she told their personal stories. She managed to portray a wide range of emotions with a talent any actress would have been proud to emulate.

Our days in Russia were very busy, mostly with teaching and supervising. Each evening we would normally be invited to dinner or the theatre by the students or teaching staff. One night we were invited to Tchaikovsky Concert Hall in Moscow to hear the Philharmonic Orchestra playing. In order to get to the theatre, we had to use the Russian metro, which is one of the most beautiful subway stations in the world. It is famous for its elegance and among the cleanest and most efficient in the world. It was like being in the entrance of a first-class hotel, lined with beautiful artwork and elaborate chandeliers. We made our way from one destination to the next weaving our way through the crowds. A far cry from the rickety old car we had previously had the displeasure of experiencing earlier in the week, but not as funny!

Of course, we had to pay the Kremlin a visit. Because of how busy we were through the day and early evening we eventually arrived at the Kremlin in Red Square at midnight. The atmosphere of this place, even at these late hours was still vibrant, as people busied around the streets. The police on duty looked scary, very like in the old-fashioned films with their flat, fur hats, and very straight laced faces. I'd hate to meet one in a dark alley. While we were at the Kremlin a voice shouted from across the street, "Is that Marion McNally?" It was one of the students who Marion had taught in Russia the previous year. It is hard to believe you could bump into someone you know thousands of miles from home at midnight. And they say it is a small world. Every night when we arrived back at the hotel the students would arrive with presents and more alcohol. Just as well I was not drinking at this stage in my life; as if I had not been an alcoholic before I arrived, I would certainly have left as an alcoholic.

Alaska

Although nothing spectacular happened on this trip it has to have a mention in order to give you an idea of the scenery. It was the most beautiful place I had ever seen, and by this time I had done a lot of travelling to numerous countries. As I flew over Greenland and into Anchorage, I was awestruck at the sight of the magnificent snow-covered mountains. I joined the luxurious cruise ship sailing from Anchorage to Vancouver. The ship hugged the coast line as it sailed hundreds of miles through the ocean. Glaciers and mountains ran for miles, dolphins and whales swam alongside the ship leaping in and out of the water. The ship seemed to squeeze its way through the fjords, as I sat awestruck at the sights that continued without end for miles and miles. I watched the salmon swim upstream and spotted brown bears as we went. A sight engrained in my mind was as the ship drew up close to a glacier. When we were a distance away it looked a couple of feet tall; as we drew closer it was clear that it was as tall as a sky scraper, as it rose magnificently into the air. You could hear the roar like thunder as the ice broke away from the main glacier; it tumbled down like rocks in an avalanche and crashed into the sea. The force of the ice hitting the water created a mountain of a wave, which came speeding across the sea like a bolt of lightning. The impact as it smashed into the side of the ship created a massive spray of sea water which rocketed right across the ship decks. Obviously with no regard to the poor souls, including me, who were so mesmerised by the sight that we did not have time to dodge the torrent of water as it landed on our heads. That beat any power shower!

The towns and villages in Alaska were remote and sparsely populated, in many there would be less than 700 residents; it was a bit like going back through time. As I walked through places I did like to see the husky dogs sitting peacefully on the doorsteps. One thing not to be missed was the incredible Alaskan Art and Native American Totem Poles. These were in the downtown area, in museums, and totem parks.

After leaving the ship I spent a few days in Vancouver before travelling through the Canadian Rocky Mountains. Vancouver must be one of the most beautiful cities in the world: surrounded by mountains, it is a bustling, vibrant, cosmopolitan, ethnically diverse city, with a thriving art, theatre and music scene. The year I was in Vancouver, Stanley Park won the 'most beautiful park in the world award'. I must say it was spectacular, with the most colourful displays of flowers, shrubs and trees I had ever seen, even though by this time I was a regular visitor to beautiful gardens and country parks.

Now as I was travelling through the Rocky Mountains people kept saying, "You must visit Banff, it is so beautiful." Banff did perfectly fit the criteria of beautiful, but what they failed to tell me was that a train goes through the town every hour in the middle of the night. This is one of those trains that toots really loudly to warn everyone it is coming! One night in Banff was enough.

DUBAI

When I booked my trip to Dubai, I was excited as well as a bit worried; I imagined lots of Arab men with oppressed women, wearing niqabs with only their eyes showing. It was somewhat refreshing when I arrived and found that Dubai was a vibrant cosmopolitan country. I booked into my hotel and went to the bank to get some money. No chance, I had forgotten to let my bank in England know that I would be in Dubai on these dates. Could I really be so stupid? Yes, of course I could, this is me! Fortunately, my hotel, bed and breakfast and return flight were paid for, so at least that was one consolation. Down hearted I entered the dining room for breakfast the next day; as I tucked in to a hearty full English I

2.   273

started to rant on at God in my head. Just as well I kept it in my head, or I might have been arrested for insanity. My internal dialogue went something like, '*Well now God, I can return to the buffet to get more food, to try to fill myself up for the day, or I can trust that you will feed me while I'm here. Look God, I am going to trust that you will make sure I don't go hungry, so I will not go back up to the buffet to eat enough food to feed a horse.*' I got up, spoke to the receptionist for a couple of minutes and stepped into the lift. A man in a suit and tie, carrying some files under his arm, also stepped into the lift. I asked him what he was doing, me being shy and all that. He said they were running a business course in the hotel. I said, "I can teach business skills, which would really complement your course. Would you be interested in me delivering some training?" Remember we are in a lift, so I am having a very fast conversation. "I suppose we can ask the course director." He said, as I stepped out of the lift with him. We walked along the corridor and into the room where the training was just about to begin. I was introduced to the course director and a couple of professors who were teaching on the course.

He asked me a few questions about my background, my qualifications, and what I taught, which I answered with great hope in my voice. But not too much hope, as I did not want to look as though I was needy, even though I was. After I convinced him that I would be an asset to the training; he asked if I would like to join the university faculty for the week. I could get involved with the training and give a presentation for the course participants later in the week. Well I was absolutely delighted. Well done me.

When lunch time arrived, I was asked if I would like to join the rest of the staff in the restaurant. You could guess my answer to that question I'm sure. This was a classy five-star hotel with an excellent restaurant. In the afternoon I was invited to join the group on a tour of Dubai. I boarded the private tour bus with the other staff and about thirty students. We went past all the marina's skyscrapers and the towers of the Jumeirah Beach Residence and the villas on Palm Jumeirah island also passing the Burj Khalifa, the world's highest tower and the famous seven star hotel, where we spent some time on the beach. We stopped off at the shopping mall with over 1,200 shops, 150 restaurants, an indoor theme park, ice rink, and huge indoor waterfall. Inside the mall is one of the largest and most stunning aquariums in the world. There is a 10 million-litre tank at the aquarium and underwater zoo, which contains more than 33,000 aquatic animals.

We arrived back at the hotel at about 8pm; I walked into my room wondering what I was going to do for something to eat as my choices were certainly limited – nothing or more of nothing. The telephone rang and the course director asked, "Would you like to join us for dinner?" "That would be lovely." I responded and skipped as I went along the corridor to the lift, quickly regaining my composure as I entered the restaurant, where I was invited to order anything I wanted from the menu. Well this set the scene for the remainder of the week. I joined the training, was taken on a rather grand tours each day, including the river cruise on the 'elegant Bateaux'.

This offered: *'a bespoke experience to explore the waterways of Dubai Creek while enjoying freshly prepared gourmet cuisine in the comfort of this glass-enclosed, air-conditioned luxury vessel. With panoramic views of Dubai, a four-course à la carte culinary journey, including an extensive selection of fine beverages, contemporary live entertainment and their signature personalised service.'*

Well you know something, if I'd had any money, I couldn't possibly have prepared a better itinerary, or had a more interesting time. I couldn't believe my luck as I sang and danced the night away. On the last day of my stay, and the last day of the course I was asked to complete two exams relating to the material that had been taught on the course. The university was holding their graduation ceremony that evening; guests were arriving from all over the world. The faculty staff were called to be fitted for their academic dress, this including me! I was issued with a red and white robe, the matching hood and a black bonnet. I felt ever so pleased with myself as I made my way for the photo shoot with all the other staff on the faculty. This was followed by a brilliant evening; I sat next to a 'Nigerian Prince' with a sense of humour to match my own. Adding to the perfection of the evening we indulged in a very fine seven course dinner. Now back to the point of this story. If I had gone back up to the breakfast buffet I would not have met the man in the lift, and then I would have been in quite a dire predicament for the week ahead. I certainly think God had listened to my internal rant and delivered the goods! Don't you?

Bangkok

At the back end of 2013 I made a trip to Bangkok in Thailand, part business and part sightseeing. Bangkok is known for its ornate shrines and vibrant street life. I did all the touristy things and visited the royal district, which is home to the very opulent Grand Palace and its sacred Wat Phra Kaew Temple. Throughout the Royal District there was a never ending stream of massive statues of demons and ornate statues of Buddha, the whole area was adorned with beautiful artefacts.

ESCAPADES AROUND THE WORLD

Unbeknown to me I had landed in Thailand during the 2013–2014 political crisis. Anti-government riots were frequently taking place all over the city. Not long after arriving I was walking around the city taking pictures; I soon came across some rather serious looking soldiers. I thought a photo of the soldiers behind barricades of barbed wire would add nicely to my memorabilia. I rather stupidly stood in the street, waving my camera saying, "Smile." Unbeknown to me, a few yards away, they had shot dead five citizens and injured another 50 people. Although I knew the commotion was going on, I did not realise what had happened until I listened to the BBC world news that evening. Yes I was standing feet away from this atrocity, and given I couldn't speak Thai I did not have a clue what had happened as I rather ignorantly continued to take pictures of the soldiers.

That same night when I arrived back at the hotel it was quite late as I'd had another very busy day. I had two appointments scheduled for the following day; one at the British Embassy with the trade and investment manager at the UKTI. The other meeting was with the executive director of the British Chamber of Commerce. I was in the hotel lobby when the bell-boy called for me to say there was a telephone call from the British Embassy. Well now, I felt terribly important that the British Embassy were contacting me. It did not matter that it was just to tell me that my appointment had been cancelled due to the killings and riots so could they reschedule for the next day.

During my stay, I went to Terminal 21, this is a one floor one theme shopping mall. It is decorated based on well-known streets in cities such as Rome, Paris, Tokyo, London, the Caribbean, Istanbul and San Francisco. The sections allocated to each cities were set up as replicas of that city, selling similar types of goods in the shops in that language. I have some great photos of "London" yet I still couldn't get my coffee with cream in "London" and eventually had one in "Tokyo". I ventured onto the Sky Train for the experience and then had a very harrowing experience trying to flag down a taxi on a road similar to our motorways. I got back to the hotel flustered but unscathed.

Now negotiating the traffic in Bangkok was not for the faint hearted; and that is just trying to **walk** around the streets. I had a number of near misses, and on one occasion was standing in the middle of an island while heavy traffic including dozens of motor bikes were whizzing by me all beeping their horns as they went. I was clearly badly informed when it came to road safety and did not realize I was supposed to use the flyover and not the traffic islands. After eventually making a run for my life to get to the other side, I was told that it is against the law for pedestrians to be on the islands in the middle of the road. It was difficult to work out which was the worst; either getting arrested on a pedestrian charge or suffering exhaustion as I made my way up the stairs of the flyover in a pair of high heels in temperatures soaring into the high thirties. A difficult choice I must say.

There were pictures all over of the King of Thailand who has great status and was revered by many of the people. Everywhere I went there were lots of decorations and flowers. There was also gentle piped music in most public areas. I really enjoyed my experience in Bangkok both business and pleasure and went out exploring the city whenever I get the chance.

One night I diligently wrote the address I was going to on a piece of paper, 'Yes' I thought, 'that will do the trick, I will now get to where I'm going'. I walked out onto the street and as I stepped into the taxi, I proudly handed my neatly written piece of paper to the driver - he looked totally confused. In my haste to be 'brain of Britain' I had failed to take into account that the taxi driver could not only not speak English, but they certainly couldn't read it either. Well that burst my bubble; I eventually found someone passing who could translate to the driver where I was going. Well done me!

ESCAPADES AROUND THE WORLD

Egypt

I was with a friend as uninformed as myself when we decided to book a trip to Egypt. After booking the trip, you know when you tell everyone, 'I'm going on holiday to Egypt?' They'd just look at me as if I was really stupid. "Catherine do you know the country is at war?" Well no I didn't, or I would probably not have booked the holiday. In fairness, the holiday was enjoyable, and the people were as nice as they could be, given a huge part of their economy relies on the tourist industry. Nevertheless, this was an opportunity to see yet another great wonder of the world, 'the Pyramids' which were quite some sight, as well as enjoying a luxury boat trip on the River Nile.

The most notable signs of the war were whenever we travelled by taxis or cars. There were lots of armed soldiers on the streets with their rifles looking rather threatening. The vehicles we travelled in were always checked for bombs as they came and went. That is, the car was stopped while a device was run underneath and around the car to pick up any signs of bombs. Because of the war and problems with the infrastructure the streets and highways were used as dumping grounds for household rubbish. It looked dreadful when we went anywhere and the sidewalks and highways were littered with black bags full of garbage.

Me being so discreet with my camera, I did find out quickly that the soldiers on the streets were not 'smiling' when I tried to take their pictures. I came close to being arrested as an angry soldier started shouting at me. If it had not been for the quick-thinking guide escorting us, who spoke quickly, then made a very quick exit from the scene I'm unsure of what would have happened. He did tell me in no uncertain terms to keep my camera out of eyeshot of the soldiers unless I wanted to spend some time in an Egyptian prison. Not an experience I would relish! Fortunately, we got home in one piece.

India

Now India must have a mention. No one can prepare you for the culture shock on arrival, both positive and negative, but without a doubt a myriad of surprises, shocks and an education in itself. I booked a tour travelling alone to India's Golden Triangle which comprises Delhi, Agra and Jaipur; it is called 'golden' because of the extraordinary wealth of cultural and historical splendour to be seen in each city. I was bedazzled by the vibrancy of colourful clothes worn by the native people. There were bazaars and markets all over the city, with cows walking through the stalls with as much right to be there as the local population. That is cows are considered sacred in India and appear everywhere you look. I was surprised to learn that

2.

the cows go out in the morning from their homes and go back in the evening, rather like our dogs used to do when I was young. I was gob smacked to also see wild boar lying in the streets with their young, sometimes the city streets appeared more like a farmyard than a city.

The traffic was very like the traffic in Africa and Cambodia with whole families out on a motor bike; not unlike watching a circus act in the middle of the street. This was combined with all sorts of animals pulling carts including: ox, camels, horses, donkeys, asses and cows. Then throw into the mix: trucks, wagons, cars, rickshaws and bikes. Without a doubt the mind boggled at the utter mayhem.

Another shock to the system was when we were catching a train at 3am in Delhi. There were hundreds of people wrapped in blankets, and to equal this there were also hundreds of rats all over the station. This scene certainly opened my eyes to the poverty which was prevalent in India. Nevertheless, a trip to India could not be complete without a visit to the majestic Taj Mahal. You guessed, I had to have my picture taken in the same position and place as Princess Diana. Regardless of the poverty and mayhem there is some amazing architecture and beautiful sights to see, certainly worth a visit. Believe it or not I didn't get Deli belly! Perhaps my childhood had blessed me with a constitution like a horse.

ESCAPADES AROUND THE WORLD

Italy

I visit very few countries more than once, as I think there is so much to see on this magnificent planet. On this occasion it was coming up to a friend's birthday and her family asked her, "If you were on a desert island and could only choose one person in the world to be with who would you chose? Guess who she said? Yes, me. Her family organised a surprise trip for us to Rome overlooking the Trevi Fountain with all expenses paid. This was her dream holiday where she had always wanted to go; I had already been a few years earlier. As the myth goes if you throw three coins into the fountain this action is supposed to ensure that you will return to Rome in the future. It had obviously worked. That was a memorable week where we spent our time admiring the superb architecture and the ancient ruins of the Colosseum as well the Vatican City. She said she chose me because I was the most uplifting and fun person she knew. Wow!

Two very close calls in New Zealand

Well after smashing the top of my arm in two I thought I deserved a special six-week holiday, given the excruciating pain I had experienced for months. No point sitting around moping, so I booked my holiday and set off to my first stop in Sydney Australia. I spent a few days exploring the city and booked to see the Sydney Philanthropic Orchestra at the

2.   284

Sydney Opera House. I had packed a couple of elegant evening dresses for special occasions should they be required so I thoroughly enjoyed getting dressed up for the evening, wearing a large pale blue silk shawl draped over my shoulders to enhance my long sleeveless dress. This was certainly an orchestra of world standing and the highlight of my stay in Australia.

My next stop was Auckland in New Zealand where I was spending a few nights before heading off on the remainder of my trip. I headed up to the Bay of Islands which exceeded all my expectations even topping my cruise trip to Alaska. I took a ferry out over the bay and found the scenery mesmerising, as we travelled for miles around the bay avoiding all the huge rock formations which protruded hundreds of feet into the air from the sea floor. One formation looked like a giant elephant and the ferry we were in went through the cave like entrance of another formation. This was extremely rocky as the waves crashed against the sides of the archway like cave. The Bay of Islands is a subtropical micro-region known for its stunning beauty & history. It did not surprise me to learn that it was found to have the second bluest sky in the world, after Rio de Janeiro as this was certainly evident in the pictures I took.

I returned to Auckland ready for the remainder of my trip, travelling through the north and south islands on the "Stray" bus. The Stray bus goes further off the beaten track than most of the other busses, with a travel route to nine National Parks, including highlights like Abel Tasman, Queenstown, Rotorua and many other special places which are exclusive to Stray. I need to tell you that the average age of the passengers travelling on the bus is twenty-six and for most of my journey I had a twenty-two-year-old driver who drove like a twenty-two-year-old driver. On a number of occasions many of the passengers feared for their safety, especially as we navigated around hairpin mountain bends at speeds that even put the fear of God into some of the young people on the bus. He also partied like a healthy twenty-two-year-old, sometimes dances and parties going on to four in the morning. In short he liked a drink.

On the brighter side the bus drivers always took us to our accommodation which consisted of: hostels, hotels, retreats, wilderness lodges, cabins, motels and a night in a Maori village. Some places were brilliant and some left a lot to be desired, but none were boring

I must let you know the precedence I set from the very beginning of my journey. I had stood at the bus stop for 20 minutes when others started to arrive, mostly in pairs or groups. When the driver arrived he locked the doors while booking everyone's luggage on the bus. Because my broken arm was still not strong, the young ones got their luggage booked onto the bus before me. While I sorted mine out, they obviously walked straight to the front of the bus to be now first in the queue. Well I had other ideas, I walked right to the front of everyone standing in the queue, to be immediately confronted by a young, long haired blonde, leggy, goby woman. "You can't walk straight to the front," She screeched at me, "I'm first." I was quick to enlighten her in no uncertain terms. "I was standing in the queue for twenty minutes before you even arrived and I'm getting on this bus before you or anyone else." She knew she had met her match and shut up fast. I got on the bus first, and of course chose the best front window seat. You will not believe it, but throughout my whole journey I had the best seat on the bus. That was some accomplishment for a five week journey, where there was a daily fight for the best seats. I just seemed to thrive on the challenge and to be fair, no one was my match. I'd done well and made a reputation for myself very quickly; I also made sure I had the best rooms or accommodation on the whole journcy. Surprise! I think I came across like someone not to be messed with, although I was probably the oldest person on the bus for most of the journeys. I was well pleased with myself as even at sixty-five I certainly hadn't lost my ability to stand my ground with whoever I met. Even two young German women who tried it on, got short shrift. Don't get me wrong, I was not in any way nasty, I was just straight as a die and as a result I made friends easily and met some great people.

On arriving in Hahei, where we were going to stay for the next two days, I got talking to a woman, probably in her mid-thirties. She came from Sweden and looked like one of those Swedish models; she was tall, slender and her thick flowing blonde hair framed her heart shaped face. We decided to make our way over to Cathedral Cove, this is where the beach scene in the Narnia movie was filmed. The heat was overpowering on this four mile trip as we meandered up and down along the cliff edge with very little protection from the sun. When I reached the cove I walked straight into the sea fully clothed and soaked myself from head to foot; otherwise there was no other way I could have made the journey back. My new found friend demonstrated her powers of agility, as she dived into the waves and swam like a mermaid. Now I really couldn't come close to matching that!

As we made our return back to the accommodation our bus driver, ex chef was busy cooking the most extravagant barbeque. I must say, he was a far better chef than he was a bus driver. Everyone on the bus had given him twenty dollars to buy the food; there was steak, chicken, pork, lamb, sausages, burgers, vegetarian foods, salad and a selection of

2.   288

sweets. After a generous scrumptious meal, the drink flowed merrily with music and dancing. This went on to the early hours in the morning, thus setting the precedence for most of our trip. I'd ended up with a bus driver who had a reputation for having more parties and encouraging more alcohol consumption than any other driver known to the Stray bus company or any other bus company for that matter.

The next day everyone on the trip made their way down to the hot water beach for a natural beach spa. In groups of about seven we dug through the sand to let the very hot water flow into the sand holes we had made so that we could lie and relax in our beach spas. The water was red hot as we lay there for about an hour, just getting to know each other. As I relaxed in the soft warm atmosphere, my attention was focused on a huge rock protruding about twenty feet from the sea. I was watching the spectacular sight as the waves smashed into the rock and rocketed three times its height into the air.

When I'd had enough of my hot water spa I went to play in the sea while I washed the sand from my body. I was playing quite happily, jumping in and out of the waves by myself. I do remember thinking these waves are quite strong, when suddenly I was picked up and swept sideways across the sea. Within seconds I was smashed into the same rock I had been watching earlier as I lay on the beach. I tried to grab onto the rock as the waves smashed my body against it. It was impossible I could neither grab the rock nor touch the sea floor with my feet. I tried to shout for help and felt my voice disappear under the roar of the waves. I was now immersed completely in the scene I had been watching only half an hour before. The waves were now smashing into me as I tried desperately to cling to the rocks. After each wave smashed me into the rock, it went on to pull me off the rock and down into the water. I absolutely thought I am a goner. No one could see me or hear my shouts for help. I'd never felt so close to death in my life and I knew it. I felt like a feather getting thrashed around in a whirl pool. For the first time in my life I could feel my insignificance. I was desperately asking God to help out. I actually could see myself dying and no one knowing what had happened to me. I had images of my body being washed up on the shore or worse still never being found. I started to panic like I have never panicked before, I couldn't get my breath as I felt myself getting weaker and weaker with each wave that battered into me. I could feel my face, body, arms and legs as each wave smashed them into the rocks. I desperately tried to breath in air before the next waves crashed over my head, repeatedly smashing me into rock. It was getting harder and

2.

harder and I was almost out of strength altogether as I felt myself going further down. I was so weak by now, I thought God I'm going down I can't keep coming back up, I haven't got the strength.

Just as I had given up all hope of surviving this ordeal a man some distance away from me, turned around and he knew as soon as he seen me that I was in great danger of drowning. It was by sheer chance or more likely the grace of God that he spotted me as he was swimming in the opposite direction. He knew he would not be strong enough to safe my life himself as the waves smashing the rocks were too ferocious. Fortunately, my companion from the night before who swam like a mermaid was close by. He shouted for help from her and they both joined up as a team. In union, they swam towards me, each taking one of my arms and swimming with difficulty away from the huge rock and back to the sandy beach. They checked me over and although somewhat battered, cut and bruised by the rocks I was otherwise fine on the surface. I was immensely grateful for their courage that day and could not thank them enough. They were modest about their deed although they knew they had really saved my life and I would not have survived without their courage. I know that day will stay with me for the rest of my life as without a doubt I was minutes away from going under and staying under. As we walked across the sands and things quietened down I burst into tears. The tears were just rolling down my face as I sobbed uncontrollably. It is very rare I cry, but the event had left me completely traumatised, the tears were tears of relieve that I had survived the ordeal.

I did learn later that when you are near protruding rocks the currents can crisscross and are much more powerful. Apparently I was caught in a rip current which are apparently one of the most dangerous natural hazards in the world. I was also not informed by our bus driver that there had been several deaths in the exact same location. He did apologise and say he had mentioned it to a couple of people as we walked to the location. I was angry that this had not been made as an announcement on the coach for everyone's ears, rather than the handful of passengers who were tagging along with him. I remain completely traumatised and now quite frightened of the power of the sea.

Now given I have just told you about one of the worst experiences of my life I am now going to tell you about one of the best. Yes, I flew a small plane over Lake Wanaka and Roy's Peak. I can honestly say it was one of the most wonderful experiences I'd ever had. I can't quite describe the feeling, as we flew over the mountains. It felt as though I was sort of floating in the air, I could hardly feel the plane moving forward, bit like being suspended in the sky. You know when you dream you are floating through the sky well it felt like that. There just seemed to be a complete calm in my whole mind and body as though I had escaped the earth and left everything behind. When I brought the plane into land there would have been nothing more I'd loved to have done, if I had been younger, than book flying lessons when I returned to the UK. By the way there was an experienced pilot sitting next to me, giving instructions; plus I did get a certificate to say I'd completed my first flying lesson. But a more important piece of memorabilia was that I flew my first plane at 65, the same day I got my state pension! Now that's memorable.

The following day we continued on our travels, it would be too much to tell you all the exciting things about this holiday, so I will just tell you a few of the things I think will interest you. I won't tell you about all the awesome glaciers, mountains and lakes, as travelling through New Zealand was a Wow on every corner. I will tell you that my first interest in New Zealand came after watching the Lord of the Rings, I was mesmerised by the beautiful places caught on film. So obviously while there I had to go and see the place that caught my interest from the beginning. So I booked on a trip to the Hobbiton Movie Set where the Lord of the Rings and The

Hobbit Trilogies were filmed. The film set is exactly what you see in the trilogies but so much more. In 2009, Sir Peter Jackson the director, writer, and producer of The Lord of the Rings returned and left the beautiful movie set behind. There are 44 permanently reconstructed Hobbit Holes, and an abundance of movie magic nestled inside the fully operational farm. Certainly worth a visit.

A trip where we had some hair-raising moments was at the Blue Duck Station which is a conservation project on the banks of the Whanganui River. It is a sheep and beef farm as well as a conservation project that also offers bush accommodation and unique activities in rural Whanganui. In order to get there we came off the main road and onto a one track road, through the mountains. This road must have been thirty miles long. My heart was in my mouth, as our young driver sped around corners with the bus wheels screeching on the narrow gravel road beneath us. On a number of occasions the bus skidded, leaving everyone on board frightened for their lives. The drop over the side of the mountain was terrifying, you know when you close your eyes and pray God please let us reach our destination. Well I think a number of the passengers were certainly saying a private prayer as they watched the bus hurdle from one hair pinned bend to the next. Several times we had to get out of the bus and clear the roads of rocks. There had been heavy rainfall in the area causing several landslides. When we reached our destination one young man came up to me and said, "Catherine I was absolutely terrified, I was going to ask him to stop the bus and let me out. I'd have felt better walking the thirty miles."

While at the Blue Duck Station a heart racing moment occurred when I was out walking by myself. Seven horses decided they wanted to befriend me; I had other ideas as they trotted towards me at quite some speed. Given I did not want to reciprocate the feeling I started to run away from them, I skidded down an embankment, jumped over a dyke, and you have never seen anyone scale a fence in such an undignified manner. I shot over the top going upside down as I hung on to the fence rather like an extremely badly preformed cartwheel. I did have a smirk on my face as I looked back at them. I might not have smirked so much if I'd realised how much mud I'd collected on my way down the embankment, my walking boots were like lumps of clay. I think that about sums up the journey to the Blue Duck Station although the place itself and the walks were awesome.

You know how most sensible people go on tours to see the glow worms, well you might have guessed by now that would have been so contrived an experience for me. So one night I decided to do the walk with another woman, to see if we could spot any glow worms. We'd heard there was a forest on the edge of a town we were visiting where glow worms could be seen. I'd heard such a lot about them, and how they were worth seeing, that I was definitely game for a venture into the dark forest! As we walked through the woods in the pitch black to accomplish our mission we were both scared as we tried to stifle our giggles. You know when you are really scared and you laugh to hide the fear, it was a bit like that. I don't know how many times we grabbed each other when we were startled with some eerie noise. One of the important things we were told before we left our accommodation was that if we made a noise the glow worms would switch off. It was therefore imperative that in order to spot the worms we had to stifle our screeches. Do I need to tell you our trip was well worth it? We spotted thousands of glow worms as we made our way through the forest. I'd never seen glow worms before and was delighted to see all these tiny shiny lights, like Christmas lights shining in the dark. I must say I was well pleased.

We stopped for a few days in Queens Town, the adventure capital of the world with more than enough to keep me entertained for a few days. There was bungee jumping, ski diving, jet skiing, speed boats, jet boats, gliding, go cart tracks, a swing which went right across the canyon, a gondola, white water rafting, kayaking, horse trekking, and gliding. Now that's a lot to be getting on with. I was with a woman who worked in the law enforcement industry from the UK who I met on the coach. She was great company and we had some right laughs

I now have to tell you about yet another hair raising experience where I thought I once more was not going to survive. All the ferries from Wellington to Nelson had been cancelled because of the stormy seas; that is until we arrived, our ferry was the first one running for a couple of days because of weather conditions and high winds. After we left the port it was not too long into the journey before our ferry was being thrown around on the sea like a matchbox. It was like a scene from the Titanic. The dishes were falling out of the cupboards, smashing to the floor, the tables and chairs were sliding up and down the floor, people were being thrown around and falling down as though they were mortal drunk. The woman in front of me, slid across the floor and badly injured herself. It was like trying to ride a bucking bronco, I positioned myself crunched up with my arms wrapped around my legs, in a corner where the seat was fastened to the wall and a fixed table in front of me to stop other furniture from bashing into me. I prayed fervently as I watched the horror in people's faces, even the staff were frightened as all work stopped and they had to find somewhere safe to stay. The waves were lashing over the sides of the ferry, it was so bad there was no one even attempting to take pictures. I watched a man walk along the floor and as the ferry tipped up, so did he, it was really peculiar he sort of fell over on a slant, smashing into the floor! Needless to say we did get eventually get to the other side.

Well now in Christ Church ready to set off for home tomorrow, via a couple of days in Dubai. I have had a fabulous time and rolled with laughter dozens of times with the people on the "hop on hop off" Stray bus. I must say I am ready for home, because changing my accommodation every one to two days for six weeks has kept me very busy, although it has been so beautiful travelling through this country I don't think I could have chosen a better way to travel. Apparently we have travelled about four thousand miles around New Zealand alone. That is not counting the seven thousand miles trip to get here and I have a twenty hour trip tomorrow just to Dubai as there is a four hour stop over.

Nevertheless the day after I left Christ Church I had just arrived in Dubai when it came on the news about that horrendous shooting. Two consecutive terrorist attacks occurred at mosques in Christchurch. The death toll was 51, and 40 other people were injured, everything was put into lockdown and flights were stopped in and out. To think that only 24 hours before I had been in the botanical gardens only feet away from the Mosques where those shootings took place. In a funny sort of way I really do think Him upstairs keeps looking out for me! He does seem to have a full time job though.

Now there a few more things I'd like to mention briefly that are included in my repertoire of experiences while travelling. In China, I visited the Terracotta Army, as well as walking part of the Great Wall of China and going on a Yangtze river cruise. In Iceland I swam under the stars in the Blue Lagoon, saw the Aurora Polaris, better known as the northern lights and watched geezers shooting hundreds of feet into the air. I paid a trip to the Canadian end of Niagara Falls, and when in America had the awesome experience of a visit to the Grand Canyon as well as visiting the Hopi Indian Reservation in Arizona. I spent a day in Disney World and a New Year in the Swiss Alps. The bleakest experience I ever had while travelling was a visit to Auschwitz concentration camp in Poland. I think that about sums up some of the more important experiences and escapades as I travelled the world.

Don't worry, I have left the last paragraph to mention our own beautiful countryside and coastline. I never fail to be awestruck by the magnificent scenery we have in England,

Scotland and Wales. The sights I see close to home remain nourishment to my soul, they never fail to leave me mesmerised with their magnificent splendour and tranquil surroundings. And believe me I have had many an escapade here, but that would be another book in itself.

MY SPECIAL GRANDCHILDREN

Now my book wouldn't be complete without mentioning two of the most important people in my life, my grandchildren. In this chapter I am just going to tell you about these two-special people. When my son reached a certain age, I started to think about how wonderful it would be to have a grandchild. I was beginning to lose hope as the years were passing by; he was now twenty-seven and still no sign of the patter of little feet. Then one day he brought his girlfriend to meet me. It was not long before they came and told me that Sandra was pregnant. I was thrilled to bits, but I did have some reason for concern. Sandra had some learning disabilities, so when she was carrying the baby I secretly thought when the baby is born she will allow me to look after him or her. In my head her baby was becoming mine. What a shock I was building myself up for, without even realising.

The night she was born, my son David rang at about 2am to say she had weighed in at 8lb 8oz. He said she had problems with her legs but not to worry. I lay back down and worried, there was no way I could go back to sleep. I got up and rang the hospital and asked about her legs. The nurse on duty said, "Yes she has deformed legs, they are the worst I've ever seen." I'll never forget those words, as they struck a chord of horror right through me. Can you imagine what that was like? David had asked me not to go to the hospital that night. I lay all night with the tears rolling down my face and just couldn't stop crying. In the morning I pulled myself together and went to the hospital. I held this beautiful baby in my arms; and as I did I just fell in love with her. I don't think anyone can prepare you for that moment of being a grandparent. As I held her, Sandra gently pulled back the small blanket covering her legs to reveal the most tangled mess of a pair of legs I had ever seen. They were horrendous, her knees and hips were dislocated, so her feet were going the wrong way and her legs were pointing upwards instead of downwards. I hid my shock, as I did not want to offend David and Sandra, but I was shocked. I imagined she would spend her life in a wheelchair and never walk. Once more I was upset with God, but this time it was different, I didn't stop speaking or praying to him. I just kept repeating, "Why God why?" I was absolutely distressed and failed to understand what sort of God would do this. So yes, God had once again dropped out of my favour, but on this occasion, I had not given up on Him. I continued to reverently pray for the healing of my granddaughter's legs, as if they would miraculously heal overnight. Did He hear?

I called into the hospital a few times to see how they were getting on. My son seemed to be taking control and handling everything in his calm, steady manner that reflected his personality, very unlike my own. Before they left the hospital, my granddaughter's mother Sandra said she did not want me to come and see them. My heart sank like a stone, I was absolutely gutted. She went on to say she had to put some distance between me and the new family unit, as she had to remake the relationships with my son and her child. I had to wait until I was invited to go and see them. I was devastated, it was as if all my dreams were just shattered. Once more I was thrown into the loss of a baby, but this time I had no alcohol to protect me from the pain. Sandra would take Louise to see her mother and never bring her to see me. I hated her mother, I was so jealous, although the woman had done nothing to deserve my resentful dislike for her. It was the best I could do to hold a brief conversation without displaying my inner world of thoughts and feelings which would have shocked anyone to the core. Just as well they weren't written across my brow!

In fairness, I have never felt as much emotional pain in my life; I cried uncontrollably for months. I talked obsessively about the pain to my therapist, who said, "You are grieving the death of your baby." I called her an idiot - still lacking tact. How could I be grieving the death of my baby 20 years later? At first I really couldn't see it, but eventually it made sense. Louise's birth and the way her mother had severed our relationship had replicated the same experience as losing my own baby twenty years earlier. I often used to say to clients, "Psychotherapy will always be played out on the streets of life." Meaning that all our undealt with issues will be triggered at some point by life's events. I was certainly seeing this in action, as I was catapulted into my own undealt with past. As the months continued the pain didn't lesson, nor did my massive over-reaction to the situation. I talked to anyone who would listen, as I struggled to get through this period.

My son was also now dealing with some of his issues regarding his childhood and had found himself a new family which he liked. You've guessed, I certainly didn't like them. I felt as though he was deliberately punishing me, as he was now playing happy families with his newfound in-laws.

This was also a time when I prayed, but shame on me, as my prayers would have been more fitting for a mobster's crew than the good Lord Himself! "Please heal their souls and make them allow me to see her, or please kill them and I will get her for myself. In a better fettle I might have prayed for the healing of my own soul along with theirs. Either way my prayers were as fervent and confusing as my state of mind at that stage.

We did have some contact during this period but it was very brief, of course they held all the 'power'. They had something

MY SPECIAL GRANDCHILDREN

I wanted, I had nothing they wanted, therefore placing me in a very weak and powerless position. Nevertheless, they told me that Louise's legs were being put in plaster casts to try and straighten them. As soon as they did this she stopped eating and lost over a third of her body weight. As soon as they took the cast off, she started to eat again. As the months went on our relationship did eventually improve; Sandra got pregnant again and they started to allow me to have Louise overnight every weekend. When my grandson was born, after a few months he also stayed with me every weekend.

I taught them both to swim at a very young age. I slowly introduced them to the swimming pool while allowing them to play wearing armbands. This progressed to putting them in the water without armbands, and as they tried to grab my swimsuit to prevent themselves from sinking, I would step away. Automatically this would make their other arm come up to grab my swimsuit, and as I kept walking backwards, they made a swimming stroke. We would go through this time and time again. Eventually they were both excellent swimmers from about eighteen months of age. I was so proud of myself! When they came to my house and played together my home was now filled with the most raucous laughter you could ever hear. My heart danced with joy as I could not stop laughing when I listened to the fun they were having. I had never before felt my heart grow but believe me every time they walked through my door my heart seemed to grow in my body. It was a feeling which seemed to set my body aglow like no other experience I'd ever had.

Now both my grandchildren were born with learning difficulties and attend a special school. When I tell people this, they usually say something like, 'Oh how sad'. or 'Poor you'. In all honesty they are two of the most delightful, funny, easy going, children I know; and I would not swap them for all the children or money in the world. They have brought more love and laughter to my door than anyone has ever done.

Although at first I wondered how having children with learning difficulties would affect my life and how I would deal with this. Well first let me tell you both children look perfectly normal, well they do to me. However, they have personalities that complement one another; Louise is the trouble maker and Allen is the peacemaker. He seems to work so hard at keeping some equilibrium in their lives as Louise spends her time causing chaos. Actually, a bit like my relationship with their dad. I caused constant chaos as he maintained some equilibrium.

I think, as a result of her troublesome personality, Louise seems to be very well known. No matter where I take her she is recognised. We travelled 200 miles to a Butlin's camp, and

2.

the day we arrived someone was shouting, "Louise Louise" this happens all the time. If I take her to the shops, theatre, parks, cinema, restaurants, horse racing, stately homes, I will guarantee someone will shout on her to get her attention. For instance, I was at a business meeting in Newcastle and arranged a meeting with a woman who I met regarding marketing my business. She arrived at my house a few minutes early. I opened the door and with my best polished voice said, "Could I ask you to take a seat in the living room as I just finish off this telephone call?" When I walked into the living room she looked at me and said, "You are not Louise's grandmother are you?" Well I could have fallen through the floor. I lost my grand polished voice and blurted, "Yes, do you know her?" "Yes" she said, *"She is the bane of my life. My son idolises her and I have to listen every night to a list of all the antics she has been up to at school, she also hits him. When I meet her I see that glint in her eyes that says, 'How can I really wind you up to get your attention?"* Yes, that sounded like my granddaughter's personality captured to a tee. This woman had recognised a picture of Louise on my cabinet. Not so long ago I was invited to a wedding by a college in Harrogate with an extended invitation to my grandchildren. While we were there I thought I would treat them to an afternoon tea at Betty's tea rooms, someone stopped us who knew them both and said, "You two look very smart." We were almost 100 miles away from where they live.

Another time I was looking after Allen while Louise was in hospital having an operation on her legs. We were out walking with a friend of mine when I said how much I missed Louise. I was explaining that everywhere I go people know her. I could see her thinking, 'you're exaggerating and given we are in Jesmond now no one will know her here'. Well we walked into a coffee bar, and had no sooner sat down when in walked two women. They walked up to our table and said, "Hello Allen where's Louise?" I was chuffed to bits. I am sure I have a direct line with Him upstairs. What do they say? When God wants to remain anonymous, He's called coincidence.

It does not matter where I take the kids, they have an amazing appreciation of life. They love going to the theatre and live shows, often sitting mesmerised throughout. I couldn't get them to leave the theatre after watching Tchaikovsky's Nutcracker. "We not go home, we stay here." People who meet them often say they have never met two such happy, loving children.

Nevertheless, life hit the children a hard blow when their mother walked out leaving them with David. Louise was seven and Allen six years old; they were both devastated, as they had a strong attachment to her, even though she seemed sadly lacking in decent parenting skills. She used to encourage Allen to kick people, smash things, slam doors, and bang his head, she laughed if they swore and were cheeky. Regardless they absolutely loved her; it took a few years to get their behaviour under control after she left. I insisted that David take control at this stage, or Allen would grow up strong and completely out of control. The boundary had to be placed with love and firmness. After a few dedicated extremely stressful and frustrating years we got there. When Allen went into his rages, which was often, David had to hold him firmly around his body until he calmed down. I was so proud of how he never smacked the children, just held them until they were calm. Allen now knows mostly where to draw the line.

Without a shadow of a doubt this was a heart-breaking time for the children. Each weekend when they came to stay Louise would suddenly stop playing, climb onto my knee, lie her head on my chest, and just sob and sob uncontrollably for between twenty to thirty minutes. When she was finished, she would climb down and start playing again, without saying a word. She had no language which could express the depth of her pain, but I know the pain created from her loss went as deep as any pain could possibly go.

During this period the school or afterschool club had to frequently send for David because Louise had hit someone or would not do as she was told. She was lashing out at everyone and anyone, struggling to contain her anger with the world, and lacking any emotional control. She would often also hit the teachers and after school club staff.

Explanations of why it was not appropriate to hit people did nothing to deter her behaviour. It also did not matter what sanctions we put in place, Louise would continue to lash out at people. I think this was a result of her mother previously encouraging this behaviour, combined with the emotional pain she felt after her mother left. I also think the fact that she underwent several operations on her legs did not help the matter. It wasn't just the operations. No, I used to get really upset when I watched her legs being bent back as far as they would go, while the callipers was fixed in position. This was the evening procedure for many years to improve the bend in her legs. There was no way I could do this to her when she stayed overnight with me, it would have broken my heart. Yes, I am sure that in her mind the world was certainly hurting her, and she was fighting back the best and only way she could.

One person she wasn't fighting with was her brother. Yes, Louise and Allen were a team who worked in close harmony with one other. When they played together Louise was the dictator and Allen, well he just fell into place and obeyed her every order without question. She would push him on the chair and say, "Sitty doon dere an litn." After falling into the chair he would just sit and listen. She would even tell him what he had to say. "Yu say ....., and a'll say ....." I struggled to understand why he just obeyed her every command and said to him, "Why do you put up with her? He looked surprised at such a ridiculous question and responded with "Cos a luv her grandma, a luv her." What could I say? One thing for sure is that they have an amazing bond and would protect each other at all costs. I am often the wicked witch of the west, more so when I have to discipline one of them. One day, as I was disciplining Allen for doing something wrong, Louise standing with her hands on her hips said, "Tek nay notice tu hu just liten tu me." I could do nothing but laugh inside, but I would never let her know this, as I gave her a telling off for being cheeky!

At other times they would both chant together, backing each other up, as they insisted I was the one in the wrong. They both clearly think it is me who has the learning difficulty. O how far would a bit of insight go? Perhaps that would make life boring. Nevertheless, I might be full of fun and love to have a good time with them, but I won't allow them to be cheeky or get the upper hand. This certainly keeps me constantly on my toes, I have to be one step ahead all the time. Louise constantly pushes the boundary, whereas Allen now knows mostly where to draw the line.

MY SPECIAL GRANDCHILDREN

Now it is not often I give up on something, but I have given up trying to teach them the rules of games, as Louise always knows best, she makes up the rules as they go. I have never seen children play such ridiculous, nonsensical games perfectly happily for hours mesmerised in a world of their own. Of course, the only rules would be those she puts in place depending on the day, and Allen just goes with the flow. Just to give you a better understanding of their learning difficulties neither of them have any concept of money. If they find a penny, they think they are millionaires, "luk Granma, luk at wha a have, can we spend it?" I just smile, as after seventeen years I am not going to explain that a penny has limited spending power. I gave up years ago trying to teach them to add up even small sums. I would ask, "What is five and two?" They had no confidence that each hand always contained five fingers, so they would diligently count each finger just to make sure. I eventually realised that this task was way beyond their mathematical ability. Well done me! Allen said the other day I could buy the woman's house for two pounds. She lacked a sense of humour!

When Allen was about seven years old he needed an extra two pence for something he was buying. I said I would loan him the two pence but wanted it back when we got home. He had left his money in the house. Not a lot to learn there! When we arrived home, I asked him for my two pence, he really could not understand that he owed me any money and started to cry as he thought I was stealing his money. I told him I was taking the money, as he had to learn that if you borrow money you pay it back. I put his two pence on the bench with quite a lot of other money including pound coins, fifty pence's etc. About an hour later I looked, and the two pence was missing, all the rest of the money was still there. Now that is theft on a grand scale!

We used to go through a similar situation every weekend with their clothes. They would arrive in the clothes they were wearing, as you do, and the next day they had to change their clothes, socks and underwear. The obvious thing here was that I would wash the dirty clothes they took off and have them ready for the following week. Well you would not believe the crying match I had every weekend, as they could not understand that they were going to get their clothes the next week. They wanted to take the clothes they had taken off back home, and really did think I was keeping them for myself. No matter how much I explained that not only did they not fit me, but that I was only washing them. Allen in particular used to go into rages, shouting, sobbing and breaking his heart. It took a long time to get them to realise that when they returned the following week their clothes would be waiting for them.

MY SPECIAL GRANDCHILDREN

These are two children who not only have no understanding of money, but also have no understanding of time. So, when they were small, they used to get up when the sun got up. I would beg them, "Please go back to sleep" in my half-awake groggy voice. Much to my dread, I would get a bright and breezy response, "No Granma the sun is up." That was it, I had to drag myself out of bed at these unearthly hours and keep them entertained. I eventually had the good sense to buy blackout curtains for their bedrooms.

Just to really capture their ability to understand time I'll tell you about another incident which happened a couple of weeks ago. I was out shopping with them, when Louise spotted some watches, "Grandma will yu buy me a watch?" "No, I've told you umpteen times I will buy you a watch when you can tell the time, and in any case, you have a watch that someone bought you." "It's broken, and I can tell the time I have learned at school it is quarter past two grandma." "Don't be ridiculous" I almost snarl, secretly laughing inside. "I have grandma, I have learned it is quarter past two." "Louise what time is it on my watch?" I show her the watch. "I told you grandma it is quarter past two." I rest my case, as it is four twenty-five.

Well it isn't just money and time that they have an issue understanding, there are other areas of life that would be too complicated to even begin to explain. Like the night I went out for dinner with friends and family, and as we are all sitting around the table enjoying our meal Allen said, "Granma tell them about all the people you sleep with." Well I could have fallen through the floor. As I struggled to recover, I gasped, "Sweetheart I don't sleep with lots of people." He looked right into my eyes and said in his sincere innocent voice. "Oh Granma just tell them about the people who you sleep with." I did not know what to say, this was one of the rare occasions I felt completely lost for words. I just sat there trying to work out where he got it that I was sleeping with lots of people. I heard a burst of laughter from further up the table and fortunately my friend clicked on to what he meant, the tears were rolling down her eyes with laughter. I had moved into a block of flats, and Allen thought all the other people in the block were sleeping in my house!

Recently Louise told me she had a boyfriend. I asked her how old he was, to be told he was twenty-one; that is three years older than her. I said, "I think he is too old." "Don't be silly Grandma I'll catch up." I rather stupidly tried to explain that as she gets older so will he. She looked at me as though I am absolutely stupid, and patiently explains to me, as though I have the learning disability, how she gets older and catches up. What can I say?

MY SPECIAL GRANDCHILDREN

One day Alan came in from school and said he had been talking to a man outside. I shouted David through, and asked if the children were told not to speak to people on the street. Indignantly he responds, "Yes mam they have been told about 'stranger danger' at school." We both tried to have a serious talk to Alan about speaking to strangers. He kept repeating, "But he spoke to me first." There was no way we could get him to understand what stranger danger meant. His rational was, that because the man had spoken to him first, he was no longer a stranger. We quite wrongly had assumed that because they had learned about stranger danger at school that he knew what it meant. He clearly had no concept of what it really meant.

I must tell you that Louise now walks reasonably well, certainly well enough to get around. I really do thank God for this and hope it was another desperate prayer answered! Nevertheless, she almost died last year with pneumonia and sepsis; the hospital said they could not find anything wrong and discharged her. Fortunately, David kept insisting that she remained very unwell, and eventually exasperated with the poor response, he took her to another hospital. They asked for the x-rays from the previous hospital which showed a massive shadow on her lung which they had missed. If he had not persisted, she would not be alive now. She is a tough little soul who has dealt with a great deal of pain and seldom complains. She prides herself on being able to endure the pain from needles and operations. "I'm brave Granma, aren't I?" I just want to hug her, as she does not need to be brave for me! My special grandchildren are truly special.

AN ABUNDANT LIFE

I was now well along that road, and although often very bumpy I now possessed the coping skills to negotiate most of the bumps. Almost every aspect of my life had now improved, I had built up a brilliant private practice as a psychotherapist and was making good money in a job I thoroughly enjoyed. I put my heart and soul into working with my clients. I am sure they put their heart and soul into working with me too. I now worked helping people to get in touch with their deep-rooted pain from the past, so that they could move on. Now doctors, professors, university lecturers, the rich, famous and everyone else was coming to see me. This surely was a turnaround for the books. At first, I felt intimidated by their status; I believed they would know more than me and be much more intelligent. However, as people began to share their personal stories, it soon became apparent that they were sitting in front of me because I was helping them, and for no other reason. I always said, people vote with their feet, and if you are good, they come back, and if not, they don't. I built up one of the busiest private practices in the area. Eventually I was unable to take on all the clients who were recommended to me and ended up referring hundreds of clients a year onto other therapist.

AN ABUNDANT LIFE

Clients often came to see me for several years. It was really satisfying to watch people grow as human beings and move on with their lives. I now felt as though I was doing a really worthwhile job; a job which provided people with the 'rich soil' to help them to grow. There were never two clients alike, and everyone needed something different from me. I prided myself on my work and read every book on the market relating to mental health problems: depression, anxiety, post-traumatic stress disorder, attachment theory, neuroscience, abuse, personality disorders, and anything else I could find. I wanted to be the best that I could possibly be. I think this was the remnants of that show off personality I was blessed with as a child. It was also the remnants of my addictive personality!

In twenty-five years, I never cancelled a session, and by many of the companies providing counselling services for their employees I was known as the best provider of therapeutic services in the region. When I worked in doctor's surgeries the receptionists frequently said, "You are the only therapist whose clients always turn up." Many a client climbed high heights during our work together. The best part of this was that they always acknowledged the role the therapy played in their lives. They would ring up years later and ask to see me, usually just to say how well they were doing, and how much the sessions had influenced their lives. When I moved to a new house recently I had over two hundred thank you cards and letters. No present in the world could beat the pleasure I felt from reading their words of gratitude. With this work I had the honour and privilege of being a part of someone's journey through heartache and tears. I felt like a millionaire when my clients came out the other side feeling more able to cope and happier people. I hope they did too!

After graduating as a psychotherapist, I attended a Professional Development Group (PDG). I had been going for a few years when it was suggested by the facilitator, a woman who I held in great esteem, that I should get involved with the profession by being active on professional committees. Wow! She believed in me. Yes, it was not long before I joined my first committee. Believe it or not, it was an ethics committee and I was soon writing the ethical standards for the committee with the help of another colleague. Fortunately, I didn't lose any of my old coping skills, as on the way to my first meeting on a dark winter's night my car broke down on the A19; I 'safely' hitchhiked the remainder of the journey and sorted my car out the next day.

Nevertheless, with the encouragement and words of wisdom from the PDG I thrived, as they, like many others who I now had in my life had the greatest belief in my abilities. It is truly amazing what you can do when others around you believe you can do it.

As the years continued, I was being asked to sit on more boards and committees for various professional bodies. I was on committees with our local psychotherapy department where I did my training, the United Kingdom Council for Psychotherapy the European Association for Counselling and a subcommittee for the British Association for Counselling. I felt so proud of myself; I was now playing another important role in the profession.

However, on many an occasion I felt out of my comfort zone when it came to knowing the correct protocol or etiquette for situations such as: dress codes, (my Levi 501s weren't cutting it in the professional world) digital etiquette, walking into a meeting or conference with composure (poise and posture), making introductions, dining out, and all those things which are noticeable when you don't know them. As a result, I attended etiquette training with an elite school of etiquette in London. My confidence in social and business situations grew, along with my knowledge in the use of the correct etiquette for most situations. I must say I found this very liberating in every aspect of my life, as I no longer felt like the only one in the room who didn't know the correct way to behave.

AN ABUNDANT LIFE

After working for over twenty-five years as a psychotherapist I decided it was time to stop and create a 'happy business'. Yes, just like that. It was not long before my 60th birthday; I had to think hard about what would be a 'happy business'. I decided that since I had completed numerous courses in etiquette, and enjoyed learning about the history and formalities, that I should set up a school of etiquette. This made good business sense to me, as there was also nothing remotely like this in the North of England.

Every time I mentioned my idea to anyone, I got a response which went something like, 'Don't be stupid, no one wants to learn about etiquette, its old fashioned.' Or, 'You are not the right person, etiquette teachers are posh and from privileged backgrounds.' Yes, who on earth was I to teach etiquette with my background? 'You are too old to start a new business.' Cheeky! Or, 'You have a brilliant business already where you make good money, so why on earth would you want to change?'

Another challenge was looming, with everyone doubting my sanity. Their doubts did not deter me, I was determined to go through with my new idea. As you'd expect, I did also have a reason for wanting to set up a school of etiquette. I believed teaching people etiquette would improve their self-esteem and confidence and provide them with the ability to feel

3. **322**

comfortable in any situation. Now, from what you know of me so far, I am not deluded enough to think that you can imagine me as an etiquette teacher. But never mind, because I did know that in order to succeed it would mean making a lot of changes to my life. That is, I would have to look and behave like a credible etiquette consultant. Can you imagine that?

My life was now at a point where it was no longer just about making money, not that it ever was, as even while on the drink I would not do a job which I felt was not ethically sound. I remember a company asking me to collect for a well-known cancer charity. When I found out I was supposed to keep part of the money I collected I was horrified. I could not bring myself to collect for a charity and put the money that the unsuspecting public thought was going to help someone with cancer, into my pocket. I suppose I had to get paid somehow, but I did not think it was right to do it like that.

Nevertheless, I was now going to take a leap of faith and drastically change the work I was doing, enough hopefully to pay for a reasonable life style. I also believed there was a market out there for people like myself who wanted to improve their social and business skills. I laboured over a name for my business; after much deliberation I chose a very grand name. What did Norman Vincent Peale say? 'Aim for the moon and if you miss you will fall into the stars'. Now that is a good idea.

Being very conscientious, I decided to book onto one more etiquette course, just to make sure I was ready. So off I went back to London to my elite school of etiquette. After I told Tammy, the founder and lead consultant of the company what I was thinking of doing, she asked to meet me for a coffee. We met in a little coffee shop in Buckingham Palace Road, where she said something along the lines of, *'It has been our policy to not allow anyone from the UK to be involved in the training within our company, however, as I have got to know you over the years I love your enthusiasm and really respect what you stand for. I would like to ask if you are interested in joining us?'* Well shoot me with a feather, could I believe what I was hearing? Sure enough, I was now being asked to train as a teacher with this elite school of etiquette in London. As we parted company we shook hands on this. A few days later I received an email from Tammy saying she had spoken to the company advisers and they would have to put three conditions in place. Two of the conditions were fine, but the third conditions said I would have to agree to only work in the Newcastle region. Well you guessed it, I wrote straight back and said, "I would feel like a bird with my wings clipped - I am going to teach worldwide so we have no agreement."

AN ABUNDANT LIFE

I was now ready to start preparing for my new life. That is my 'newly designed happy life'. I began by researching and preparing my training material. I worked all day as a counsellor and psychotherapist and then spent hours each evening (until at least midnight) writing up my training materials. Being me, I would not do anything half-hearted and wanted my courses accredited. This was no mean feat, and a lot of hard work, but it paid off when I was successful in getting all my courses accredited.

Three years later I was now ready to teach etiquette around the world. However, I might have been ready to teach, but how was I going to let the world know I was ready? I decided I would build my own website and learn how to make the best of website optimisation and social media. I was ploughing through a minefield of information and felt as though I was doing the equivalent of a degree in marketing and social media. I also started to attend network meetings and prepared my two-minute spiel: "*I offer training in business and social etiquette including areas such as: poise and posture, how to make introductions, skilful communication, digital etiquette, dress codes, table manners, interview skills plus a lot more.*" Tuned to a fine art, I may add. I published my books on Amazon. However, I put them on the American Amazon, which was really annoying as it had taken me days to write all the descriptions and link my books to the site. It did not help that I was getting bills from the American tax man.

Nevertheless, not long after my website went visible, I started to get enquires. I will never forget my first client; he was from an Asian background and had been brought up not to look into anyone's eyes or smile. He wondered why he was unable to get work or accepted onto a course at university. So, the irony was, that I ended up using all my psychological knowledge to fulfil the remit of building his confidence in social situations. By the time we finished the sessions he was accepted onto a university course and had a part time job. Well done me!

Shortly after this I was contacted by a man who was very concerned about how his daughter walked. He said she walked with a stoop, as she was quite tall. She was also flat footed and stomped her foot as she walked, which made her look odd; the other children at school were mocking her because of this. This man drove his daughter on a five hundred mile round trip for a session in poise and posture. When I watched her get out of the car and walk towards my door, I was also concerned about how she was walking. As I watched her flat footedly stamp her way up my garden path I thought, 'What on earth have I let myself in for here, how am I going to get her to walk elegantly in a couple of hours?' Take note here of the thinking process. I was not thinking, 'I haven't got a hope in hells chance of getting this young woman to walk elegantly.' No, I put a positive slant on my thoughts, even though it was a stretch of the imagination.

It was agreed her father would leave and come back in a couple of hours. I was now left with a sixteen-year-old full of 'attitude'. When I asked her to walk across the floor she tutted and flung her hair back. I was not impressed, and very directly asked, "Do you want this or not?" She looked shocked, got up and walked across the floor. We spent the session using two mirrors so that she could see what she looked like as she walked. At the beginning of the session the emphasis was on what was going wrong, and then practicing a method to rectify this. When her father returned, she was as excited as they get. "Dad watch me, watch me!" she commanded enthusiastically, as she elegantly walked up and down the room. When her father paid me my fee, he said, "You have given me more than money can buy." A very happy father and daughter left my house that day - much to my relief.

The business was progressing in different ways to how I imagined. I was inundated with phone calls from people wanting to join me, or to buy my courses and deliver the training. I lost count of the offers I had to collaborate with other businesses. However, I was unwilling at this stage to share my training material, as I had put so much work into it.

AN ABUNDANT LIFE

After working for a while in the UK I started getting overseas enquires, this felt really exciting. I was now going to do what I set out to do, which was teach etiquette around the world.

My first overseas trip teaching etiquette was with the United Kingdom Trade and Investment (UKTI); this trip really built my confidence in the overseas market. I was invited to deliver a talk about etiquette in Kuala Lumpur which is a beautiful city, surrounded by mountains. It was my 60th birthday and delivering a workshop at the British Education Suppliers (BES) Asia Forum at the Malaysian Convention Centre felt like a dream come true.

After delivering my talk I felt like a celebrity; dozens of people were asking if they could have their photographs taken with me. How my world had changed! I was also told later that I was the only person at the conference who got a standing ovation. Didn't I do well? After the talk there was an event planned at the home of the Director of Trade & Investment in Malaysia. Most of the other presenters from the conference were there enjoying the food, drink and good music. A few nights later we were invited to the British High Commissioner's residence and had a brilliant night with lavish food, rich surroundings, and great company. I was now rubbing shoulders with a different caliber of people; engaging in a lifestyle I never dreamt was possible. These houses without a doubt must have been worth millions, the interiors were exquisitely decorated, and the outdoor areas were vast with patios for hosting large numbers of people and beautiful gardens.

On returning home I received a phone call from someone in France, who told me he was meeting, 'Heads of State'. He wanted to arrange to do a course in fine dining. I agreed to meet him at the Train Station in Newcastle. An extremely handsome man in his early thirties, over six-feet-tall, walked up to me, bent down, and kissed me on both cheeks. Can't be bad! As we walked into the restaurant, I instructed him to attend to seating me before himself. He pulled out my chair and placed it slowly back as I lowered myself into it. Well this was a far cry from being knocked unconscious into the chair, what an amazing life I had made for myself.

My travels while teaching etiquette took me to some fantastic places and situations. While in Cambodia, another country which has had its share of conflict, I met up with Sheila South who founded a large modelling agency in Cambodia. We discussed possibilities for the etiquette market as I was invited to join her in a hotel for a: *'Night of fun & fashion featuring the Cambodian Model Look finalists walking in Victoria Secret, inspired designs by Phka Kn'Jay, Ambre & Jasmine.'* This event was filmed to go out on the television in Cambodia

and America. The tuc tuc ride to the venue was not as
inspiring, we bumped our way through the mayhem of traffic
with several near misses. I hung on to the sides like grim
death, as I almost lost my fingers in a collision which knocked
a woman from her bike. She just picked herself up and set off
again, obviously a common occurrence in the hustle and bustle
of the streets of Cambodia.

Not long after getting back to England I was contacted by a
woman called Uka who asked me to deliver some training in
Lagos, Nigeria. "Yes I'll do that." After numerous
negotiations, flights, visa and hotel sorted, I'm on my way. As
I got on the plane to go to Nigeria, I asked the airhostess a
question. She said, "If you sit down, I will find out, and get
back to you. I will recognise you by your hair." Well I thought,
she's a bright spark, given I was not only the only woman on
the plane I was also the only white person on the plane.

I arrived in Nigeria and was met by Uka and two other
Nigerians, who cushioned me as they pushed their way
through all the hustle and bustle going on outside the airport. It
was as though everyone in Lagos, which is one of the most
populous cities in the world, had turned up in the middle of the
night to welcome the plane. I kept close to my escorts, as I was
told before leaving the UK that white women are often
kidnapped, and that Nigeria can be a very dangerous place. I

really would benefit from a few more reservations, but caution has never seemed to rate highly in my repertoire of behaviours.

My trip to Lagos was also just before the Boko Haram extremists kidnaped 276 schoolgirls in April 2014 from Chibok in northern Nigeria. Perhaps if this had happened prior to my trip I might have hesitated in my decision to go, but probably fortunately I was not blessed with the gift of foresight. We made our way to the car, which crawled through the swarm of people and eventually we drove through the dark streets of Lagos lined with prostitutes. I arrived at the hotel which was surrounded by an eight-foot metal fence and huge metal gates which were opened and closed as the vehicles came and went. Actually, I could easily have mistaken it for a high security prison. All the soldiers on the streets were well armed with what I think were machine guns, but my knowledge in this area has some limitations, although I did know they weren't hand pistols!

After a peaceful night in the hotel I waited at the entrance, as I was being picked up by Uka in a chauffeur driven car. After a thirty-minute journey through the busy streets of Lagos we arrived at the venue where I would be delivering the training. The staff at the company were waiting patiently on our arrival. I was going to be delivering the etiquette training for ten days in different companies and schools. I loved teaching the Nigerians, they were open, dynamic, respectful and receptive.

Nevertheless, just in case you didn't know, they are notorious for their scams and non-payment of debts. Uka the woman who had invited me over to teach, had promised me I would receive my teaching fee before I started work on the Monday morning. Do I need to tell you it was not there and came with another promise? "You will get it by the end of the day." By this time I was certainly getting long in the tooth, and a lot less likely to be taken to the cleaners. This is where I really had to hold my own and make it clear that I would not continue for another day until I was able to see all the fees in my bank account. They continued to hum and haw, "Well this is how we do business in Nigeria and you will get your money." "Well this is how we do business in England and you either put the money in my bank account or I do not teach another day." "You mean you don't trust us?" I find it insulting when people think you are stupid enough to fall for this type of manipulation. "Yes, that about sums it up, the only person I trust is myself." They knew by the tone of my voice I certainly wasn't kidding. Fortunately, Uka's husband worked in a bank, and although they had all closed, some of the staff were still working. At 6pm we were allowed to enter the bank, I remember being asked to squeeze through a set of doors which scanned my body to ensure I was unarmed. As if! It took a while, but I was eventually able to witness the money being transferred from their account to my account. Yes, I was now happy, as this was a weight off my shoulders, and stress I could well do without.

In all fairness I loved my time in Nigeria, even though it could be a pretty scary place. I was also invited into numerous schools to deliver talks to the children during my stay. The first school was a primary school and the small children were so sweet, they sang songs for me about etiquette and manners, and almost every child in the school wanted to touch me. They screeched with delight as they fought to get close to me. As I entered the schools a man sat at the gates with a long bamboo cane, which was used to whip the children if they tried to leave the grounds. When out in the school field surrounded by hundreds of teenagers with a microphone in my hand, I almost caused world war three when a child asked, "Do you believe in corporal punishment?" Without a second thought I responded with, "No it's abuse." Well I have never been surrounded so fast by adults in all my life. I was told that I was not allowed to say this, as I would influence the children against corporal punishment. How bad would that be? Talk about feeling as if I had committed a cardinal sin, could I redo the damage? A weak attempt at going against my integrity failed drastically. It was clear from my voice that I fully believed what I had said, as I stuttered out a pathetic explanation. The best that would come out of my mouth was, "It is important that children respect their elders." All this was happening as the children were loudly chanting my praises. In reality I was so proud of the children who were trying to fight against the corporal punishment embedded in their culture. Nevertheless, I'd certainly hit the top of the popularity list with the children and the bottom with the adults.

Everywhere we went there was a car and driver to escort us; I felt like a millionaire with my own personal chauffeur. When I first set up my etiquette business, I joined an organisation called 'Toastmasters International'. This is an organisation which helps to improve people's public speaking and leadership skills. They hold their meetings all over the world. On the Saturday a driver arrived to take me to a toastmaster meeting thirty miles outside the city. When I entered the meeting, a woman walked up to me and said, "How do you do," as we shook hands. I was somewhat taken aback, as this was the first person I had met with such impeccable manners. I wonder why. Would you guess that she had attended my etiquette training a few days earlier, thus explaining her impeccable manners? I was delighted to see the training executed to such perfection. Hadn't I done well?

AN ABUNDANT LIFE

Now negotiating the back streets of Lagos was one of those experiences etched in my memory. I was asked to visit the father of one of the trainers I was working with. As we made our way through the back lanes the streets were squalid. It was like being on an American film set. Youths hung out on the street corners, others stood by their rickety old cars, with one foot on the front bumper, while smoking joints and staring at me as if to say, "What the f… is she doing in our area?" You are right in thinking I certainly didn't fit in, not in my beautifully cut classic clothes, and Italian leather briefcase.

I was guided off the street through a narrow old stone alley, to an upstairs apartment. As I entered the sparsely furnished living room, with no carpets and bare plastered walls, a load of youths jumped up, obviously waiting on my arrival. We did 'fist bumps' as opposed to shaking hands. Yes, on this occasion I decided it would be wise to refrain from partaking with any of my newfound knowledge as I joined the family for a mug of tea.

On my last Monday morning in Lagos I walked into a room to deliver the training and found they started the first Monday of the month with an evangelist preacher. I was invited to join the employees, as they gave thanks to the Lord for all the great gifts of life bestowed upon them. Well what a great start to the day, as the energy in the room rose to crescendo level. He repeated "Praise be to the Lord" time and time again between sections of his very powerful service. Well I am sure the service must have achieved what it intended to achieve, which was to set the tempo for the rest of the month and lift the spirits. It certainly lifted mine, as I had never experienced anything like this before in the work place.

Later in the week I was teaching at another company. One man, you know the sort, full of his own self-importance, said in a dominating voice, "I'm here to learn and you are here to teach me." I looked at him and said, "We are going to have fun while you learn, and you are going to enjoy the training." I learned, that their idea of learning was a teacher standing at the front of the room spouting facts, while they sat and listened, without interaction.

With my new found assertiveness skills, I graciously made it clear that if anyone was more interested in their mobile phone, than what I was teaching, they could leave the room and would not be given a certificate at the end of the training. Now we could get down to business; as the training got underway, we rolled about with laughter, and nearly got thrown out of the hotel for laughing, as we practiced walking elegantly down the stairs on the hotel staircase. The same man in his testimonial at the end of the few days training wrote, "I did not want the training to end or to go home as I could not believe how much fun we had or how much I learned." I was pleased, but I must tell you this story. During the training we were discussing the correct way to ask for the toilet when out and about. I explained that it is not etiquette to ask for the 'toilet' as that is considered inappropriate. Another etiquette teacher taking the course told me that in England we ask for the 'water closet'. I said, "I don't think so." He said, "They do, I have read it." I said, "And I have lived there for 61 years and never in my life have I ever heard anyone ask for a water closet." He said, "The toilet doors in the UK have WC written on them. (He'd read this too) So they do! "Excuse me could you direct me to the water closet?" "Eh what's that?"

Nevertheless, while delivering the training in Lagos a reporter from one of the biggest national newspaper joined the training and reported. *"The globally renowned Catherine Ellison comes to Lagos……The participants said it was the best training they had ever had."* What an accolade!

After I returned home, I often received enquiries from clients who lived in china, but at first nothing amounted to much, given my expenses and fees were too much for most individual clients. It was not until I received an email from someone in London who wanted me to train a student to teach my etiquette courses in Shanghai that I eventually agreed to go to China. This felt really exciting, again I was on an all-expenses paid trip. From leaving my home to getting back to the UK I never put my hand in my pocket.

When I arrived at the hotel I was surprised to find that it was acceptable to order food from local restaurants and have it delivered to the hotel. The hotel room was also used to hold our business meetings. Once more the man who invited me over to Shanghai tried to get me to accept a contract which was not acceptable. I refused to move forward until everything was sorted out to my satisfaction. People seemed to think I could be railroaded into a contract I did not agree with if I was in their country. Well they certainly had a lot to learn about the English.

I found the Chinese very different from the Nigerians and much more reserved. Nevertheless, I did enjoy teaching in China - the students took what they were doing very seriously. Their culture tends to be more reserved in expressing appreciations or affection toward others. They are not forthcoming with feedback or compliments which I found strange at first. Nevertheless, I had read about this prior to leaving home, so should have been prepared.

We had a lovely venue in a select area of Shanghai, surrounded by ornate gardens. When I arrived at the venue where the training was taking place, I was surprised to find this huge picture of me right across the entrance to the venue. Two hours were put aside for photo-shoots, as people queued up endlessly to have their pictures taken with me. Once more I felt like a celebrity. I must say I did like that feeling. After the event we were invited to a big dinner party by the owner of a hotel in Shanghai. I was their 'guest of honour' which meant I was given all the privileges that go with that position in China. I also enjoyed listening, as they explained the Chinese customs and etiquette.

My host Jackie, the young woman who I was training, took me to several places while in China. We walked along the Huangpu River bank which flows through Shanghai. It was first excavated and created by Lord Chunshen, one of the Four Lords of the Warring States. It is also the last significant tributary of the Yangtze before it empties into the East China Sea. The Bund and Lujiazui are also located along the river, the views of the skyline were spectacular especially at night as was walking through the city with all the fabulous ornate Chinese buildings.

We had dinner and visited the Yuyuan Garden at night. This is an extensive Chinese garden located beside the City God Temple in the northeast of Shanghai. I found the Chinese gardens extremely tranquil and gentle on the eye. We hired a long boat although only three of us were on this very long rowing boat with a Chinese man rowing the boat, it was an extremely memorable trip. We wove our way through the narrow river banks, watching and listening to the sounds of exotic bird and wildlife. There was steam coming off the river and the lotus flowers were just dying back. It was the most peaceful serene boat trip I'd ever experienced. We even had a cup of green tea!

Jackie also took me to West Lake which has influenced poets and painters throughout Chinese history for its natural beauty and historic relics. It has also been one of the most important sources of inspiration for Chinese garden designers. It was made a UNESCO World Heritage Site in 2011, described as having "influenced garden design in the rest of China as well as Japan and Korea over the centuries" and reflecting "an idealized fusion between humans and nature". There are many romantic and fairy tale stories about the West Lake.

While in China this time, that is I had previously spent two weeks on holiday travelling through China, I noticed that people continue to slurp their food and clear their throats to hock. This is common practice in China, and felt to be inappropriate in most Western countries, my opinion entirely. Although more recently, that is January 2018, I was teaching some Chinese students visiting the UK at St Hugh's College at The University of Oxford. When I mentioned this behaviour, they looked repulsed and said, "Any person doing this must not come from a good home." Now that was something I didn't know, I just thought this was done in China regardless of the type of home the person came from.

Apparently, it is rare when a foreigner is invited into the home of a Chinese person. Yes, you have it, I was one of the chosen few to have this experience! Jackie asked me if I would like to spend a couple of days with her parents. On arriving, after removing my shoes, I entered a sitting room and was greeted with a beautiful smile and a present. Jackie's parents were lovely and couldn't have done enough for me. They made a huge dinner for my arrival and a very unusual but delicious Chinese breakfast. Before I left they took great pride in showing me their rooftop garden which was lovely. Jackie's parents went out of their way to make my stay as comfortable as they possibly could and it was so appreciated.

While travelling overseas it was important that I learned the code of etiquette for each country I visited; otherwise I would have been disrespecting their culture. Can you imagine me trying to shake hands with someone who by the nature of their religion is not allowed to touch a woman? No that wouldn't do. Nevertheless, I was now rubbing shoulders with high officials: Executives, High Commissioners, Governors and Diplomats from all over the world. This was an amazing time in my life; I was staying in the best hotels, eating in the best restaurants, while meeting all kinds of people; and realising that there was a whole new world out there which I had not experienced before. I also made a point of going to some of the top hotels in London; The Savoy, The Dorchester, The Ritz, and I was now a regular visitor to the theatre and West End shows. I was also now sitting on a few boards and committees for businesses.

The main one being the Federation for Small Business (FSB). The best time I had with the FSB was when they asked me to go as one of the representatives for the North East Region to their conference which was held at Birmingham's International Conference Centre. This was an all-expenses paid trip, and one of the biggest conferences in the FSB history. We were given an opportunity to quiz top politicians from the three major political parties ahead of the 2015 General Election. The speakers were: Labour leader Ed Miliband, Chancellor George Osborne and Liberal Democrat leader Nick Clegg. We mainly just wanted to know what their intentions were towards small business in the UK. The entertainment and food over the weekend were five star; they even had a very grand black tie event which was exceptional on every level.

Although now doing a lot of oversees travelling, I was also teaching in companies throughout the UK. This involved a lot of travelling to many of our cities, some of which I had never visited before. People also came to me from other countries for the etiquette training. Including one young woman who came from Russia to train with me for five weeks. Every day we dined in the best restaurants, while travelling the UK to see the sights. Money was no object, as her partner owned businesses around the world. He paid for everything she wanted, while I went along to instruct on the etiquette for each situation. She was a lovely, refined, unpretentious young woman who loved country walks and nature, a woman of my own heart. Her manners were impeccable, and to be fair I am sure she could have taught me etiquette! We did have fun ordering oysters at the Lockfine restaurant in Gosforth and laughing, as I demonstrated the correct way to eat them. After about seven, she had it down to a fine art.

By now my reputation was building up, I would get telephone calls every week to speak on the radio, this was both locally and nationally. They would ask my opinion regarding features in the newspapers, or issues which had hit the news headlines in connection with correct behavior. Often the person on the end of the telephone assumed I came from some elite privileged background. They projected onto me how they thought I should be. *"Could you come onto our morning programme? There has been an article in The Times about*

*swearing in pubs and we know how much against swearing
you will be, so we would like your opinion."* or "We know that
you will hate tattoos." Or, "Someone has said …. on the TV."
It never failed to make me smile at the way I was perceived.
People imagined what I should be like, rather than getting to
know what I was really like. I was even contacted to comment
on a faux pas made by Prince Charles. I oozed with pride at the
thought! Can you hear me keeping Prince Charles right in
regard to his manners? I was also well pleased with myself
when I was contacted by Woman's Hour, but unfortunately, I
was away that day. Now that really would have been a feather
in my cap.

I was now also being asked to appear on numerous TV
shows, however most of the time I was too busy travelling the
world to get to the studios. At first, I must say I was quite
nervous speaking on the radio or TV. This usually was a result
of being confused about my view point, as I tried to maintain
my integrity. A huge task indeed, given I usually swayed
between two viewpoints depending on which part of my head I
was listening to. I mean, how could I say in front of thousands
of people that I thought swearing was terrible, when my own
language in the past had left something to be desired?
Regardless, I knew that this was what was expected from the
presenters of the show. As time went on, I got a bit better at

finding some middle ground, but still felt as though I fell short of how I would have liked to come across. Never mind, so long as I'm not dead anything is possible.

It was June of 2015 when I was contacted by the Head of the university who I had previously done some work for in Dubai. They asked me to go to Benin in Africa to teach business etiquette. Everything was booked, I sent my passport away for the visa, the flights and hotel were paid for. It was a Sunday, and I had eaten more than my fill, as you do on Sundays. As the evening progressed, I began to feel ill with pain in my chest. You know when you try to ignore the reality of what you are feeling, and keep telling yourself it will be alright shortly? Well believe me this pain was not reducing, it was increasing.

I eventually telephoned the NHS helpline, and after quite a frustrating phone call with someone who repeatedly asked me how I would rate the pain, I eventually lost my temper and said, "How many times do you want me to tell you I'm in intense pain, and what do you not understand about 8 out of 10? Not too long after losing my temper I heard the ambulance siren going, as it came into the street. The paramedics were lovely and took me to the Royal Victoria Infirmary where I was told I was having a heart attack. "No" I said, "I have probably wrenched something in my sternum as I was being sick and belching." Of course, I would know better than the doctors. "No" they said, "The blood tests confirm you have had a heart attack."

They kept me three days before sending me to another hospital to have a stent placed into an artery in my heart. Now I had never had an operation while I was awake and did not know what to expect. That was just about to change! As they started to push a stent through the artery in my arm the pain rocketed to a 100 out of 10. I'd heard someone say it was like a burning hot poker going up your arm, well that was a very accurate analogy.

I kept sitting up, which did not impress the nurse, she kept pushing my head down as she said, "Will you lie down and shut up?" What! I don't think so, as up I went once more saying, "Look I'm dying." I could feel the blood pumping out of my artery; soon there would be none left! During the operation my arm went into convulsions, as it was in so much pain. They injected me with something to calm down the convulsions. As I lay there, I remember one tear rolling down my cheek and thinking, 'Oh God I need you now.' The poem "Footprints in the Sand" saw me through the operation. I lay there and imagined God carrying me through this ordeal. I couldn't remember all the words at the time, but the gist of it was enough. I have Googled the poem below just for those who would like to read it.

Footprints in the Sand.

One night I dreamed a dream.

As I was walking along the beach with my Lord.

Across the dark sky flashed scenes from my life.

For each scene, I noticed two sets of footprints in the sand,

One belonging to me and one to my Lord.

After the last scene of my life flashed before me,

I looked back at the footprints in the sand.

I noticed that at many times along the path of my life,

especially at the very lowest and saddest times,

there was only one set of footprints.

This really troubled me, so I asked the Lord about it.

"Lord, you said once I decided to follow you,

You'd walk with me all the way.

But I noticed that during the saddest and most troublesome

times of my life,

there was only one set of footprints.

I don't understand why, when I needed You the most, You

would leave me."

He whispered, "My precious child, I love you and will never

leave you

AN ABUNDANT LIFE

Never, ever, during your trials and testing.

When you saw only one set of footprints,

It was then that I carried you."

Author Unknown

Well I got through the operation and that evening I was full of myself again, when the nurse asked, "What would you like for your evening meal?" I said, "I'll have feta cheese, green olives and avocado salad, followed by fillet steak medium rare, mushrooms and chips served with fried onions and cherry tomatoes. I'll order the pudding later with my coffee and cream." "O" she said, "We have a comedian on the ward."

Naturally the heart attack had a detrimental effect on me for a while; although I tried to ignore the fact that I'd had a heart attack at all. This was difficult, as I could feel my heart was not as strong as it had previously been. I was sent to cardiac rehabilitation classes which were fun, rather like going to dancing lessons! Oh, I forgot to mention that the week I had the heart attack I also had 14 tons of garden materials delivered to my caravan in the countryside. I was preparing to do some landscape gardening. The doctor made it very clear that I must not do any heavy work. My grandchildren were gems at this time in my life, I think they were frightened in case I was going to die and could not do enough to help me.

3.

They shovelled quite a bit of the gravel between them and every time I asked them to stop, they just kept going. When I tried to help, they would shout in chorus, "Granma am tellin me da yu mutn't do tha."

As I'd been forced to slow down a bit, I stopped for a whole two weeks to rethink my future. Although the training and experiences around the world had taken me to another level, I was ready to make more changes. For a number of years now I dreamt of being able to touch a lot more lives but wondered how I would accomplish this. Years ago, I had started writing my life story after constantly being told, "Catherine you must write your autobiography." I now decided that it was time to finish my story. That would achieve my goal to help and inspire others. Of course, I knew it would be very exposing writing a book about my life, but knew in my heart that this was the way forward. However, how would I reconcile continuing to teach etiquette and writing such a revealing book? Would it be the making of me, or the ruin of me? God only knows.

I knew it would take me a few years of hard work to write a book worthy of reading. So now would be a good time to tell you I got involved with Women Against State Pension Inequalities, (WASPI). This is a campaign group that fights the injustice done to women born in the 1950s regarding the changes to their state pension age. This cohort of women, many of whom left school at fifteen, were supposed to collect their state pension at sixty. A couple of years ago the government changed the goal posts twice, providing very little notice regarding the changes, thus forcing them to work until they are almost sixty-six. I have been to numerous protests in London and campaigns throughout the country with thousands of women to get the government to make fair transitional arrangements.

Can you remember the opening paragraph in the first chapter regarding the inequalities experienced by girls and women during the 50s? Well this continues in 2018. These women started their working life with disadvantages which have continued throughout their lives. Many of these women, including me, have worked for over 47 years while paying our National Insurance and taxes; we are entitled to every penny the government has taken. As a result of the financial insecurity caused by the age increase in the state pension, I decided to sell my five bedroomed house and downsize so that I had the money to do whatever I wanted, within reason!

Have I stopped fighting? No, life constantly throws situations where it is necessary to fight. In fact, I am probably doing more fighting now than I ever did. However, my fights are not some drunken brawl like they used to be; yes, they are much more sophisticated. I now also have the hindsight to realise that fighting takes up an enormous amount of negative energy, which whenever possible I would rather spend on something positive.

Nevertheless, life constantly throws stuff at you which needs dealing with. A couple of months ago I stepped off an unmarked step in the middle of a hairdressers shop in South Gosforth, and as I fell I smashed my arm on their reception desk and snapped the top of my arm in two. As I lay on the floor screaming in pain, calling out to God for help, (I think He was busy that day) the ambulance crew arrived. When they cut my top off, the paramedic said, "God your arm is really badly deformed."

After an operation to insert metal plates, and a ten- inch scar from my elbow to my shoulder, I spent months in agony unable to do everyday tasks. I was unable to cook, wash, drive, hug, get on a bus or see my grandchildren. I was even unable to write or use my computer. Any touch at all sent shock waves of excruciating agony rocketing through my arm. Even lying in bed was agony. Just before the accident I had been looking after my son and grandchildren. He'd had an operation and was quite poorly, so he could not bring the children to see me. I went into a depression and just wanted to die, I felt so bad. Never mind, this too shall pass! It is amazing how events soon become history.

I need to say that I have changed my life considerably on an unforgettable, remarkable journey. Although in the past I felt trapped in a life without hope, destined for poverty, violence and misery and often wished I was dead. I eventually turned that around to build an abundant, worthwhile life with a great family, a selection of good non-abusive friends, and plenty of good food. I can honestly say there has seldom been a dull moment in my life, whether that is good or bad. What more could I want?

There is one more chapter - read on.

DO MIRACLES STILL HAPPEN?

Now in this chapter I want to tell you a couple of stories that happened in my early 20s. This means that chronologically this chapter fits into my life after the second chapter. However, I did not think it was appropriate to bring it in at that point, as it would have interrupted the flow of my story. As you know, throughout this book I have told you about some strange spiritual experiences and other strange phenomena; well I believe these next two events were miracles. I also need to add that I understand that not everyone would interpret my experiences as divine intervention or miracles; well that is fine by me, as this is a matter of personal choice. Nevertheless, I have no doubts that my experiences went beyond the ordinary and into the realms of the extraordinary, and if we add God to the mix that amounts to miracles.

My first experience was after my son was born in 1972. I was eighteen at the time, and had eclampsia, which is convulsions during the birth. For years I wondered if the convulsions might have been caused by my friend Barbra telling me that giving birth was the same as, "Passing broken glass." I only recently learned from another friend, who reviewed this book, that eclampsia is not caused by someone telling you something, it is a medical condition. Oops! One learns something every day. Nevertheless, it was a terrifying thought, especially given I was already six months pregnant. If she had told me before I was pregnant there might not be a little David. A lesson in tactful conversational topics, appropriate for the situation, would not have gone amiss for this seventeen-year-old with a young baby of her own. Nevertheless, she was the font of all knowledge on what it was like to have a baby. My auntie with eleven children, what would she know?

After David was born, I was unconscious for a few days, when I came around, I asked if I could see him. I was told I was not strong enough and would have to wait. I created such a fuss, they were pleased to take me to see him. He weighed four pounds and was in an incubator. He had very dark hair, looked quite thin, with dark slanted eyes. I was just so pleased he was all right.

When David was two years old, he was still unable to speak, he used to grunt and point to what he wanted. I responded to him either with a yes, no or total confusion. In fact, I was beginning to get a bit worried, as his development seemed quite slow. He was not doing a number of things that the children his age were doing. Other people had also brought this to my attention and were quite concerned.

I explained my concerns to our doctor who arranged for David to see a specialist; who then referred him on to a professor at the Royal Victoria Infirmary (RVI). After the professor examined David, he said he suspected that he had Downs Syndrome. We were admitted to Leazes Baby Hospital in Newcastle for tests. They said he had a straight line across the palm of his hand, and a fold in his eyes, as well as other distinctive features, which suggested he had Downs Syndrome. We were admitted to the hospital for two weeks while several tests were carried out. They x-rayed his bone age, took bowel samples, blood and urine samples, and did other tests. They also made observations of his behaviour, intellectual, mental and emotional progress. The professor who was dealing with my son was really quite sure that his diagnosis was accurate. He talked to me about what to expect for the future in terms of David's ability to learn, or not learn, as the case may be.

From first being told he might have Downs Syndrome I never stopped praying. I did not know how to say the more formal type of prayer, but someone told me that when you pray you must say it through Jesus Christ, so that is what I did. 'Our Father through Jesus Christ….' and that was how all my prayers started for years. After his admission to hospital I had to wait two months for the test results.

I incessantly worried during this period, and if I saw him with chocolate on his face I imagined that this was how he was going to be for the rest of his life. I spent time with him teaching him all the things the professor had asked if he could do. He asked him to hop and he couldn't. I played football with David which improved his ability to balance on one foot. As he learned to kick the ball, and balance on one leg the task of hopping became much easier. I was pleased with myself! I taught him to read very small words, such as: "at" "hat" "mat" "cat" and so on. I'd bought him one of those Fisher Price houses with the magnetic letters which stick on the roof, therefore making the learning into a game. We all know that when learning is fun it is so much easier, and this was no exception. Although quite young at the time, I was not that stupid that I thought all the teaching in the world was going to change a diagnosis of Downs Syndrome. I also knew that it was a chromosome defect, and not a problem which could be rectified by any medical intervention or playing football and reading. Nevertheless, like most mothers who are told there might be a problem with their child I think it is second nature to hope and pray that the professionals have got it wrong. It might be that 99.9 % of the time they are right, but no mother wants to accept that their child might have a serious physical, emotional or intellectual problem.

During that period, health visitors came to see how we were doing. On their visits they talked as though there was no doubt whatsoever that David had Downs Syndrome. They discussed the type of special school he would have to attend, and his restricted learning capacity. I felt devastated that the bleak picture they painted was to be our future. Nevertheless, when I returned for the results after my two months wait I was told that all the tests came back to say that David was perfectly normal. By this time, I had taught him to do all the things the professor had asked him to do while we were in the hospital. He could now fasten his clothes, read small words, talk more clearly and hop! The professor dealing with the case found this difficult to believe. He said, "I

take my hat off to you, you have done really well with this child."
I told him how much I prayed that David would be all right.
People think you are stupid if you believe your prayers have any
effect on life, and I don't think he was the exception to the rule.

He asked me if I could bring David back for research, so that
they could find out why he was normal! Yes, I did say normal. I
struggled to control my temper, as I felt so insulted that they
wanted to conduct more tests to try to see why he did **not** have
Downs Syndrome. This did not make a lot of sense to me. I don't
think so, I told him not so politely. One thing was for sure, I was
furious at the amount of distress he had caused me, although
absolutely delighted with the result. I did stop and say my thank
you to Him upstairs. I now had a certified perfectly normal son,
whatever that might mean.

I am going to tell you now about an extraordinary story which I
believe was also a miracle. It was 1973 and I was twenty years old.
This was the year my sister went missing; my brother reported that
she had allegedly just walked out of the house and never returned.
The police did everything within their powers to try to find some
trace of her. They sent out lost person leaflets with a photograph of
her all over the UK and Europe. There were frequent broadcasts on
local and national television with her picture. Articles were placed
in the local and national newspapers. They even broadcast and
searched in Europe. Whenever they got a telephone call, they
followed it through. Of course, the telephone calls were usually

from people saying she was hidden in someone's attic or buried in their garden. This did not place us at the top of the popularity list with the local residents, as the police searched their properties.

As the months went by the search efforts were reduced; eventually they sent for me and my family. We were told there was very little chance of ever finding my missing sister alive. As a nationwide search had failed to find any trace of her, they said, "The probability is, your sister's body will eventually be uncovered under a heap of rubble to reveal she has been murdered." Can you imagine what that was like? It was certainly a shock to the system and sent us reeling, as it would. I could be wrong, but I think at the time they suspected my brother but did not have any evidence. We were told to prepare to expect the worst. It was hard to hear that they were ending the search to find her; as I think we all held some hope that they would find her somewhere.

Months later we were told the police thought they had a sighting of my sister in London. They were not a hundred percent sure if it was her, as they intended to fly her back up to the north east when she disappeared again. If my sister was alive she was making sure she was not going to be found to be returned to our home town. At that time I was unable to do anything, as I did not have the financial resources, or anyone to look after my son. Months later, I was working for British Rail in a Hotel. I told everyone I was going to go to London to find my sister. They all said things like,

DO MIRACLES STILL HAPPEN?

'Don't be stupid it will be like finding a needle in a haystack,' or, 'you have no chance, don't be ridiculous.' 'If the police can't find her, there is little chance of you finding her.' Their responses did not deter me, at twenty I was invincible, as you are at that age. I'd now set my mind on this mission.

My now three-year-old son was being cared for daily by a registered child-minder while I was at work. This put me in a better position to go and look for my sister. I asked the child-minder if she could take care of my son until I returned. She was happy to do this. I got a reduced fare train tickets, as I worked at the Royal Station Hotel in Newcastle, which in those days was part of British Rail. I had never been to London before and felt quite excited. In fact to be fair, at this age I had never even had a holiday, not even to a caravan park or camping. I had a very limited image of London, probably as realistic as Dick Whittington's. It was where all the rich and famous lived, along with; gangsters, alcoholics, drug addicts and down and outs. Nevertheless, cities fascinated me, even though I had only been to Newcastle!

I set off on an overnight train from Newcastle to London. These were the days when trains had sleeping compartments. You often hear that trains make comforting sounds which sets the scene for a peaceful night. Well it didn't for me; the sound unfortunately did nothing other than keep me awake, obviously resulting in very little sleeping and more tossing and turning.

DO MIRACLES STILL HAPPEN?

After making my decision to go and look for my sister I spent a lot of time praying. That night on the train I prayed earnestly most of the journey. "Please God through Jesus Christ let me find my sister…." When I wasn't praying, I would imagine all sorts of frightening scenes where I would attempt to rescue my sister. I'd find out where she was staying and knock on the door. Some foul man holding her captive against her will would threaten to beat me up and refuse to allow her to leave. What would I do? I could see the scuffle as we struggled; me probably being the loser but at least putting up a fight. If I was persistent enough, he might even call it a day. Worse still she might not want to leave! She would be so brain washed by the guy she was with that she would be unable to make a wise decision. Well now that I have shared with you my bizarre thought processes I am shuddered back to reality, as the train pulls to a stop at Kings Cross. Pulling myself together, I thought, in all fairness she could be dead; the police seemed to think she was dead, so why should I think she was alive, and not only alive, but that I could find her!

When I arrived in London everything seemed so fast, as people went about their daily business engaged in the hustle and bustle of life. So, I set off on my mission. I made my way to the metropolitan police station in King's Cross, where they said they thought they had seen my sister. I was armed with a tiny photograph taken in a picture booth. They checked their files and said there had been a possible sighting of my sister. However, they could not be too sure of the person's identity, as whoever it was made a speedy departure before her identity could be confirmed. I was told by an officer that many people who are homeless arrive in London and end up in squats. The officer gave me a few addresses, as he explained they would be a good place to start my search.

Off I went again to search the streets of London in the hope of finding my sister. Even though I had experienced violence most of my life, for some reason I never seemed to have any fear of dangerous situations. I found my way to the area the police had suggested would be a good place to start my search. That was of course after stopping and asking numerous people for directions. I lost count of the buildings I entered and the doors I knocked on, but always got the same negative response. No one knew anything. My search took me to some really squalid areas, the buildings looked quite derelict, the bare uncarpeted wooden staircases were decorated with graffiti, and smelt old and stale. In some of the buildings, youths hung around the doorways with their cigarettes hanging out of their mouths. You know that image. Strangers beware, this is my territory and I'll run you down if you take another step. Amazing imagination!

After the days fruitless searching I booked into the Mount Pleasant Hotel; it was quite a nice hotel and after a good night's sleep I had a hearty breakfast. I was now into my second day in London, and as I made my way around the squats, I combined it with as much of a sightseeing tour as was possible under the circumstances. There was no way that I was going to go too far off track, as I knew I had to keep my focus if I was to find my sister. All day I knocked on doors and got the same response. No one had seen my sister; I had a weary day and had to think about my accommodation for that night. My finances were limited, and I might have quite a long haul ahead of me, as I was determined to give this my best shot. These were the days before credit cards, and wages were low for women, so to be fair I was doing really well considering things.

I was now on day three of door knocking with the same gusto with which I had commenced my search. I eventually arrived at another dilapidated block of flats, and again made my way around proudly presenting my little photograph. Once more most people just said a brief "No" and closed their doors. I wore my long hair tied up in a sophisticated, rather unusual style. Some older friends of mine taught me how to put my hair in some really fancy styles when I was a teenager. I was now putting these skills to good use. I still have a black and white photograph which was taken in Trafalgar square during this trip, although I have my hair down on the picture. I was wearing a smart white blouse; an arran knit brown tank top, and a brown classy looking skirt about two, or maybe three inches above my knees, with a pair of platform shoes. These are now back in fashion forty years later, and the young of the day think they invented these!

DO MIRACLES STILL HAPPEN?

Again, I knocked on a number of doors with no success, but not prepared to give up, as I had spoken to God. God obviously having quite a busy agenda must have tired of looking down on my unfruitful search of the London backstreets and decided to give me a break. Eventually a woman, probably in her mid-twenties answered the door. I asked her, "Do you recognise the person in this photograph?" She asked me in a very suspicious voice, "Are you from the police?" I hastened to say, "No I'm her sister." She said, "Yes, I know her, there were a few of us who were quite friendly. Your sister was friends with a young lad called Bill Watson who lived in Aberdeen." After a more in-depth, but brief conversation while standing on this woman's doorstep she gave me his address. She told me that they had both gone up to Scotland. I did thank the woman and God as I was delighted with my success. You know, when you punch the air, well just imagine me "Yes" as I clench my fist and raised my arm into the air at rocket speed. I was absolutely over the moon.

It would have been so much easier if we had owned mobile phones in those days, but I'm afraid this would have been science fiction in the 70s. So off I went to Aberdeen, again on an overnight train, and I didn't forget my prayers, even though they were no more than a string of consciousness to God, with the words 'through Jesus Christ' scattered throughout. This was a 540 mile trip so it took quite a few hours; I arrived there early in the morning. I made some enquiries and negotiated the streets of

DO MIRACLES STILL HAPPEN?

Aberdeen to find the address I had been given by the woman in London. Do notice there is not a doubt in my mind that the woman was not telling the truth, it didn't even cross my mind.

I went to the house and knocked hopefully on the door, a dishevelled elderly woman answered the door probably in her mid-forties. After all I was only twenty, so anyone over thirty looked old. I asked her if Bill Watson was at home, she shouted his name Bill with a harsh bellow from the door. He arrived wearing a vest and pulling his trousers on over his underpants. Again, I had to convince him I was not the police. The police were obviously not very popular. He was not as difficult as my first informer. He said, "Yes" he knew my sister, they had been good friends when they met in London. He told me that she had left Aberdeen after a short stay and was now working in a hotel in Glasgow. Off I went again to Glasgow, I wanted to surprise her. I could visualise our reunion and felt really excited. When I arrived at the hotel she had moved on again. I felt disappointed and disheartened.

Nevertheless, I was given another address in Saltcoats in Ayrshire. Once again there was no telephone number, it was the address of a house. I found my way there negotiating the public transport system in Scotland, and eventually arrived at a cul-de-sac on a sunny evening. I knocked on the door wondering what sort of person I was due to meet now. Was this the time I would need to slay the enemy to free my sister from some fiend who had kept her prisoner? The door opened, and there in front of me stood my father; who I had not seen for many years. I was shocked, as this was certainly not what I was expecting. I thought he was dead, in fact I just told everyone he was dead, as it was easier than telling them that he was alive and did not want to know his own children. I stepped back, hoping to hide my identity in the shadows of the house. I coldly asked him if he knew the whereabouts of Marion White; while not identifying my relationship with her, in the hope that he would not recognise me. He said, "No I don't." I turned and walked away.

No, I didn't fall into his arms and break down sobbing on seeing my long-lost father. Instead my thoughts were overcome with anger. I was angry that he had deserted my mother, and siblings without looking back to give us a second thought. I also saw the other woman's children poking their heads around the door to see who was there. These were the children he had swapped us for. They had their mother and our father. We were left to fend for ourselves with no parents and my youngest sister was only eight years old when my mother died. As I walked away, he shouted after me, "Is that Catherine?" I answered, "Yes," He asked me to come back and invited me into the house.

I put on my best phoney smile, as I turned around slowly and walked back to his house where I met his new partner and her two children. I felt a sense of betraying my mother's memory for speaking to them. I was as pleasant as I could be, but did not ooze with joy at this reunion. Nevertheless, I wanted to know where my sister was, and I imagined he had the next link, so I had to be civil. I didn't tell the woman that she couldn't tie my mother's shoe laces, or that she was no oil painting, or that my mother was a good-looking woman. No, this was one of the rare occasions that I thought it better to keep my thoughts to myself. However, I did not really wish to engage in small talk as I was hiding my bad feelings towards him and his new family. My father gave me an address in Dunblane at the Hydro Hotel and a telephone number. He said, I could go to a public telephone box to ring her, and if she came to Saltcoats we could go back to his place to talk. I thanked him rather reluctantly, acknowledged his new family and left.

This time I telephoned the hotel and asked to speak to Marion. Yes, this time she was actually there and came to the telephone. This was a very emotional telephone call. She couldn't believe anyone could possibly have found her, as she had been so careful to cover her tracks. She started to cry, and said she was really pleased I had found her. She did not think she could have ever returned to her family or home town because of the way she had just disappeared. I had done it, I had accomplished my mission, I was absolutely delighted, another air punching moment.

My sister was so pleased to hear from me, she said she would get the next train through to Saltcoats; we agreed I would meet her at the train station. I felt very excited as I negotiated the streets in this seaside town. I asked a man for directions and he kindly said, "Oh, I am going that way, I will take you." I thanked him and walked along with him in my normal trusting manner. When we arrived at the railway station, he was following me in. I said it was ok I could manage from there, but he said he needed to go to the station too. As we were passing a door, he pushed me into an old derelict dark room. He started to punch me in the face and dragged me to the floor. He tried to rape me, but I fought like hell. I was also screaming my head off trying to attract attention. A safety pin saved my life that day. The button on my trousers had burst earlier, and I'd put a safety pin in to keep them together. As he held me down, he couldn't neither rip the trousers nor undo the pin. I eventually broke free and ran. There was a man walking passed with his head bowed down; I knew he had heard my screams and chose to ignore them. I wondered what he would think of himself when he looked in his mirror the next day.

Needless to say, I had missed the train and was in a terrible state. The nails on my fingers were bleeding from clawing him as I tried to fight him off; I was badly bruised and ached all over. I did not go to the police, as in those days it was customary to blame the woman and say she was 'asking for it.' With some difficulty, given my lack of direction I found my way back to where my father lived; I knew that is where my sister would have gone when I was not at the train station. Although she would think it was odd me not meeting the train when I had put so much effort into finding her. Before arriving at his house, I tidied myself up and collected myself. No, I was not going to ruin this important moment telling them what had happened, that could wait till later. As you can imagine this was one of the loveliest moments of my life. My sister did eventually return to the North East, married and had children. Do miracles still happen? Well they still happen for me, and I hope to God they still happen for you.

Just to let you know I have just written a book called: *God! Not Cancer*. It is quite controversial given I stop my chemotherapy and use a number of alternatives, not to forget my prayers.

Can I please ask if you have found my book useful would you be kind enough to leave me a review? You see, if a book is well reviewed this proves its credibility and helps other readers to know if this book is right for them. I also think there is a lot of really good information in this book which could help other people.

Thank you so much for your time and for joining me on my journey.

Printed in Great Britain
by Amazon

60986367R00208